WITHDRAWN

# Side Effects

# *Side Effects*

A Prosecutor, a Whistleblower,
and a Bestselling
Antidepressant on Trial

## ALISON BASS

ALGONQUIN BOOKS OF CHAPEL HILL 2008

Published by
Algonquin Books of Chapel Hill
Post Office Box 2225
Chapel Hill, North Carolina 27515-2225

a division of
Workman Publishing
225 Varick Street
New York, New York 10014

Library of Congress Cataloging-in-Publication Data
Bass, Alison.
  Side effects : a prosecutor, a whistleblower, and a bestselling
antidepressant on trial / Alison Bass. — 1st. ed.
      p. cm.
      Includes bibliographical references and index.
      1. Spitzer, Eliot — Trials, litigation, etc.   2. GlaxoSmithKline —
Trials, litigation, etc.   3. Products liability — Drugs — United States.
4. Antidepressants — Side effects.   5. Paroxetine — Side effects.
I. Title.
KF228.S685B37 2008
346.7303'8 — dc22                                    2008007345

10 9 8 7 6 5 4 3 2 1
First Edition

# Contents

# Contents

## Author's Note

IN NOVEMBER 1995, when I was a reporter for the *Boston Globe,* I received a message from the city desk. A woman had called with an anonymous tip, something to do with the misappropriation of funds from the Massachusetts Department of Mental Health, the state agency that oversees the care of people with mental illness. The phone message was forwarded to me because I was the *Globe*'s mental health reporter. When I called the number on the message slip, a woman named Donna Howard answered the phone. She said she worked in the psychiatry department at Brown University and had found evidence of wrongdoing by researchers in her department. Clinical trials were not being conducted properly, and her boss, Dr. Martin Keller, chair of Brown's psychiatry department, was collecting funding from a state mental health agency under false pretenses. Would I be interested in meeting with her? I would.

It was the beginning of a series of stories I wrote that opened my eyes to the way medical research was being conducted in this country. The first story, which ran in the *Boston Globe* in January 1996, reported that the financially strapped mental health agency in Massachusetts was paying the psychiatry department at Brown University School of Medicine hundreds of thousands of dollars for research that apparently wasn't being conducted. I followed that story up with several articles about other research and billing controversies in the psychiatry department at Brown.

At the same time, I was also covering the astonishingly successful emergence of a class of new antidepressants called SSRIs (selective serotonin reuptake inhibitors). These psychoactive drugs—Prozac, Zoloft, Paxil—were fast becoming blockbusters, earning their manufacturers billions of dollars in sales. However, there was growing concern about their safety. In 1990, Dr. Martin Teicher, a psychiatrist at McLean Hospital and Harvard Medical School, together with two colleagues, published the first case report linking Prozac to suicidal thoughts and behaviors in some patients. Their case report came under heavy fire from the pharmaceutical industry and prominent members of the psychiatric community. I remember interviewing Teicher at the time and thinking that he was either very brave or unusually foolhardy to buck the wave of excitement sweeping his profession over these new antidepressants. The mishaps that befell Teicher in the years after he questioned Prozac's safety are part of my narrative.

Then in 1999, I received another anonymous tip: Martin Keller, still Brown's chief of psychiatry, was earning hundreds of thousands of dollars in personal income from the very companies whose drugs he was touting in medical journals and at conferences. That tip led to a front-page story in the *Boston Globe* on Keller's extensive financial ties to the pharmaceutical industry. Martin Keller declined to be interviewed for this book despite numerous requests left with his office and with the Brown University public relations office.

The story continued to unfurl after I left the *Globe*. In 2003, the New York State attorney general's office began investigating the pharmaceutical industry. The investigation, led by a spunky newcomer to the AG's office named Rose Firestein, focused on drugmakers' widespread practice of disclosing only positive results about new drugs and withholding the negative research outcomes. What Firestein and her colleagues found raised serious questions about the veracity of Glaxo-

SmithKline's claims that Paxil was a safe and effective drug for children and adolescents. In this book, I recount the story of how Firestein found and assembled the clues that Martin Teicher, Donna Howard, and other whistle-blowers had left before her. My narrative tells the larger story of how pharmaceutical companies and their partners in the research community pulled the wool over the public's eyes with tacit assistance from the Food and Drug Administration, the premier agency in charge of protecting the nation's health.

All of the people written about in this book exist. There are no imaginary scenes or characters. When I describe someone as feeling, thinking, or recalling something, the emotion, thought, or memory was explicitly described to me by the person to whom it is attributed. In the case of key scenes, I was nearly always able to contact others present to confirm that my subjects' memories were accurate. The names in this book are real, although I have used one person's middle name.

The material for this book was culled from dozens of interviews with primary sources and key experts and from thousands of pages of university, corporate, and government documents. In addition, I reviewed transcripts of government meetings, disciplinary hearings, and legal proceedings and collected hundreds of relevant newspaper articles. Many of these documents are cited in the Notes.

Alison Bass
2008

# Side Effects

## Prologue: 2004

AT SIXTEEN, TONYA BROOKS was painfully shy, with long blond hair, round cheeks, and blue green eyes that changed color with the light. She earned decent grades at Pflugerville High School, twenty minutes outside Austin, Texas, but she was too uncomfortable around other kids her age to take part in extracurricular activities. Instead, she would come home after school every day and do her homework or watch television. She noticed a commercial on TV for a drug called Paxil. It showed a teenage boy, who, like her, felt self-conscious all the time, as if everyone were staring at him. After taking Paxil, the boy changed; he became confident and carefree, and wherever he went, friends flocked to him. Tonya wanted to be like that. But she didn't say anything to her parents about her longings or her fears.

One day when she was almost sixteen and a half, Tonya drove to her favorite Subway to get a six-inch ham sub. As she pulled into the parking lot, she saw a group of kids she didn't know. I can't do this, she said to herself, and drove home. When her mother asked her where her sub was, Tonya started crying. "I can't go out anymore; I can't go anywhere," she said. "I don't know what's wrong with me."

Her mother suggested they go and talk to the family doctor about Tonya's anxiety. Tonya asked the doctor about Paxil, and the doctor said it might help. So in January 2004, Tonya began taking Paxil. But instead of making her feel better, it made her restless, agitated, and unable to sleep. It also made her mean.

Tonya used to care about her schoolwork and feel guilty when she didn't do well. Now she just didn't care. In fact, she didn't give a damn. And if her mother so much as asked how her day had gone, she would yell, "Don't talk to me. I hate you!"

Tonya had always had a bump on her left elbow, but she had never given it much thought. A month or two after she started taking Paxil, she decided that the bump should be removed, so she asked her father how he would remove such a bump. He kidded that she could use an X-Acto knife. He thought Tonya was kidding too.

She wasn't. She found her father's X-Acto knife and starting digging out the bump on her elbow. It started bleeding badly, and her dad put some Band-Aids on the wound. That evening, as Tonya was lying in bed unable to sleep, she realized that the cutting hadn't hurt. In a weird way, it had made her feel better.

Around this time, Tonya went back to their family doctor, who prescribed Ambien as a sleep aid. It didn't help much: she'd lie awake at night and think about how awful she felt. One afternoon, at her part-time job at the OfficeMax in Round Rock, five miles away, another employee there accused Tonya of stealing some money, which made her feel bad. On her break that day, she noticed that someone had left a box cutter lying around in the back of the store. She took it into the bathroom and cut into the underside of her wrist—not enough to open a vein, just enough to bleed. It didn't hurt, and again, it seemed to make her feel better.

After that, she always cut herself in the same place, to keep the wound fresh. She covered the cuts with her watch and told no one. She didn't confide in anyone, mostly because she was afraid they would take her medicine away. She kept hoping the Paxil would start working, that it would make her feel better about herself.

[2]

One evening, Tonya was counting the money in her till with another employee, a kindly gentleman in his sixties. "What happened to your wrist?" he asked. Tonya lied and said she had been working in the garage with her father and had been cut by a tool. "That's a weird place to get cut," the man said. "Are you sure you didn't do that on purpose?"

She told him no, she was fine.

As Tonya's cutting became more and more frequent, she felt so depressed, especially at night, that she started thinking seriously about killing herself. She began planning her own funeral, picking out tapes she wanted played. To her relatives, she would say strange things like, "I want you to be happy when I die."

Cheryl Brooks, Tonya's mother, saw the radical change in her daughter but didn't understand what was happening. "She got mean, very sharp," Cheryl told me years later. But she had no idea Tonya was mutilating herself or that she felt suicidal. "I've got two older children and I didn't see it," Cheryl said, her voice pungent with regret. "I just didn't put two and two together."

On the evening of May 30, 2004, Tonya swallowed all the pills in her Paxil and Ambien bottles. That night, she crawled into bed with her parents, thinking that she wanted to be near them when she died. Several times that night her mother had to take Tonya to the bathroom because she had the dry heaves. "I thought it was the flu," Cheryl said. "She was really, really sick."

But she didn't die. On her way to work the next day, Tonya had a car accident. "She hit the curb on both sides of the road and blew out her tires," her mother recalled. "We had to pick her up and bring her home."

That evening, Tonya's mother discovered the empty Paxil and Ambien bottles and confronted her daughter. Tonya lied and said she must have accidentally taken all the Paxil after she had taken the Ambien, when she was half-asleep. Her mother let it go.

Three days later, Tonya took her daily dose of Paxil and Ambien and went to bed. It was June 2, the very day that Eliot Spitzer, the attorney general in far-off New York State, filed an unprecedented lawsuit against GlaxoSmithKline, the maker of Paxil, accusing the British-based pharmaceutical giant of consumer fraud. The action was a gamble, some might say an act of sheer chutzpah. No lawmaker had ever before accused the drug industry of fraud for deceiving doctors and patients about a new drug. The lawsuit was the brainchild of a newcomer to Spitzer's office, a feisty litigator named Rose Firestein, who knew a thing or two about loneliness and despair. Firestein had made a career out of defending the rights of vulnerable children, traveling all over the country to provide legal counsel on their behalf. In the past few years, though, she had lost much of her eyesight, making travel difficult. Instead of quitting and going on long-term disability, as her doctors counseled, she found a spot on Eliot Spitzer's team in lower Manhattan. There, she began investigating the way powerful psychoactive drugs such as Paxil were being tested and marketed for uses not approved by the FDA.

By 2003, millions of Americans were taking Paxil and other antidepressants in the same class (such as Prozac, Zoloft, and Celexa), and these bestselling drugs were earning the pharmaceutical industry billions of dollars in profits. For many people, the drugs worked. They lifted the fog of despair from adults who had been crippled with depression for years; they eased the anxieties of others hobbled by self-doubt; they may have even kept some people from killing themselves. But the drugs also seemed to exert a paradoxical effect in some patients, particularly children, making them *more* agitated and suicidal, not less. At the New York State AG's office, Firestein and her colleagues were not interested in making a medical judgment about the value of these drugs. The question they posed was this: in its rush to create a bestselling drug, had GlaxoSmithKline deliberately suppressed important information about the safety and effectiveness of Paxil in children?

Thousands of miles away in Pflugerville, Texas, Tonya Brooks had no idea who Eliot Spitzer or Rose Firestein were or what they were up to. All she knew was that she was feeling sad and agitated and she couldn't sleep and she wanted to cut herself again. In the small hours of the night, Tonya propped up her left leg and started digging into it with a needle and her mother's cuticle scissors. Then she grabbed a paring knife from the kitchen.

She sawed off some skin with the knife and discovered that it didn't hurt. Then she realized she didn't want to get her bed dirty, so she went into the bathroom. The wound got bigger and bloodier. It felt as if somebody else were doing the cutting.

Suddenly, something in Tonya snapped. Sometime around two in the morning, she stumbled to her parents' bedroom and banged on the door. When Cheryl answered groggily, Tonya yelled, "I want my dad. Please tell Dad to come here."

A few minutes later, her parents found her in the bathroom, blood all over the floor and a huge, gaping hole in her leg. Her mother screamed and fell to the floor. Her father grabbed gauze and tape to try to stanch the bleeding. He half-carried Tonya to the car, and they sped to the hospital, Cheryl driving like a maniac. Tonya lay bleeding in the backseat, her head cradled in her father's lap.

# 1. Martin Teicher and the Wonder Drugs, 1988–89

The rhododendrons were in full, blush pink bloom as Martin Teicher hurried up the path to his lab at McLean Hospital in Belmont, Massachusetts. The psychiatrist paid no attention to the flowering bush or the magnificent maple tree that shaded the courtyard outside of the Mailman Research Center, making it such a hospitable spot for staff and patients to linger. All Teicher could think about was the startling admission that his patient had made in their weekly therapy session that afternoon. Ms. D., as he had taken to calling her, suffered from a depression so disabling that she could no longer work, although she had once been a successful business executive. When the thirty-nine-year-old woman first came under his care, Teicher had tried her on a potent antidepressant known as an MAO inhibitor. While the drug lifted her mood, it caused an extremely uncomfortable rash. So Teicher prescribed another antidepressant known as a tricyclic (for its three-ringed molecular structure), but this drug did nothing to dispel the woman's lethargy and sense of gloom. Electroshock therapy worked for a few months. Teicher then tried his patient on yet another tricyclic known as amitriptyline. Although the drug helped, it gave Ms. D. a ravenous appetite. Her weight ballooned and she stopped taking the medicine. Ever since, she had lapsed into a deep despondency, sleeping all the time and withdrawing from family and friends.

In the spring of 1988, Teicher decided to put Ms. D. on a new anti-depressant about which he'd heard great things. Launched in the United States just a few months earlier, Prozac was a selective serotonin reuptake inhibitor (SSRI), so named because it blocked the uptake of a neurochemical called serotonin. Brain cells communicate by releasing "transmitter" substances into the space, or synapse, between them, and serotonin is one of the brain's key transmitters. Research indicated that in people with depression, the levels of a metabolite of serotonin appeared to be low. Some researchers theorized that if the surrounding brain cells were blocked from absorbing serotonin, the chemical would build up around the nerve endings of the brain and help alleviate depression. That hypothesis would later be discarded as too simplistic, but not before it became a compelling rationale for how Prozac worked.

Yet the buzz about Prozac went beyond theory. A number of Teicher's colleagues had experimented with the drug before the Food and Drug Administration approved it for official use in January 1988, and several had experienced such good results that they'd taken to calling Prozac a wonder drug. It was easy to see why: The SSRI was the first new antidepressant to come along in a decade, and unlike older antidepressants, it could be prescribed in convenient one-a-day twenty-milligram capsules. Most important, it seemed to have none of the nasty side effects of the older drugs. Perhaps, some psychiatric researchers speculated, that was because Prozac influenced only one neurotransmitter in the brain; older antidepressants (such as the tricyclics) acted on several key neurotransmitters.

In time, this theory would also prove to be flawed. The brain's circuitry is amazingly complex and interconnected, and dramatic changes in serotonin levels can trigger ripple effects in other important neurotransmitters, such as norepinephrine and dopamine. As many people would soon discover, Prozac and other SSRIs could cause far more dangerous side effects than their manufacturers initially let on.

NONE OF THIS, however, was in the air in 1988, when Prozac arrived in the United States. Many clinicians, Teicher among them, were eager to try a new weapon in the fight against depression, particularly a "clean" drug that appeared to target only one transmitter system in the brain with no serious side effects.

By the spring of 1988, Martin Teicher had been at McLean for six years, first as a psychiatric resident and then as a staff psychiatrist and neuroscience researcher. Along the way, he had picked up a number of private patients, such as Ms. D., whom he saw in his office on the second floor of the Wyman House, a stately brick building tucked away in the rear of the campus (a brisk ten-minute walk from the Mailman Research Center) and named after Dr. Rufus Wyman, the first superintendent of the McLean Asylum. At thirty-six, Teicher, known as Marty to his colleagues, was a compact, soft-spoken man with wavy black hair and a serious demeanor. His colleagues admired him for his innovative approach to research, his passion for learning, and his willingness to put in long hours. At McLean, it was expected that an ambitious young psychiatrist would see hospital patients, conduct lab research, *and* have his own private practice. But Teicher eclipsed even those expectations. He was a workaholic, devoted to his patients, his research, and his career. In July 1988, his hard work would pay off with his promotion to director of the hospital's newly endowed developmental biopsychopharmacological research program.

When Teicher had first come to McLean, fresh out of Yale Medical School, he had been too busy—what with thirty-six-hour shifts crammed with clinical care and lab work—to dwell on the incongruity between the hospital's beautifully manicured setting and the strange ailments of the patients treated there. With its mix of handsome colonial and Jacobean revival buildings, the 232-acre campus could easily have been mistaken for an Ivy League university. Over the last century, McLean had become famous for catering to wealthy Brahmins and celebrities in need of "rest." And yet the patients Teicher saw in his daily rounds were worlds away from such highbrow clientele. They suffered all manner of mental torment. One woman believed that worms and maggots were eating her brains and repeatedly bashed her head against the wall in an attempt to rid herself of the vermin. Others lay coiled in fetal positions for hours at a time, unable to move a limb. One of his private patients had multiple personalities, including one flirtatious alter ego named Sue, who fantasized about having sex with Teicher, and a second persona who gruffly demanded that she kill herself.

Teicher was fascinated by these patients, even more by the question of how the wiring in their brains could have become so crossed and tangled. And there was also the satisfaction in being on the staff of New England's preeminent psychiatric hospital, with a faculty appointment at Harvard Medical School.

ON THAT LATE spring afternoon in 1988, Teicher had returned to his lab at the Mailman Research Center to check on an experiment before leaving for the day. But he couldn't concentrate; he was too distracted by what his patient had told him that afternoon. It had been three months since he had started Ms. D. on twenty milligrams of Prozac. When her depression didn't abate, he followed standard medical procedure and gradually increased the dose—first to sixty and then to eighty milligrams. Her mood, however, continued to worsen, and she started drinking again after eight years of sobriety. Even more worrisome to Teicher, she became preoccupied with thoughts of suicide.

During that day's therapy session, she told him that she was thinking of buying a gun to kill herself with. She referred to Prozac as that "deadly drug." Teicher knew that his patient had attempted suicide on two previous occasions, but he saw those overdoses largely as calls for help: she had phoned someone almost as soon as she crammed the pills in her mouth.

This time, however, she confided to Teicher that she was sure that Prozac would enable her to finish the job. As Teicher listened with mounting unease, he suddenly remembered that two of his other patients on Prozac had also exhibited a growing preoccupation with suicidal thoughts. And then it struck him: What if this was something more than a worsening of their depression? What if this obsession with self-destructive thoughts (one of his other patients had even put a loaded gun to her head) had something to do with the antidepressant itself? There is something very weird going on here, Teicher thought as he locked the door to his lab. He would have to ask around and see if any of his colleagues had had similar experiences with the new "wonder" drug.

IT WOULD TAKE Martin Teicher another six months to begin to understand what he was seeing in his patients. In the fall of 1988, he and two colleagues at McLean began putting together a case study of six patients, including Ms. D., none of whom had been seriously suicidal before taking Prozac. After taking the drug for several weeks, all of them developed an intense and in some cases violent preoccupation with suicide. One of these six patients, a nineteen-year-old college freshman, repeatedly lacerated herself on her forearms with a knife, requiring emergency room care. She was taken off Prozac, and her self-destructive urges abated. Teicher and his coauthors, Dr. Jonathan Cole, the head of psychopharmacology at McLean, and Carol Glod, a respected nurse-practitioner at the hospital, observed the same phenomenon with the other five patients in their case report. They submitted their clinical observations to the *American Journal of Psychiatry.* By January 1989, the prestigious journal had promised to publish the case report with some revisions. In May of that year, Teicher took a break from revising the paper to attend the annual meeting of the American Psychiatric Association in Montreal. He was eager to hear about other practitioners' experiences with Prozac.

As TEICHER TOOK the wide concrete steps of the Montreal Convention Center plaza two at a time, a flurry of activity in one corner of the plaza caught his eye. A small group of people were chanting and waving signs. Some signs read PROZAC KILLS; others, PROZAC = VIOLENCE. As Teicher drew closer, he noticed a large man standing in the center of the group with a lowered bullhorn in his hand, deep in conversation with a woman who appeared to be taking notes. That woman was me. As a reporter for the *Boston Globe,* I was covering the APA's annual meeting in Montreal that year. I too had noticed the demonstration and had gone over to investigate.

Teicher immediately recognized who the noisemakers were: Scientologists. The Church of Scientology had been founded in 1953 by a science fiction writer named L. Ron Hubbard, who had written books attacking psychiatry as the dark art. Hubbard was now deceased, but in the past few months, Scientologists had taken up the supposed ills of Prozac as part of their campaign to discredit psychiatry.

Teicher knew that Prozac had disturbing side effects in some patients. He and his colleagues had observed the drug triggering persistent, obsessive, and violent suicidal thoughts in the six patients in their case report. He also knew that Prozac had a particularly long-lasting effect on the body's metabolism and that many patients harbored self-destructive urges even after they stopped taking the drug. Two weeks after Teicher took Ms. D. off Prozac, she attempted to kill herself, consuming a lethal combination of Valium and alcohol, and this time she would have succeeded had her sister not discovered her and rushed her to a nearby hospital. Even so, Teicher and his coauthors suspected that these suicidal behaviors occurred only in a small subset of people on Prozac. For his case report, Teicher had totaled up all 170 patients that he and Cole had treated with Prozac as outpatients and estimated that suicidal ideation occurred in perhaps 3.5 percent of them. It was a very rough estimate, he realized, but whatever the real percentage of people who developed suicidal thoughts on Prozac was, it certainly didn't constitute a majority of those treated with the drug.

The McLean researchers had made it clear that their purpose in publishing the case study was to bring this occasional phenomenon to the attention of doctors and patients so that they could be on the lookout for its emergence during the first weeks of treatment. None of Teicher's own patients had responded well to Prozac, but according to anecdotal reports from his colleagues, the drug really did help many patients, particularly those whose chronic depression had not responded to other antidepressants. He himself intended to keep prescribing Prozac when he felt it was warranted. He wanted nothing to do with an extremist group whose mission was to destroy the very credibility of his profession. He walked away.

LATER THAT EVENING, Teicher joined a few colleagues for dinner at the Bistro à Champlain, an expensive French restaurant in Montreal with an Old World flavor. With its wainscoted walls and the rich cigar smoke wafting through the air, the restaurant reminded him of a private men's club. Teicher was seated next to Bruce Cohen, a well-regarded psychiatrist who would later become the president of McLean Hospital. Also at the table were Carol Glod, Teicher's coauthor, and George Zubenko, a psychiatrist and an old friend who had trained with Teicher at McLean and would soon take an appointment at the University of Pittsburgh. As Teicher savored his dessert, he became aware that a group of men at the next table were chattering excitedly about the buzz surrounding their new drug and the rave reviews it had received at the APA conference that day. They were sales representatives from Eli Lilly, the maker of Prozac, Marty realized, and they were raising their drinks in a toast. One of the men stood up and said, "To Prozac! May its side-effect profile never change!"

As he watched the men laugh and clink their glasses in unison,

Teicher leaned over to Cohen, who had also noticed them. Thinking of the case study already accepted for publication, he whispered, "I'm afraid it's going to change." Only later would Teicher realize just how prescient his off-the-cuff comment had been. Lilly's fight to make Prozac a blockbuster drug would haunt Teicher's own life in ways the ambitious young psychiatrist couldn't begin to imagine.

## 2. Rose Firestein v. New York City, 1989

**B**leary-eyed, Rose Firestein looked up from her computer screen and the messy sheaf of papers on her desk. It was after 1 a.m. and she'd been working for close to sixteen hours on a brief for the Legal Aid Society of New York. At this hour, there was no one else in Legal Aid's cramped offices on Park Row in Lower Manhattan. Even the cleaning women had come and gone. The place was silent and shadowy, but Firestein didn't mind. This was when she got her best work done. A few years back, she had pulled an all-nighter while preparing the initial filing for a mammoth lawsuit against New York City's Social Services Department. On the way home the next morning, she'd fallen asleep on the F line and missed her stop in Queens. She wasn't going to let that happen again, Firestein vowed as she rode the elevator down from the twenty-first floor. This time, she'd find a cab. Hopefully.

When Firestein first joined Legal Aid, some of her new colleagues hadn't taken her seriously. Rose Firestein didn't look particularly formidable. She stood all of five feet one inch in her stocking feet and had silky, white blond locks and hazel eyes. This wasn't the first time others had underestimated her, and it would not be the last. In her second job out of law school—for the Indiana Center on Law and Poverty— Firestein had been working on a race discrimination case on behalf of several young black men who were hired part-time for below-normal wages at a small manufacturing plant in Elkhart, Indiana. After months of dickering back and forth, the middle-aged attorney for the manufacturing company told Firestein to craft a draft proposal for a possible settlement and he'd see what he could do. A few days after she turned in her proposal, a treatise that ran to many pages, the company attorney called her up and said admiringly, "Rose, you've been hiding your light under a bushel!" In the settlement, not only did Firestein's clients receive back pay, but the company hired them full-time and put in place its first-ever affirmative action plan.

After her stint in Indiana, Firestein moved to Savannah, where she worked as a senior staff attorney for the Legal Services of Georgia. There, she and several colleagues sued the Tattnall County Board of Education, accusing county officials of resegregating Tattnall's schools in the way they tracked and separated black and white students. "They assigned black kids with borderline IQs to classes for mental retardation while the white kids with the same measured IQ were assigned to specific learning disability classes," Firestein said. She and her compatriots won that case and went on to sue the Georgia State Department of Education and twelve counties for the same discriminatory practices. The statewide lawsuit stirred up a hornet's nest. An attorney representing one of the school systems, an elderly man from a white-shoe law firm, told her, "You're trying to ruin my way of life!"

Rose Firestein had not set out in life with that goal in mind; it just wasn't her nature to back down in the face of resistance. She was stiff-necked that way, just like her father, a Jewish grocer's son who had pulled himself up out of poverty to become a respected cardiologist in South Bend, Indiana. Her father had raised all four of his children—three girls and one boy—to be independent adults who could make their own way in the world. Rose's older sister, Janice, was an information technology manager for Merrill Lynch in New York City; her brother, a corporate consultant. Her younger sister worked as a paralegal in a law firm. Rose herself was a workaholic, pale from spending so much time indoors. At the office, she was known for being among the first to arrive and last to leave. One time, her boss, only half-joking, told a visitor, "Thank goodness Rose works twenty-four hours a day."

With her glasses and small stature, Firestein was not the kind of woman who automatically drew a second look. At the office, she dressed conservatively, in a tailored skirt or pants suit and shell top. So co-workers who didn't know her well were caught by surprise when she opened her mouth. Firestein had a salty way of expressing herself. When something wasn't going well, she could be heard to mutter an "Oh, hell." One time when a colleague asked her how she had unearthed a document that turned out to be crucial to their legal case, Firestein responded, "A little song, a little dance, a little something in your pants." Her associates sometimes couldn't believe the things that came out of Rose Firestein's mouth. But she made them laugh—that was the important part.

Firestein had never been shy about expressing herself. It came from being the third child in a big family: you had to make noise to get noticed. She was also quick to rise to the defense of the injured party when she perceived an injustice—sometimes too quick. Once, when she was just starting out as an attorney, working for the Indiana Civil Rights Commission, she and her boss, the executive director of the commission and the only African American in an executive position in state government, had looked around and observed that blacks were significantly underrepresented in the state's workforce. They decided to do something about it, so they served an extensive subpoena on the State of Indiana's Department of Personnel, seeking records that would document the situation.

A few days later, they were called in to see the then governor of Indiana, Otis R. Bowen, who very politely said he understood their concern about diversity. However, this was not the way to go about things. After the pair left Bowen's office, they were pulled aside by one of his aides, who was not so polite. The aide lambasted them for not going through the proper channels. What Firestein remembered most vividly, though—the memory that stayed with her some thirty years later—was that excruciatingly long walk across a large blue rug to reach Governor Bowen's desk. Every step had seemed an eternity.

Over the years, Firestein learned how to curb some of her Don Quixote tendencies. By the time she began working for Legal Aid of New York in 1984, she was a seasoned litigator who understood the value of thinking things through. In less than a year with Legal Aid, she was named lead attorney on one of its biggest class action suits ever, *Doe v. New York City Department of Social Services.* It was at the height of the crack epidemic, and many of the children removed from their homes were being kept overnight in the department's field offices and moved on a nightly basis from one office to the next. There were simply not enough home placements for all the neglected and abused children flooding the foster care system. Legal Aid's lawsuit was an attempt to force the city to provide the resources necessary to get these foster children into decent long-term placements.

What Firestein saw while collecting evidence for the *Doe* lawsuit made her want to go out and hurt someone, bad. During visits to the DSS field offices, she observed the empty eyes of foster children kept overnight with no place to go. She smelled the tangy odor of their unwashed bodies. But what horrified her even more were the stories she gleaned from family court files of children who had been put on potent psychoactive medications—drugs designed to alter the very chemistry of the brain—with no one to monitor their condition or watch for the drugs' often dangerous side effects. One child, who had been removed from his home after being abused by his mother and remanded to his father's custody, ended up in foster care at the age of twelve when his father died of an overdose. "Victor" had been placed at the St. Christopher's group home, but the facility had kicked him out after a month, claiming he was "disturbed and uncontrollable." At that point, Victor had been put on Haldol, a powerful antipsychotic drug, and transferred from one DSS facility to another, often staying somewhere only a single night before being moved again. By the time a court-appointed psychiatrist caught up to his case, Victor was beginning to suffer from involuntary muscle tics, a common side effect of Haldol.

Rose Firestein was not a squeamish person. Having accompanied her doctor father on occasional house calls and worked as a nurse's aide in a South Bend hospital, she had seen her share of sickness and death. She cherished the memories of driving to house calls with her father; they were among the only times she had had him to herself. She had even toyed with the idea of following her father into medicine. Of all her siblings, Firestein most resembled her father, a brilliant man who was passionate about medicine but had many other interests: wood-working, gardening, reading. Firestein too was fascinated by the medical sciences. But as a child growing up in the nation's heartland, she had heard President Kennedy's call to make the world a better place. Social justice became her passion, and Rose Firestein decided that the law would provide her with a better means than medicine of pursuing that cause.

Even so, reading Victor's file and others like it turned her stomach. In one of the court filings on the case, a psychiatric expert had testified that Haldol, with its severe side effects, should not have been prescribed to a teenager, much less a twelve-year-old who had just lost his father. It was only intended for use in extreme cases of psychosis. Maybe this particular boy needed Haldol; Firestein knew she couldn't make that call. What bothered her was that so many of these children seemed to be drugged so they wouldn't make problems for their caregivers. Drugs like Haldol were being used as chemical straitjackets. Yet there was no one around to supervise this usage, to make sure these children didn't overdose or develop potentially dangerous side effects. And that, to Firestein, was the real crime.

LEGAL AID WON a preliminary injunction with its lawsuit, and after a week-long trial that embarrassed Mayor Ed Koch and other city officials, the city finally agreed to stop the practice of keeping foster children overnight in field offices. But many children were still being held in DSS field offices during the day—the court order stipulated only that they had to be moved to an overnight placement by 11 p.m.—and conditions in those offices had not improved much. Firestein could remember her horror at walking into field offices in Bedford-Stuyvesant, the South Bronx, Queens—it didn't matter—and finding cockroaches, expired baby formula, inadequate care for the HIV-positive children, even multiple babies in one crib.

As an accomplished cook, Firestein was especially disturbed by the bad food these children were served: hot dogs, baked beans, and potato chips were staples, often washed down with sugar-laden fruit drinks. There was no security in the field offices, and one time, a neglected baby who had been removed from his mother's custody was snatched back in broad daylight. Other times, Firestein and her colleagues would arrive at the Bedford-Stuyvesant field office only to find some of the kids hanging around outside in an area reputed to be the hub of the neighborhood's drug and gang activity. The department's caseworkers were as upset about the conditions and lack of resources as Firestein was, but no matter how many times she or another of the Legal Aid attorneys called to complain that the department was in violation of its court settlement, nothing seemed to change.

So in 1989, Legal Aid decided to file a legal motion to have the city and its Social Services Department held in contempt of court. Firestein and her colleagues worked on the contempt motion around the clock for weeks. They set up a booth in a diner right around the corner from the Emergency Children's Services office on Laight Street in Soho, and one by one, caseworkers from ECS would drop by after their shifts and spill the beans on what was going on in the field offices. The caseworkers had the express permission of their union representative to talk to

Legal Aid; all it took was a slice of pie and some sympathetic questions to open the floodgates.

BY THE TIME Firestein pulled her working-into-the-wee-hours maneuver, she and her team had collected dozens of affidavits from these employees. The contempt motion was almost ready to be filed.

As Firestein walked down Broadway looking for a cab, she wondered when she would get her life back. After moving to New York from Georgia, she had looked forward to meeting men who didn't view her as a carpetbagger, an opinionated Yankee who didn't even know how to flirt. But although she had dated on and off during her first few years in New York, her job at Legal Aid had become all-consuming of late.

Firestein felt a sudden frisson of anxiety. It wasn't just the late hour; something else nagged at the edges of her consciousness. And then it hit her. She'd been mugged not far from here a few months earlier. She'd come into work especially early that morning, and the sky was just turning a pearly gray when a scraggly-looking man rushed up and demanded all her money.

"I have a gun," he threatened. Firestein squinted at the man. She didn't see any gun. So she reacted instinctually. Instead of handing him her purse, she started screaming. An employee from a nearby bagel shop heard her and came rushing out. He chased the man away, and Firestein bought a bagful of bagels in gratitude.

Now, a cab finally pulled up to the curb. Firestein jumped in and told him where she wanted to go.

"Sorry, lady, I don't go to Brooklyn," the cabbie said.

"Oh, c'mon, please? It's late and I'm really tired," Firestein pleaded with him. It wasn't the first time this had happened to her. At that hour of the night, many cab drivers didn't want to go to Brooklyn, even though they were legally obliged to, because they knew they wouldn't find a fare back to Manhattan.

"Nope."

Firestein didn't have the energy to write down the cabbie's medallion number and report him. She knew from experience that it wouldn't do any good anyway. Feeling fatigue in every bone of her body, she slowly slid out of the backseat and slammed the door shut. Damn! What was she going to do now? There was no way she was going to take the subway and switch trains at this hour. She began trudging back up Broadway, holding one arm in the air as she walked. Just as she was about to give up and turn back down Park Row toward the office, a taxi careened to a stop in front of her. Firestein got in and gave the cabbie her address, holding her breath. This time, the driver merely nodded and took off. Firestein settled back into the ripped leather seat and promptly fell asleep.

# 3. Donna Howard's Quest to Help Her Adopted Daughter, 1990

**D**onna Howard could tell that Maria was awake, even though her daughter's bedroom was down the hall from the kitchen. Maria was slamming doors as she moved between her room and the bathroom. It was a hot Saturday in August and Howard had been hurrying to finish a grant proposal before her fifteen-year-old daughter woke up. Howard's job was to develop outreach programs for Coastline Elderly Services, a nonprofit group that assisted senior citizens living on fixed incomes in the poor, heavily immigrant New Bedford area of southern Massachusetts. She found she had a knack for writing grant proposals that brought in much-needed funding to the organization. Today, she was up against a tight deadline. But she had the feeling she wasn't going to get any more writing done.

A few minutes later, Maria stormed into the kitchen.

"It's fucking hot in here!" she raged. "What's wrong with this place?"

Howard sighed.

"You're right," she said. It didn't pay to argue with Maria when she was in one of her moods. "It really is hot."

Maria's dark, brooding eyes fell on the thermostat on the wall next to the doorjamb. With an angry lunge, she reached over and grabbed the round, glass-covered dial. Howard tried to intervene, but too late. With a strength that belied her slender, five-foot frame, Maria ripped the thermostat out of the wall, threw it on the floor, and ran out of the house. Howard gazed numbly at the hole in the wall, the plaster crumbling around it.

She felt hopeless at times like these. Maria, whom Howard had legally adopted in 1988, had been growing steadily worse over the past few years, and now she was out of control. The child of a Cape Verdean woman who was mentally ill and a Nipmuc Indian father who had abandoned the family, Maria, along with her two siblings, had landed in foster care after their mother had a breakdown and was taken in a straitjacket to Taunton State Hospital. Maria ended up on Donna Howard's doorstep on a hot July afternoon in 1984. A social worker with the Massachusetts Department of Social Services, who knew of Howard's experience as a foster parent for special-needs children, had called her in desperation.

"Please, you've got to help me," the social worker said. "A foster family has just dumped an eight-year-old girl here. They've refused to take her back, and I have absolutely no place to put this kid. She's bounced out of every placement I've put her in. I'm desperate. Can you take her for just one night?"

An hour later, Maria was standing at Howard's door, clutching a grubby stuffed animal. Skinny and petite, with belligerent eyes and silky black hair, the little girl demanded to know what Howard's rules were. And she reminded her that she was only staying for one night.

That had been six years ago, and Maria was still with Howard. Donna had long wanted a child of her own. Thirty-five and unmarried, Howard was a statuesque woman with expressive green eyes and a silvery laugh. Both her parents were deceased, and she'd been on her own for some time.

When her father, a British-born sailor for the U.S. Navy, was still alive, Howard had won his respect by being the first in their family to earn a college degree. Her mother had died when Donna was only fourteen, and it was her father to whom she looked for love and approbation. He spent weeks away at sea, but when he was home, he was her biggest fan. He would take her and her older sister shopping for clothes, and he cooked them dinner. Although he didn't have much money, he helped Donna pay for college and the graduate-level courses in public administration that she excelled in. Hired as an outpatient coordinator at an acute care hospital in New Bedford, she rose quickly, becoming first the patient services supervisor and then the hospital's admissions manager, in charge of a staff of thirty people. But there was emptiness in Donna Howard's heart. Her father was often gone, her older sister had left the state, and Donna wanted a family of her own. Somehow she doubted she would ever meet the right man. In June 1984, she left the hospital and accepted a job directing an alternative education program for low-income children. In her spare time, she took in foster children with special needs. Then Maria turned up on her doorstep.

By the time Howard adopted Maria, she understood that raising her would be no picnic. At elementary school, Maria regularly picked fights with her teachers and classmates. She couldn't seem to sit still or even stay in a classroom for a fixed period of time. She would periodically run outside and hide. School officials, exasperated by Maria's behavior, kept trying to expel the child. Howard had to threaten to take the school district to court to keep her daughter enrolled. Life with Maria seemed to be crisis after crisis.

Howard soon discovered that the one thing that seemed to soothe her daughter's spirit was water. Maria loved to swim, and while other girls her age played with Barbie dolls, Maria fantasized about being a mermaid. She would spend hours in the huge claw-footed bathtub in their old Victorian house, contentedly splashing around in flippers. In 1989, Howard moved them to an abandoned beach cottage in southeastern Massachusetts that was surrounded by water and marshland. The cottage sat right on the edge of a tidal marsh, where the Nasketucket

River emptied into the bay. Howard fervently hoped that being lapped by water might calm Maria's inner demons.

It didn't work. Shortly before her twelfth birthday, Maria's emotional state worsened. She was by turns agitated and full of restless energy and then severely lethargic and depressed. She talked of killing herself. And there were rages, when Maria would spiral out of control over the smallest things. She often ran outside to escape the voices in her head, taking long walks on the beach with her dog, exhausting herself against the roar of the wind and the waves. On several occasions she had run outside in the middle of winter in her pajamas, and Howard had been forced to call the police. Another time, Maria attacked one of the Windsor dining room chairs that Howard had inherited from her grandmother. Even though Maria weighed less than eighty pounds, she had grabbed the wooden spokes in the chair and torn them out. Howard had to call the police again because she feared for Maria's safety. By the time the police arrived at the isolated cottage, the chair was a pile of toothpicks on the floor and Maria was sitting next to it, looking dazed.

Over the years, Howard came to know the local police quite well. She also dragged Maria to one expert after another—psychologists, a neurologist at Massachusetts General Hospital, a psychiatrist at Children's Hospital, a learning specialist, more psychiatrists. Maria had been hospitalized several times and prescribed all manner of psychoactive medicine. Along the way, she had collected twenty-seven different diagnoses. Post-traumatic stress disorder, depression, oppositional defiant disorder, attention deficit disorder, borderline personality disorder, psychosis undifferentiated, schizophrenia—the list went on and on.

The summer that Maria ripped the thermostat out of the wall, she was seeing a child psychologist and a child psychiatrist who worked together in New Bedford. The psychiatrist had recently prescribed Prozac, a new antidepressant that was getting rave reviews. If anything, though, the drug seemed to make Maria more agitated and violent. As Howard sat at the kitchen table that Saturday morning, she stared hard at the hole in the wall where the thermostat had been, as if it would somehow yield a clue to the mystery that was Maria.

A FEW WEEKS LATER, Howard finally wangled a fifteen-minute consultation with Maria's psychiatrist. His practice was on the first floor of an elegantly appointed historic mansion that he owned in downtown New Bedford.

When Howard told the psychiatrist about the incident with the thermostat, she noticed that he quickly glanced around his office, which was filled with expensive furniture and valuable antiques.

"I'm not going to be able to treat your daughter anymore," he said. "I don't think she's treatable."

He then advised Howard to terminate the adoption, return Maria to the custody of the state, and "cut your losses." Howard sat glued to her seat in shock.

It was now the first week of September. School was about to start, and Howard was feeling desperate. Maria wouldn't listen to her, and if she so much as looked her way, the girl would fly into a rage. Howard couldn't stand the thought of another year of expulsions, hospitalizations, threats, and tears. Swallowing her pride, she called the psychologist who worked with Maria's psychiatrist even though this woman too had said Maria was untreatable. But Howard had to find a new psychiatrist. Did the psychologist know of anyone?

"As a matter of fact, a new psychiatrist has just joined the practice," the woman said. "He says he would be willing to see Maria."

Howard would remember the psychologist's exact words more than a decade later. It was the first time she heard of the doctor whose clinical skills and diligent care would help her daughter begin the long road to recovery.

Four days later, Howard returned to the historic mansion near New Bedford's waterfront. The new psychiatrist's office was in the back of the building, a modest room cluttered with boxes of unpacked books.

Alison Bass

He looked young to Howard but seemed soft-spoken and earnest. He listened intently as Howard poured out the story of her daughter's bizarre behavior. He asked a few questions, and then he put down his notes and leaned forward in his chair.

"Your daughter has bipolar disorder," he said quietly. "Here's what we're going to do . . ."

# 4. The Empire Strikes Back, September 1991

Marty Teicher leaned forward, riveted by the elegantly dressed woman standing behind the microphone. Her name was Mrs. Frederic Richardson, and she was the twenty-second speaker that morning to address the FDA's Psychopharmacological Drugs Advisory Committee. The blue-ribbon committee had been convened on September 21, 1991, in response to rising public concern over claims that Prozac caused some people to become suicidal and even violent. Thus far, the FDA had fielded at least fourteen thousand reports of patients who had experienced adverse effects from taking the drug — a far higher rate of complaint than with any other medication to date. The Public Citizen Health Research Group, a Washington, D.C., watchdog organization, had recently filed a petition asking the FDA to put a new warning on the Prozac label about the heightened risk of suicidal behavior. The Church of Scientology had also launched a massive public relations blitz against the drug. The Scientologists' campaign, however, seemed to be having a paradoxical effect: it was rallying psychiatrists and the mainstream press in defense of Prozac. In fact, just a few months earlier, *Time* magazine had run a cover story attacking the Church of Scientology as a power-hungry cult. The magazine quoted a cult expert as saying, "Scientology is quite likely the most ruthless, the most classically terroristic, the most litigious and the most lucrative cult the country has ever seen." Among Teicher's colleagues at Harvard and McLean, emotions were running high. At the annual meeting of the American Psychiatric Association that year, Teicher overheard someone refer to him as "that Scientologist from Massachusetts."

Even so, the FDA had invited him—Marty Teicher from Plainview, Long Island—to act as one of the six expert consultants for this unprecedented public hearing in Rockville, Maryland. Teicher knew he had been summoned because of his paper on Prozac. Ever since the article, titled "Emergence of Intense Suicidal Preoccupation during Fluoxetine [the generic name for Prozac] Treatment," had been published in the *American Journal of Psychiatry* in February 1990, he had received hundreds of letters from people around the world, many of them from family members whose loved ones had killed themselves or tried to while taking Prozac. His office had also fielded dozens of calls from attorneys who were interested in suing Eli Lilly, the manufacturer of Prozac. Teicher had refused to take their calls, but several attorneys had told his assistant Cindy McGreenery that they were psychiatrists who needed Teicher's advice with a patient. He had returned their calls only to find himself connected to a law office, at which point he promptly hung up.

One afternoon a few weeks after the paper's publication, his intercom buzzed. Cindy told him that a psychiatrist from Washington, D.C., was on the line, asking to speak to him about a patient. Did Marty want to take the call?

Teicher ran his hand through his combed-back hair. He felt torn. What if this was yet another attorney pretending to be a colleague? He didn't want to be dragged into legal fisticuffs with Lilly. Yet he was beginning to enjoy his new status as a sought-after expert on the subject of Prozac. There was a part of him that relished playing the role of a latter-day David to Eli Lilly's Goliath. The more some of his colleagues warned him to back off—it wouldn't be good for his career, they said—the more he wanted to run full tilt at the issue of whether Prozac caused suicidal thoughts and behaviors in certain patients. Teicher had always liked the feeling of living life on the edge, passionately engaged. In college he'd been able to pull it off. A top student, he'd also had a regular radio show, had played in his own band, and was constantly going off to late-night concerts, all the while keeping his grades high enough for graduate school.

Marty believed he inherited his passionate nature from his Italian mother, who was a gifted artist and cook. But his drive, his need to excel in whatever task he applied himself to—that, he knew, came from his father. A stern, well-read man, Marty's father had always been interested in the sciences, but his own dad had died when he was in high school, so Marty's father had been forced to drop out of school and go to work to support the large family. The senior Teicher had become the manager of a millinery supply company in New York City and had scandalized his family by marrying a non-Jewish divorcée with a young child. He moved to Long Island and commuted back and forth to Manhattan, working long hours. Even as a child, Marty sensed that his father was not a happy man. Once his own children were born, Marty's father had insisted that his wife send her daughter from her first marriage to California to live with her father. It was a decision that would prove cataclysmic to Marty's half sister, who eventually died of a drug overdose, and one for which he, as a grown man, would look back and judge his father harshly. And yet the senior Teicher loved and indulged his oldest son.

Like many kids, Marty loved building rockets and blowing things up in his chemistry lab. But he also had a sensitive, musical side. Blessed with a good ear, he learned to play the guitar at a young age. As a teenager, he would write his own songs and sing them to himself, strumming softly, late at night in his room. In college he toyed with the idea of becoming a "rock 'n' roller," but in the end he chose the vocation his father had envisioned for him: As a young child, Marty had suffered an unusual allergic disorder that prompted capillaries to burst and caused massive internal bleeding. He survived, and the illness left him and his family in awe of medical doctors and the miracles they could accomplish. By 1981, he had earned not only a PhD in developmental psychology from Johns Hopkins but an MD from Yale Medical School. He married Bev, his college sweetheart, when they were both in graduate school. She was a biochemistry doctoral candidate, also at Johns Hopkins, as bright and competitive as Marty, and determined to have both a family and a career. When Teicher embarked on his psychiatric residency at McLean, he was the father of a baby boy. But by the time his second child arrived, Teicher's full-speed-ahead style had hit a speed bump. His marriage was suffering. His wife felt that he cared more about his patients and his career than he did about his family. Teicher traced the strain between them back to the time his wife had a minor car accident while he was on call at the hospital. Their son was in the backseat, and even though neither she nor the baby was injured in the collision, Bev had been seriously rattled. She had called Marty at the hospital and asked him to come home. He did manage to find someone to cover for him, but he had felt he should go back to the hospital after a few hours. Bev had never forgiven him.

WHEN CINDY MCGREENERY buzzed Marty that day with the news that a fellow psychiatrist wanted to talk to him about Prozac, he asked, "Are you sure this one is for real?" Cindy said yes. Dr. Allen Sandler was a psychiatrist practicing in Washington, D.C.

"Okay, put him through."

Sandler sounded distressed as he told Teicher about his patient, a prominent forty-nine-year-old attorney in Washington, D.C., who was depressed but had never been suicidal. Five or six days after starting Prozac, the man jumped off a bridge and killed himself. Sandler said he had just read Teicher's article in the *American Journal of Psychiatry* and had made the connection between his patient's death and the drug he had prescribed for him. He said he felt deeply guilty and wished that he had known about this side effect before prescribing Prozac.

The man's estate, Sandler went on, was now tied up in probate because he had not executed a will. As a result, his wife was having a terrible time making ends meet. She was thinking of suing Lilly, he said. Would it be possible for Teicher to talk to her and the attorney she had retained—as a professional favor?

Teicher groaned inwardly. Until now, he had resisted getting involved in any legal action against Lilly. But this case did sound horrendous. And since the publication of their Prozac paper, he and his colleagues had come across more patients who had become agitated and preoccupied with suicide after taking the drug. Several patients had turned uncharacteristically aggressive while on Prozac; some began mutilating themselves. In a follow-up article that Teicher and his colleagues would publish in 1993, they cited the case of one woman, with no prior history of depression, who began cutting herself after taking a high dose of Prozac. Her self-mutilation was so "incessant" that it eventually required plastic surgery, the McLean authors wrote. After this patient was taken off Prozac, her self-destructive behavior and suicidal thoughts disappeared.

For its part, Lilly dismissed the McLean researchers' findings as completely unfounded. In the month before the 1990 case report was published, the drug company had flown two of its top scientists to Boston to show Teicher and Cole computer printouts of clinical trial data on three thousand patients. The results, they insisted, showed no correlation between Prozac and an increased risk of suicidal thoughts or behavior. But based on what he was hearing from colleagues and patients themselves, Teicher was beginning to believe the link between Prozac and suicidality was not as rare as he had originally thought. He was also starting to question Lilly's sincerity in ferreting out the truth about its popular new drug. He and colleagues had asked the drug company for a grant to do a more thorough prospective study that would compare

[33]

patients on Prozac with those taking a placebo pill. Teicher was eager to do the kind of rigorous research that could put to rest criticisms that his original case report was anecdotal and thus not scientifically sound. But Lilly declined to fund the study. So, as it turned out, did the American Association of Suicidology, a nonprofit group that underwrote research to understand and prevent suicide, and the National Alliance for Research on Schizophrenia and Affective Disorder, a private organization that also funded research. Both groups received substantial money from the pharmaceutical industry, but that was probably not the only reason they were reluctant to fund a controlled trial that would examine Prozac's safety in a larger population. Such a study would be extremely expensive and time-consuming, and many psychiatrists just didn't see the need. They believed in Prozac: they had seen with their own eyes the way it worked to lift the mood of some of their most severely depressed patients, people who had not been helped by the older antidepressants. Teicher himself still believed that Prozac had a place in his medicinal tool kit. His coauthor Jonathan Cole liked to tease the younger man by saying that he was going to hire a balloon to fly over Boston with a trailer that read MARTY TEICHER STILL PRESCRIBES PROZAC.

"Okay," Teicher told Allen Sandler on the other end of the phone. "I'll talk to them."

THE MORNING OF the FDA meeting in Rockville, Maryland, Teicher walked from his hotel to the conference hall with the eminent British researcher Stuart Montgomery. It was a warm, sunny day, and the two men strolled past well-groomed green lawns and a large library with an impressive marble facade. When they arrived at the Parklawn Building, the squat concrete facility that served as the FDA's headquarters, security was unusually tight. With all the publicity over the Scientologists' aggressive campaign and the media backlash against them, FDA officials feared that things might get out of hand. All the attendees were required to walk through a metal detector and present their IDs. While there were only a handful of demonstrators outside with signs that read PROZAC KILLS, it was clear the FDA was leaving nothing to chance.

The hall where the meeting would take place was huge. In the front of the room, Teicher and the other consultants sat at one wood-grained vinyl table, along with most members of the Psychopharmacological Drugs Advisory Committee. At another table presided a number of top FDA officials and the chair of the advisory panel, Dr. Daniel Casey, a psychiatrist with the Veterans Administration Medical Center and Oregon Health and Science University in Portland, Oregon.

Casey was wearing a bulletproof vest.

Fanning out from the tables on both sides were more chairs in a bleacherlike arrangement. To Teicher's left huddled the lawyers and representatives from Lilly and other pharmaceutical companies, dressed almost identically in dark suits and crisp white shirts. To his right were more FDA officials and government scientists. Facing the conference tables were long rows of chairs for the public; tall microphones had been set up at the front of each aisle.

Dozens of people had flown in to testify from as far away as Arizona, California, Florida, and even France. Teicher found himself moved, as speaker after speaker told devastating tales of loved ones who had killed themselves. Lee Ann Westover, the wife of the pop singer Del Shannon, recounted how her husband suddenly became agitated and sleepless after being prescribed Prozac for stress. "I want you to know suicide was totally out of character for my husband," she told the committee. Yet Del Shannon killed himself on February 8, 1990. Another woman, Sally Barrett, told how her seventeen-year-old daughter had shot herself to death after taking Prozac. A man by the name of Tucker Money-maker, of Halifax, Virginia, said his wife, a churchgoing Cub Scout leader, had killed both of their sons after she was prescribed Prozac for "nerves." She shot herself as well and "is now in jail for murder," Moneymaker said.

The testimony Teicher would remember most vividly involved a case he already knew something about. He had been interviewed by the FBI because the suspect in this murder-suicide had been taking Prozac and the FBI wanted to know if he thought the drug could have been a factor. The suspect's mother, a woman in her fifties, certainly thought so. In a halting French accent amplified by the microphone, Mrs. Richardson recounted how her son, a promising musician in his early twenties who managed a family-owned hotel on the French Riviera, had come home to the United States at Christmas complaining of headaches and low energy. His physician prescribed Prozac. A month after he returned to France, Mrs. Richardson said, she heard from a musician friend of his that her son wouldn't open his door to the cleaning lady. The cleaner had heard the young man singing opera at the top of his lungs and talking nonsense. "I sent him a telegram to call home immediately. The next day I called back and demanded they break into his apartment."

Mrs. Richardson had gone over her allotted four minutes, and Casey interrupted her, telling her to wrap up in the next few seconds. She began sobbing. Her son, she said, had been found dead in his apartment with a young woman friend of his. She had been stabbed to death, and he had apparently killed himself with the same knife. "His hand was completely severed on the bed. There was a knife wound on his neck, cuts all over his body; the last blow was through his eye socket that pierced his brain. He died on the floor with the kitchen knife beside him."

Mrs. Richardson had more to say, but her microphone was abruptly cut off. Ten or eleven more speakers came forward after her, and then finally Casey called a brief recess. It was time for the "scientific" part of the meeting. Dr. Paul Leber, director of the FDA's Division of Neuropharmacological Drug Products, led off. He stressed that the evidence to date from clinical trials—the only assessments "deemed reliable in the scientific community"—did not indicate an increased risk of suicidal thoughts, acts, or other violent behaviors from Prozac. The emphasis, Teicher thought wryly, was on the word "reliable," Leber having dismissed all of the anecdotal testimony with one sweep of his tongue.

Teicher suspected that Leber had already made up his mind that the link between Prozac and suicidal behavior was a chimera, a delusion on the part of all the preceding speakers, who must have confused a natural worsening of depression with the effects of a new drug. Leber's words were judicious, but the FDA official made it clear that he didn't support stronger warnings on the drug's label about its possible suicide risks. "It is very difficult to tell, from where we sit, what more needs to be done at the present time," Leber said.

Leber's attitude infuriated Teicher. He didn't understand why the FDA official, a respected psychiatrist from New York University, was being so closed-minded. It would take the distance of time for Teicher to understand what had happened that day. By then, a flood of lawsuits against Eli Lilly would force the disclosure of internal company memos from 1990. The Lilly corporate memos called Leber "our defender" and noted that "Lilly and FDA are working together on the suicide issue." Teicher didn't want to believe that Leber was in bed with the pharmaceutical industry; in all likelihood, Leber simply shared the concern of many psychiatrists that depressed patients might be scared off lifesaving drugs by publicity about their link to suicide. That afternoon, Leber concluded his remarks by saying that if a stronger warning was put on Prozac's label, "the result might cause overall injury to public health."

Two other FDA officials voiced similar concerns. And then came the pièce de résistance: a massive, two-hour-long presentation by scientists speaking on behalf of Eli Lilly. Dr. Jan Fawcett, an expert on suicide from Rush–Presbyterian–St. Luke's Medical Center in Chicago, talked about the incidence of suicide and the woeful undertreatment of depression in the United States. Dr. Charles Nemeroff, a psychiatrist from Emory University School of Medicine, gave what Teicher would remember as an elegant presentation, complete with detailed slides, on the research to date on Prozac and other SSRIs. Nemeroff dismissed Teicher's case study and a more recent finding of unexpected suicidal behavior among six adolescents on Prozac as being tainted by complicating factors.

Nemeroff concluded that "there is simply no scientific evidence whatsoever . . . that has established a cause-and-effect relationship between antidepressant therapy of any class and suicidal acts or ideation."

Nemeroff's words were echoed by Gary Tollefson, a Lilly scientist who summarized what he said were the results of the drug company's controlled clinical trials of Prozac in the United States and abroad. Using an impressive array of slides, Tollefson showed data culled from trials with fifty-six hundred adult patients who had been randomized into three groups: Prozac, placebo, and an older tricyclic antidepressant. The data, he concluded, showed no statistically significant difference between Prozac and placebo in the rate of suicidal acts or thoughts. Striking a chord with Leber and many of the other psychiatrists in the room, Tollefson concluded, "It is our feeling that the major public health concern relative to suicidality and depression is the current stigma, underrecognition and undertreatment of a very serious disease." In other words, it was not Prozac the FDA should be concerned about, but the legions of untreated Americans with depression.

As Teicher watched Tollefson throw up slide after detailed slide, it struck him that the Lilly scientist had neglected to mention what he himself saw as a major flaw in the Prozac trials: it was very difficult to pick up suicidal side effects because the measurement used — the Hamilton depression scale — wasn't sensitive enough to differentiate between occasional fleeting suicidal thoughts and constant preoccupation with killing oneself. Only one question on the Hamilton scale, question 3, asked about suicidal thoughts, and question 4 inquired about actual suicide attempts. During the discussion period a little later, Teicher saw an opportunity to make that point. He noted that one patient he knew of in the Lilly-sponsored trial had "started out with a three because she had some very, very mild suicidal thought." "Then," he said, "during the course of treatment [with Prozac, her suicidal thoughts] became obsessive and unrelenting but [she] still scored a three; it did not go to four [the code for an actual suicide attempt]." So researchers using the Hamilton scale may simply not have picked up many instances of suicidal thoughts and behaviors short of actual suicide attempts. "The Hamilton item itself . . . is a very coarse instrument," Teicher concluded. "That may be a problem in really interpreting those data."

Tollefson dismissed that idea. He noted that the Lilly researchers had also looked at other indices of depression, and none of them showed any "deviant results." Before Teicher could respond, Leber jumped in and changed the topic.

Only later would Teicher discover that Tollefson had also omitted from his talk that day information that would have been even more damaging to Lilly's defense of Prozac: One of the company's international clinical trials had indeed shown an increased risk of suicidal acts among patients taking Prozac (as compared to placebo). After seeing this data in 1984, the German regulatory authorities had declined to approve the drug's use. (When Prozac was finally approved in Germany six years later, it came with a clear warning that it could cause problems and that it might be necessary for physicians to coadminister a sedative to prevent the agitation and suicidal behaviors sometimes caused by the SSRI.)

Teicher understood that Eli Lilly had a lot riding on the advisory panel's decision that day. But he had no idea how much. No one did, not even Lilly. How could anyone predict that Prozac would soon be one of the bestselling drugs in pharmacological history? By the end of the decade, the drug would inspire several books, a *Newsweek* cover story, even lyrics to a song; and it would reap Eli Lilly annual sales of $2.6 billion. Lilly was not the only company that stood to benefit from the FDA's support that day. Zoloft, an SSRI manufactured by Pfizer, was on the verge of being approved by the FDA. (The federal agency would give Zoloft the green light in December 1991.) SmithKline Beecham (the company that later became GlaxoSmithKline when it merged with Glaxo Wellcome) had already submitted its application for Paxil, and the FDA would approve that too, in late December 1992. Pfizer and SmithKline thus had a vested interest in Prozac's surviving its first serious challenge.

Late in the day, there was one effort to turn the tide. Dr. Ida Hellander, a young physician from the Public Citizen Health Research Group who had been invited as a consultant, spoke up. She said she was very disappointed that the panel had not heard much from the three researchers—Teicher, William Wirshing of Los Angeles, and Robert King of Yale, who had reported the most cases linking Prozac and suicidal thoughts and behavior. Wirshing and King had not been invited to the hearing. But, Hellander continued, "Teicher is here and I would really appreciate it if he could have a few moments to talk."

Five minutes later, Casey turned the mike over to Teicher, who proceeded to talk about possible mechanisms that might propel patients on Prozac into a state of suicidal preoccupation. Referring to his published case study, Teicher explained, "The reason why I believed that we were dealing with a drug-emergent effect is because the symptomatology that [patients] developed during the time they were on fluoxetine was unlike anything they had experienced prior to or following—"

Casey interrupted him, saying that Teicher had digressed from the first question before the committee: whether there was evidence to support a conclusion that antidepressant drugs cause the emergence of suicidal and violent behaviors. "You are expanding onto item two [whether a particular drug posed a greater risk than others] and I would like to be sure that we stay focused on question one. I am going to ask for a vote of the committee. Do you have some more to say?"

Teicher could tell that Casey wanted him to stop talking. But he wasn't quite finished. There was too much at stake here. He proceeded to talk about a reanalysis he had just completed, which showed that patients on Prozac were three times more likely to have suicidal thoughts than those who were not. This time, it was Paul Leber who interrupted.

"Again, maybe it would be useful if you would say precisely where these data that show an excess risk for fluoxetine actually are cited or published," the FDA official said. Was there a hint of sarcasm in his voice?

"I will be happy to show you," Teicher responded. "May I show you a couple of slides?"

"I would rather not . . . ," Casey responded. When Teicher tried to explain that he was talking about published data, the panel chair shook his head.

"Let us stick with question number one," he said, shutting Teicher off. Casey went on to say that in his opinion, there was no credible evidence to support a conclusion that antidepressant drugs caused the emergence of suicidal thoughts or violent behaviors. Casey then called for a vote, and in a show of hands, the advisory panel unanimously agreed with him. The committee next discussed whether they should advise the FDA to put a stronger warning on Prozac. The drug's label, as Leber had noted, already warned that depression carries with it the risk of suicide and that great care must be taken to monitor patients closely. Leber made it clear that the FDA did not think a stronger warning was warranted. And the committee agreed, voting against a more explicit warning in a split 6–3 vote.

Teicher would recall his experience that day as frustrating and somewhat surreal. Why had he not been allowed to throw up a few slides, when each of the scientists speaking on behalf of Lilly had been permitted to present numerous slides?

An academician far removed from the shark tank of Washington politics, Teicher had no idea that powerful forces were at work in support of the pharmaceutical industry. By the fall of 1991, the FDA was under enormous pressure to expedite the approval of new drugs. AIDS activists were one group that had been demonstrating in Washington to fast-track the approval of new HIV-fighting drugs like AZT. Yet the FDA, having seen its regulatory budget slashed by the Reagan administration and then by the first Bush presidency, no longer had the staffing power to do the kind of thorough vetting of new drugs it had once been known for.

Paul Leber himself had acknowledged those pressures in calling for the approval of Zoloft for use in treating adult depression. In two memos, one in August 1991 (before the FDA hearing on Prozac) and a second in December 1991, Leber acknowledged that the clinical evidence of Zoloft's effectiveness was weak. In an August 26, 1991, memo, he wrote that "the evidence marshaled to support sertraline's efficacy as an antidepressant is not as consistent or robust as one might prefer it to be." In a memo a few months later, Leber noted that several European regulatory authorities had not been willing to approve Zoloft (the brand name for sertraline) because of the "lack of robustness" in comprehensive clinical studies of the drug. Two placebo-controlled studies of the drug, one in the United States and one in the United Kingdom, found no difference between placebo- and Zoloft-treated patients. But "given the perceived urgency" for "expediting the public's access to new potentially promising drugs," Leber argued that Pfizer's application for Zoloft must be approved. And so it was, in the waning days of 1991. (In 2003, Zoloft would become the world's top-selling antidepressant, with annual sales of $3.4 billion.)

In an effort to respond to the growing political pressure, the FDA also agreed to a new arrangement whereby pharmaceutical companies would pay the federal agency dues so it could hire more drug reviewers and approve drug applications faster. These dues, which came directly from the pharmaceutical industry, were called "user fees," in acknowledgment of the fact that the drug companies were essentially the users of the FDA's drug approval services. In 1992, Congress passed legislation legitimizing this arrangement: the so-named Prescription Drug User Fee Act

(PDUFA). The idea behind this law was to ease the burden on American taxpayers by requiring the beneficiaries of new drug reviews—that is, the drug companies—to help fund the cost of such reviews. The drugmakers, though, refused to allow their money to pay for the routine monitoring of drugs' safety once the medicines were on the market. As a result, the divisions within the FDA charged with ensuring the safety of drugs and medical devices began to shrink in importance. And as the amount of funding from the pharmaceutical industry for new drug reviews increased year after year—in the face of declining financial support from Congress—the role of the FDA underwent a not-so-subtle change. By the end of the 1990s, top FDA officials were referring to the pharmaceutical industry (not the American public) as their clients or partners. Big Pharma, after all, was paying the bills. The FDA's budget numbers tell the story: In 1993, the pharmaceutical industry's $8.9 million in user-fee money accounted for just 7 percent of the FDA's drug review budget. By 2004, the industry's allocation of $232 million in user fees represented 53 percent of the agency's entire drug review budget. Many public health advocates believe that the Prescription Drug User Fee Act ultimately ended up making the nation's preeminent health agency beholden to the very industry it was supposed to regulate.

FDA officials, however, would argue that they had no choice. By the mid-1990s, political pressure on the nation's premier public health agency had only intensified. Conservative forces led by Newt Gingrich, the Republican Speaker of the House, were pushing to dismantle the very mandate of the FDA to oversee the approval of new drugs. Pharmaceutical and tobacco companies supplied millions of dollars to fund a promotional campaign that argued that the FDA's plodding pace in approving new drugs was hurting public health. In 1996, Republican lawmakers proposed legislation that would have allowed companies to market their products without agency review, essentially gutting the FDA's oversight authority. The FDA was ultimately able to deflect this attack, but only by showing that it had significantly sped up its drug approval process. By the end of the millennium, the agency would succeed in cutting drug approval times from a peak of twenty-seven months to approximately twelve months.

That sprint came with a price tag. A flood of questionable drugs was unleashed onto the market, many of which—like the diabetes drug Rezulin, the diet drugs Redux and Meridia, and, of course, Vioxx— would later have to be recalled.

ON THAT FINE autumn day in Rockville, Maryland, in 1991, the FDA's expert advisory panel seemed far less worried about questionable drugs than about depriving patients of a promising new treatment for depression. And indeed, the press took the panel's inaction as a ringing endorsement of Prozac and its SSRI analogues. Headlines in the nation's papers at the time say it all: FDA PANEL FINDS NO HARD EVIDENCE THAT PROZAC CAUSES VIOLENCE, PANEL FINDS LILLY'S PROZAC IS NOT LINKED TO SUICIDES, and finally, LILLY REPORTS RECORD SALES AND EARNINGS FOR THIRD QUARTER.

A few muckraking journalists would eventually point out that of the nine committee members on the FDA's "blue ribbon" advisory panel, five had financial ties to the pharmaceutical industry, which required the FDA to "waive" its own standards regarding conflicts of interest. Four of the six consultants also required conflict-of-interest waivers. One of the committee members, Dr. David Dunner of the University of Washington in Seattle, had been lead investigator for Lilly in one of the four original studies that Lilly submitted to the FDA to win approval for Prozac. Dunner, Jan Fawcett, and Charles Nemeroff—the scientist who spoke so eloquently on behalf of Lilly—also had lucrative consulting arrangements with the drug company. Nemeroff even owned stock in Lilly.

The waivers these scientists were granted would become standard operating procedure for the FDA in the decade ahead. In the fall of 1991, Teicher himself required a waiver to participate in the FDA meeting. Earlier that spring, he had received an unexpected phone call from

James Young, an executive with the Boston-based biotech start-up Sepracor, which was studying the two isomers of fluoxetine. Isomers are compounds that are mirror images of each other; they have the same molecular structure, but the atoms are arranged in a slightly different three-dimensional form, as if one compound were left-handed and the other right-handed. Prozac itself was a mixture of both of its isomers, known as R– and S+. Because the original mixture of these two compounds did not dissolve easily, Lilly's researchers had reformulated it as a chloride salt. As Young explained in that phone call, Sepracor was hoping that a compound made of only one of fluoxetine's isomers might have fewer side effects than Prozac and thus be a safer alternative. Young was interested in talking to Teicher because the McLean researcher had just coauthored a paper on the isomers of another drug. Teicher's lab was also known for its capability in testing the toxicity of potential drug compounds on animals (specifically rats).

Teicher was just beginning to work with Sepracor in the fall of 1991. He had not yet received any money from the biotech, but he wanted to be completely aboveboard with the FDA. He felt it was the right thing to do. And in fact, the Sepracor contract would eventually prove to be a lucrative source of income for Teicher and his lab, one of the few bright spots in a decade marred by misfortune. Indeed, it would be easy to cast Marty Teicher's snubbing at the FDA hearing on Prozac as the beginning of his personal and professional travails.

When the hearing finally ended at 5:40 p.m., Teicher hoped to walk back to his hotel with Stuart Montgomery and discuss the day's events with him. But Montgomery was deep in conversation with the panel chair Dan Casey and didn't seem to notice Teicher as he waited patiently to one side. Finally he struck out on his own. As he emerged from Parklawn to a still-clear sky that evening, he felt disconsolate and adrift. He was too preoccupied to take note of how quiet and peaceful the grounds had become. The Scientology demonstrators had long since decamped.

# 5. Rose Firestein's Big Gamble:
## Suing the Pharmaceutical Industry, June 2004

Every time Rose Firestein emerged from the Wall Street subway stop, the devastation took her breath away. Where once the towers of the World Trade Center had crowded out the sky, a giant hole in the earth now greeted her. Firestein had joined the New York attorney general's staff nine months after the planes flew into the World Trade Center, and she'd heard all the stories: How her colleagues had rushed from the building when they saw the flames shoot out of the North Tower. How Eliot Spitzer had barely made it down from the twenty-fifth floor before the towers collapsed. The crusading attorney general of New York was forced to run for his life, pursued by a choking wave of dust and debris. When Spitzer finally made it to the governor's office in Midtown Manhattan, tired and covered in ash, Governor George Pataki was so glad to see him, he gave the attorney general a big hug.

The building where Spitzer and Firestein worked, a granite fortress known as the Equitable, was only three blocks away from Firestein's subway stop (and Ground Zero). But Firestein found she had to navigate the journey with care, sweeping her white cane in a wide arc to search out those unexpected dips in the sidewalk, the sunken sewer holes that pockmarked every block of Lower Manhattan. The cane also served as a warning sign to other pedestrians to keep their distance from the small hazel-eyed woman with hair the white blond color of corn silk.

Firestein had lost much of her eyesight three years earlier during a trip to her childhood home in South Bend, Indiana. Her mother was seriously ill, and Rose and her siblings had decided it was time to sell the house and move the frail older woman to an assisted-living facility. Together, Rose and her younger sister, who lived nearby, settled their mother in the place where she was to spend the last four years of her life. Firestein then began the tedious job of readying her childhood home for sale. One evening at dusk, she was driving back to the house after having visited her mother when suddenly everything turned blurry. She could barely see. In a panic, Firestein pulled over to the side of the road and stopped the car. Everything in her field of vision was wavy except for one or two small vertical stripes, which constantly moved around. She sat there for a long time, trying to quiet her racing heartbeat. Something terrible had just happened, but she didn't know what. After a while, she slowly drove the rest of the way home, praying there were no reckless drivers on the road that night.

The next day, Firestein flew home and went to see her eye surgeon. He took one look at her eyes and hustled her into a hospital operating room for surgery. The retinas in both her eyes had partially peeled off, and the surgeon worked desperately to reattach them. As he later explained, the retinal detachment was a by-product of diabetic retinopathy (Firestein, like her father, had type 2 diabetes). She was sent home with both eyes covered in gauze.

The operation didn't take. Firestein went back to work, although she could barely read and had to write her legal briefs in two-inch-high letters, a few words to a page. A month or so later, the surgeon operated again. And again. In all, Firestein's doctor would perform ten surgeries in an effort to save at least some of her vision.

As FIRESTEIN TURNED up Broadway on an overcast morning in late June 2004, she tried hard to focus on the terrain in front of her. In a few hours, she and her colleagues in the Consumer Frauds and Protection Bureau would be sitting down for the first time with attorneys for GlaxoSmithKline. It had been almost a month since the New York State attorney general's office had filed its groundbreaking civil suit against the London-based pharmaceutical company, and today's meeting was pivotal. Firestein would be playing a lead role. The lawsuit had been her idea, her baby. Over the past eighteen months, Firestein had spent countless hours poring over documents, searching the Web for clues, and talking to experts who understood the profit-driven jungle of drug research.

The resulting lawsuit accused GlaxoSmithKline of committing "repeated and persistent" fraud by hiding from the public the results of several negative studies about Paxil, one of its bestselling drugs. Not surprisingly, the lawsuit attracted a burst of publicity when it was filed on June 2, 2004. The press coverage spotlighted what many said was a widespread practice in the pharmaceutical industry of disclosing only the results of positive studies in order to boost the sales of new drugs.

Firestein's cane struck something hard and unyielding. She cursed under her breath. The police must have moved the barriers in front of 120 Broadway yet again, and she'd been too lost in thought to notice.

With no eyesight in her left eye and limited vision in her right, Firestein had long consigned to memory every step of the commute between her home in Brooklyn and her closet of an office on the third floor of the Equitable. But she was less sure of her footing as one of the newest members of Eliot Spitzer's team. Firestein understood that she was something of an anomaly in the attorney general's office. While Spitzer and many of his top lieutenants hailed from law schools like Harvard, Yale, and NYU, Firestein had learned law at a state school in Indiana. She had taken classes at night, working days in Xerox's billing office to pay her own bills. Worse, she had the dubious distinction of being legally blind, although the AG's office hadn't known that when it hired her. Back then, Firestein wasn't using a cane. She figured that if she ignored her disability, the attorneys who interviewed her would too. Her strategy had worked, and now Rose Firestein was sitting atop an unprecedented legal attack on the pharmaceutical industry. She was afraid it was going to blow up—in Eliot Spitzer's face. That would not be a good outcome. Spitzer was seriously considering a run for governor of New York, and the pressure on his staff to rack up legal wins was greater than ever.

IT WAS NOT as if Firestein doubted the rightness of what she was doing. She and her colleagues had been buoyed by the congratulatory phone calls that flooded in after they had filed their lawsuit against Glaxo in New York State Supreme Court. Some of these callers had been routed to Firestein, and even now the assistant attorney general could hear their voices, redolent with rage and disbelief. She had talked to parents whose children had tried to kill themselves and in a few cases had succeeded. They all asked her the same agonizing questions: How could their child have been allowed to take such a dangerous drug? Why were they not warned that Paxil could stir suicidal thoughts and behaviors in some children and adults? Who was looking out for their loved ones?

The phone calls reminded Firestein of the time she had canvassed the state of Florida on behalf of foster children who were being overmedicated on drugs like Paxil, Prozac, Zoloft, and Risperdal, an antipsychotic. At the time, Firestein had been working for Children's Rights, a nonprofit organization based in New York that provided legal counsel for vulnerable children nationwide. Children's Rights had been tapped to help out on a class action suit brought by a group of local activist attorneys against the Florida Department of Children and Families. Known as *Bonnie L.* (after the first child listed in the complaint), the lawsuit charged the Florida children's services agency with the inadequate care and treatment of foster children in its custody. Firestein's job was to help gather evidence showing that state-funded caregivers were using psychotropic drugs as chemical straitjackets to keep hard-to-manage children docile.

Her experience in Florida had opened Firestein's eyes to the sometimes disastrous effects of antidepressants on children. Even so, she found it difficult to listen to the people calling the AG's office. Firestein remembered one phone call with particular clarity. It came from a mother in Michigan whose teenage daughter had been feeling a little depressed. She'd taken the girl to her own general practitioner, who had casually written out a prescription for Paxil. Almost immediately, the girl began acting strangely; she seemed agitated and angry all the time. One afternoon, she slashed her wrists with a knife and almost bled to death. Her mother got her to the ER just in time. As she later told Firestein, "My daughter was a hairsbreadth away from death. How could something like this have been allowed to happen?"

Firestein had no easy answer for this mother or any of the people she spoke to. Not that she could have said much anyway. The case was still in litigation. She thanked the woman for calling and said she hoped the attorney general's action might bring about some needed reform, so that no other parents would have to suffer the way she had.

Privately, though, Firestein was not so sanguine. It wouldn't surprise her if GlaxoSmithKline decided to fight the case in court. From the drug company's vantage point, the stakes were high. The damage to Glaxo's reputation from fighting a high-profile case like this could be long-lasting. But settling the case also had its risks. It would mean a tacit acknowledgment that the second-largest pharmaceutical company in the world had misled the public about the safety and efficacy of one of its blockbuster drugs. If Glaxo didn't settle and then won in court, that could embarrass Spitzer at a critical time in his gubernatorial campaign. Lord knows, Firestein didn't want to do that.

Winning a spot on Spitzer's elite team had been the crowning moment in her career, something she still couldn't believe she'd achieved—and at the very same time that her doctors were counseling her to quit working. "Now that you're legally blind, you could qualify for disability," they told her. But she couldn't afford to stop working—not now that she was a breadwinner not only for herself, but for Ellie, the adopted child she and her sister were raising together. They had rescued Ellie from an orphanage in China in 1995, and although her sister had legal custody, the little girl treated Rosie, as she called her, as a second mom.

The image of Ellie made Firestein smile, and the security guard who manned the checkpoint on the Broadway side of the Equitable's vast marble lobby nodded in return. The guards knew Firestein and her white cane. After 9/11, security at the building had been beefed up considerably, and everyone who worked in the Equitable had to show a laminated identity card to the security guards stationed at the two main entrances before gaining access to the elevator banks. But when Firestein had lost her card once, they let her through anyway. They were good about things like that.

That afternoon, Firestein found herself back at the elevators, waiting for the visitors from GlaxoSmithKline. Tom Conway stood with her. Tall and ramrod thin, Conway had crisp, graying hair and a genial air. But Firestein knew that underneath his cheerful mien lay a prickly toughness, formed by decades of battling grafters, embezzlers, shoddy contractors, and the legions of other bad actors that ran afoul of New York's business laws.

When their visitors arrived, Conway led the way single file down a narrow aisle and through two locked doors into the bureau's unpretentious warren of offices. Firestein brought up the rear. The third-floor office hadn't been painted in years; its walls were a dreary government-issue gray. Dozens of cardboard boxes filled with old files were stacked in every available cranny, and the only modern piece of furniture visible was a photocopier. The consumer bureau had long been a backwater in Spitzer's high-profile shop. Most of the big news came out of his Investment Protection Bureau, which was constantly grabbing headlines in its pursuit of the banking and mutual funds industry. By contrast, the attorneys on the third floor spent most of their time going after sleazy contractors and loan sharks who preyed on unsuspecting New Yorkers. It was a mission that, while important, had pretty much kept the bureau out of the limelight—until now.

THAT AFTERNOON, WHEN Conway and Firestein finally arrived at the designated conference room with their visitors, they found Shirley Stark, an assistant attorney general and Firestein's immediate supervisor, and Joe Baker, the head of the AG's Health Care Bureau, waiting for them.

Conway, who was wearing a crisp blue shirt and navy pants, thanked the Glaxo attorneys for coming and made a joke about the drab surroundings. The conference room, which had dusty fluorescent ceiling lights and gray walls, looked like something out of a World War II interrogation room, complete with mostly empty metal bookcases stacked against the wall. The lead Glaxo attorney, whom everyone called Wick (short for Joseph Sedwick Sollers III), was a large, distinguished-looking man in his late forties with impeccably styled, graying hair. With his monogrammed cuffs and tailored suit, Wick, a partner at the national law firm of King and Spalding, looked distinctly out of place, as did Dwight Davis, who was fifty-one and also a partner at King and Spalding. Davis was wearing a respectable navy blue suit and red tie, but his attire seemed downright dowdy next to the resplendently attired Wick. The third visitor, Frank Rockhold, a senior vice president for biomedical data sciences at GlaxoSmithKline, also paled in comparison. None of the assistant AGs in the room could even remember what Rockhold looked like.

All three men sat down on one side of the conference table, their backs to the metal bookcases. Conway took his place at the end of the table farthest from the door, with Firestein next to him. Stark, a slender, dark-haired woman in her late forties, sat next to Firestein, and Baker, an affable-looking man with stylish black glasses and a receding hairline, parked himself directly across from Wick.

Conway began by talking about what the AG's office needed to see from GlaxoSmithKline in order to settle the case. The state prosecutors had already made it clear they wanted more than money on the table. Their real goal was to convince the pharmaceutical company to post the results of its clinical drug trials on a publicly available Web site. As Eliot Spitzer was fond of saying, "This case is not about money. As bad as all the Wall Street cases were, that was about money. This is about people's health, where the consequences of mischaracterizing the impact of a particular drug are dramatically more important." To prevent the kind of mischaracterization Spitzer and his team believed had occurred in the pediatric Paxil studies, they felt strongly that Glaxo should be required to post the detailed results of its clinical drug studies on a public Web site.

Smiling benignly at the visitors from GlaxoSmithKline, Conway restated that demand: there would be no settlement without a comprehensive clinical registry. He then turned to the blond-haired attorney sitting next to him and said, "Rose, you want to talk more about that?"

Firestein nodded and leaned forward. The online registry, she said, would have to include not just the results but other key data from the drug company's studies of human patients, known as clinical trials. To win FDA approval to market a drug, pharmaceutical companies first must test its safety and effectiveness in animals (usually rodents) and then determine whether the drug is safe or toxic in humans, using a small sample of healthy volunteers. They perform these Phase 2 studies to examine the drug's effects on the body's metabolism and see what kind of side effects it causes. Drug companies were required to submit their Phase 2 studies to the FDA, but they rarely published them in medical journals or otherwise made them available to the public.

The pharmaceuticals were not required to publicize any of their test results, including the large-scale clinical trials that they conducted on people to compare the effectiveness of the drug to either a sugar pill or older medicines already on the market. These Phase 3 and 4 studies had to be submitted to the FDA, of course, but the information in them was considered proprietary and the FDA rarely made the results public. So the drug companies could pick and choose which of their clinical trials to publicize and which to suppress.

But now the AG's office was demanding that GlaxoSmithKline post pertinent clinical data from all its Phase 2, Phase 3, and Phase 4 trials after a certain date on a publicly available Web site. And that wasn't all. As Firestein explained to the three men sitting across from her, the posted summaries also had to contain detailed data on adverse side effects as well as information on efficacy and other key protocols.

Rockhold, the senior VP from Glaxo, interrupted her.

"You know we can't do that," he said. "If we post that kind of detail on the Web, we won't be able to get published in the journals."

"I understand your concern," Firestein said, "but we think something can be worked out. Perhaps the data could be posted online concurrently with the study's publication in the journal."

Rockhold tightened his lips.

"Look, I want you to know that we've decided to post our registry this Friday," he said. "We've already determined what the content will be."

Firestein's mouth went dry. That was two days from now. Firestein knew that a quick posting by GlaxoSmithKline would make it harder for the AG's office to convince a judge that a truly comprehensive registry was needed. And if the case was settled without specific terms spelled out for the registry, the AG's office would have no legal standing to enforce a complete listing of all the clinical studies, those with negative results as well as those with positive. "Glaxo could easily cream the good studies and leave out the bad ones," Firestein later explained. "And if they did something that seemed reasonable on the surface, that would make it that much more difficult for a court to say they violated the law." The chance to bring real reform to an entrenched industry would be lost.

Before Firestein could open her mouth to say something, Tom Conway spoke up.

"If you post it, we'll see you in court," he said in a cold voice that carried an unmistakable challenge.

And then he stood up. Baker and Stark stood up too, and Firestein had no choice but to join them. But her insides were churning with anger and a sinking sense of despair. Firestein knew she cared too much about this case. The last time she had invested this much in a lawsuit had been in the 1980s, when, after winning that resegregation case against Tattnall County in Georgia, she and her colleagues at the Georgia Legal Services had sued the entire state. They had accused the Georgia Department of Education and school districts throughout the state of essentially the same practice: assigning black children with borderline IQs to warehouselike classes for the mentally retarded while white children with the same test scores were given specific learning disability instruction. Firestein poured everything she had into the statewide complaint, traveling all over Georgia's hinterlands to take depositions. She even camped in a tent on several occasions when she couldn't find lodging. But after all that hard work, her team lost the case in the Eleventh Circuit Court.

The defeat had broken Firestein's heart. She left Georgia and moved to New York to live with her sister in Queens, swearing never again to go into a courtroom. She took culinary lessons with the idea of becoming a chef, until one day it dawned on her that working in the restaurant business was even harder than litigating cases. Now here she was on the cusp of another monumental legal battle, and Conway was going to ruin everything with his all-or-nothing ploy. They'd never get Glaxo-SmithKline to the bargaining table again. But her boss had made his move, and she had to show a united front. Sick with disappointment and frustration, Firestein followed her three colleagues out of the room.

# 6. The Brown Connection, 1995

**D**onna Howard hung up the phone and sighed. She sat back in her chair and looked out the dirt-encrusted window of her office. Her aging Saab had been making strange noises that morning, so she had driven it directly to the Swedish Motors shop a few blocks from her office. And now the mechanic was telling her it needed a new transmission and the job would take at least three days, maybe four. That car spent more time in the garage than it did on the road! Donna glanced at her watch; it was just after 4 p.m. Maria would be home from school. Howard had left a casserole for her to put in the oven, but she knew how anxious her daughter could become when she was late.

Howard's office was in the Duncan Building, a dust-red brick edifice that was part of the sprawling Brown–Butler Hospital campus on the east side of Providence. Duncan had been built in 1846 as a mental asylum. The offices on the south side of the building had big bay windows, through which light poured in on sunny days. But on the north side, where Howard's office sat, the windows were tall and narrow, too narrow for an adult body to easily fit through. When she first came to work here, Howard had speculated to co-workers that the building had probably been designed to offer palliative care for patients at a time when real medical treatment didn't exist. The depressive patients were probably kept on the south side, where it was hoped that all that sunlight would cheer them up, while the manic patients were kept on the north side, at least until they settled down.

"I guess I just haven't settled down yet," Howard would add, almost always eliciting a laugh, particularly from people who didn't know about her own family history. And Howard would laugh too, her laugh as light and silvery as chimes. Among her colleagues at Brown, she had made no secret of the fact that Maria, her adopted daughter, had manic depression. But she had told no one of her own more recent diagnosis. Howard too suffered from bipolar disorder. In the fall of 1991, after Maria left for a boarding school in Connecticut for emotionally troubled girls, Howard felt strangely disconnected and confused, as if her brain had switched to slow. The doctor prescribed Prozac. Two months later, Donna found herself staying up all night for days at a time, her thoughts racing, her senses acutely, uncomfortably aware of every sound, every smell. Howard had had these periods before—during college, she would stay up nights to finish papers and feel extraordinarily creative and energetic for weeks at a time—but nothing this intense or disorienting. She later learned that in people who, like her, were predisposed to bipolar disorder, a sudden switch to mania was often triggered by exposure to an antidepressant. She began taking the antipsychotic Depakote to tamp down what sounded like a buzz of locusts in her brain.

Donna Howard was not the kind of person most people think of when they think of mental illness. Her colleagues saw her as a competent and levelheaded administrator. At the acute care hospital in New Bedford, she had managed a staff of thirty employees and a budget of $750,000. When her doctor diagnosed Howard with bipolar disorder, he said, "Until now, you've been a supercompetent, superresponsible person. You've been able to make your disorder work for you. But you can't do it on your own anymore. You need medication to manage this illness."

Howard had taken the assistant administrator job in Brown's psychiatry department in large part because of her and her daughter's diagnoses. She was eager to work at an institution where so much important research into the workings of the human brain was taking place.

That had been eleven months ago. Now it was September 1995, and she was desperate to leave Brown. She had already started casting around for another job. But first she needed a ride home. Who did she know who lived out her way? Howard commuted an hour every day from one of the forgotten coastal towns in southeastern Massachusetts whose residents enjoyed the same mild Gulf Stream waters as Falmouth and Martha's Vineyard, but at considerably cheaper real estate prices.

As she gazed out the window of her office in Duncan, Howard remembered what one of her co-workers had told her the other day: Alice Tangredi-Hannon, Brown's director of research administration, lived in Marion, an upscale coastal town near hers. Howard had never met the woman, but the researchers and support staff at Brown lived in fear of her. Tangredi-Hannon held the power of life and death over their research projects. It was her job to ensure that the university's researchers lived up to the letter and spirit of the informed consent rules for research involving human subjects. And she was vigilant in her duties. Howard had seen a few of the terse memos Tangredi-Hannon fired at Dr. Martin Keller, the head of Brown's psychiatry department. In one memo, in which the research director was responding to notice of a suicide attempt by a teenage patient enrolled in one of Keller's clinical trials, her tone bordered on scolding.

> We are in receipt of your memo . . . outlining an adverse event
> which took place on January 19, 1995. Please provide us with a
> copy of the full written summary of the adverse experience that
> you are required to submit to the [pharmaceutical] sponsor . . . The
> above referenced memo did not include your signature. Please sign
> any future correspondence to our office."

The woman couldn't be that bad, Howard decided, if she was willing to take on Marty K. She looked up Tangredi-Hannon's extension and dialed it. To her surprise, the administrator picked up the phone herself and sounded quite pleasant. After hearing where Howard lived, she said, "I'd be happy to give you a ride home."

"Are you sure? I don't want to impose—," Howard began. The confident voice on the other end of the phone cut her off.

"No imposition at all! It's right on my way home."

TANGREDI-HANNON KEPT her waiting only a few minutes. She pulled up to the front entrance of Duncan in a silver Infiniti. It was after five and the windows of the campus buildings glowed with the sun's dying brilliance. It was the time of day Howard loved best, knowing she was on her way home to Maria. Her daughter, who had left boarding school and was living at home again, was not doing very well. For a while, Maria had responded to lithium and then to Depakote. But Maria was what is known in the field as medication refractory: she might respond to a new drug for three to six months, but then it almost invariably stopped working. By the time she turned eighteen, Maria had run through almost every antidepressant and mood stabilizer on the market, and that summer, despite her mother's misgivings, she underwent seven electroconvulsive therapy (ECT) treatments. The ECT worked for several months, but by December of that year, her symptoms had roared back. Her doctor then started Maria on a powerful new mood stabilizer known as Clozaril, which seemed to work. She was still taking Clozaril when her mother's Saab developed its hiccups.

Howard had envisioned Tangredi-Hannon as a tall, stern woman dressed in a dark suit, her hair caught in a tight bun. Instead, a small woman with short brown hair and expressive eyes waved her into the plush leather passenger seat. As Tangredi-Hannon skillfully negotiated the curves of Route 195 high above Providence, she wasted no time on chitchat.

"God, you work for Marty Keller. That can't be easy," she said.

Howard laughed. She felt immediately comfortable with this woman.

"Oh, I hardly ever see him," she said. "I've only met with him twice."

Keller enjoyed an elegantly updated suite of offices in the Sawyer Building, a Victorian brick building across campus from the psychiatry department's more dilapidated research quarters in Duncan. He communicated with Howard and the other support staff mostly by fax. It was not uncommon for Peg Ciarlone, his secretary, and Howard to fax documents back and forth twenty, thirty times a day. But even in absentia, Keller's presence cast a huge shadow on his research staff.

DR. MARTIN KELLER had come to Brown in 1989 from Massachusetts General Hospital and Harvard Medical School, where he had a reputation for pulling in substantial grant money for multisite research studies. As head of psychiatry at Brown, Keller was tasked with building an academic research department where none had existed before. That meant bringing together often-feuding research groups from the six Rhode Island hospitals affiliated with the university's school of medicine. By the time Howard joined his staff in the fall of 1994, Keller had largely succeeded in his mission—with a few bumps along the way. He had assembled a drug research empire that rivaled anything his former Harvard colleagues could boast of, bringing in millions of dollars each year from federal research institutes and pharmaceutical companies to study mental illness and promising drug treatments. While Keller's single-minded focus on raising money endeared him to the dean of Brown's medical school and other university officials, the way he conducted business did not sit so well with some of his colleagues. A few years earlier, Jonathan Cole, then head of psychopharmacology for McLean Hospital, had sat in on a committee chaired by Keller, who was at Brown by then. Keller was principal investigator of a $1.4 million Harvard-Brown study funded by the Upjohn Company to study people who had been diagnosed with anxiety at twelve medical centers and see how they did, on and off certain medications. Cole took an instant dislike to the way Keller presided over the committee meetings. As the senior McLean psychiatrist would later recall, Keller ran the meetings "like an emperor." He would give orders and then zip off in the middle of the meeting to take phone calls. "He raised a hell of a lot of money from Upjohn and was happy to plan the study, but he didn't seem particularly interested in making sure it went all right," Cole said.

A few years later, Howard saw her boss display the same kind of cavalier behavior toward his purported colleagues. In June 1995, the research heads from the six hospitals affiliated with the psychiatry department gathered one afternoon to pick the winners of Brown's annual internal competition for research grants. The meeting was the culmination of a three-month-long process to decide which research proposals should receive coveted seed money from the university and its affiliated hospitals, grants ranging from $25,000 to $100,000. The psychiatric chiefs from Butler, Rhode Island, Bradley, and Miriam hospitals, along with other senior researchers in the department, had devoted hours to weighing the fifty applications, with the understanding that the ten top-ranked proposals would receive funding. As Keller's liaison to the group, Howard sat in on every one of those meetings, and it had fallen to her to submit the top-ranked proposals to Keller, by fax of course. As Brown's chief of psychiatry, he held the purse strings for almost all the research conducted at Brown and its affiliates. He thus wielded the final vote on grants. Yet he had not attended a single meeting, even though the group, known as ECOR (Executive Committee on Research), met every few weeks in a small conference room adjoining his office suite.

On this day, however, Keller made an appearance. As the group sat chatting among themselves, he swept in, wearing an exquisitely tailored suit. He flung the faxed list of proposals across the conference table and, striding over to the whiteboard, started scrawling down researchers' names. Howard recognized several of these new names: they were researchers at Butler Hospital, where Keller was psychiatric chief. None of them had been included in the committee's top-ranked list. She also noticed that the researcher whose proposal the group had ranked number one was not even on Keller's list.

At first, a baffled silence permeated the room, and then one of the research heads piped up.

"I don't understand. You haven't included Gary Epstein's proposal," said Ron Seifer, research chief at Bradley Hospital. Seifer was referring to the most favored proposal, which belonged to a young researcher at the Veterans Administration who was doing creative work in molecular genetics.

Charlie Marotta, a neuroscientist and the director of the Psychiatric Research Division at Brown, nodded. "Epstein is doing some very important research," he said. "He's putting in unbelievably long hours."

"We're not going to fund anyone from the VA," Keller responded. "The VA's got its own money."

Dave Abrams, the research head at Miriam, one of the Brown-affiliated hospitals, spoke up next. He was a compact British-born scientist with a nationally recognized reputation in behavioral research. In 2004, he would leave Brown to become the director of the Office of Behavioral and Social Sciences Research for the National Institutes of Health.

"I don't see Bess Marcus's name on the board," Abrams said, referring to another young researcher who worked with him at Miriam Hospital and also ranked in the top ten. "She's doing some very valuable research on the preventative benefits of physical activity."

Keller stopped writing on the board. He turned around.

"Look, the dollars have got to be divided up proportionately to the hospitals that put money into the pool," he said. "I realize this is different from how we've done it before, but this is the way it's going to be from now on."

The research chiefs looked at one another. Finally Abrams said, "It would have been helpful if we had known this before we spent all our time rating the candidates according to merit. This was a very labor-intensive process."

Keller shrugged. "I realize that," he said. "But the rules have changed."

A few minutes later, he left the room.

In the silence that followed, Howard could feel the anger rising among the men around the table. They waited until Keller's footsteps had receded.

"We really got screwed over here," Seifer said.

Marotta, who had worked with Keller at Harvard, jerked his head in agreement.

"If I had known this, I would have advised my people to not even apply," he said bitterly. "This is just the way it was at Harvard."

Now, GLANCING AT the woman steering the car beside her, Howard wondered how much Alice Tangredi-Hannon knew about the enmity between Keller and the hospital chiefs. Probably a good deal. She struck Howard as politically savvy. As the decaying textile mills of New Bedford flashed by, Tangredi-Hannon chattered about the house she and her husband had just finished building in Marion. It was the dream getaway that they had worked hard toward all their lives.

"We don't have kids," she said, as if to explain why she was spending so much money on a house. "We have cats."

She paused, biting her lower lip. "Or rather, we have one cat. My Persian died last week. It was horrible!"

Howard knew exactly how her companion felt.

"I'm so sorry. It's awful to lose a pet," she said. "They're like part of your family."

Tangredi-Hannon nodded but kept her eyes on the road.

"I love cats." Howard paused, wondering what the other woman would think of her pet menagerie. "We have three cats and two dogs. Maria loves animals."

"Maria?"

"That's my daughter. I adopted her—let's see—seven years ago."

"How wonderful!" Tangredi-Hannon's voice radiated warmth. "She must bring you a lot of joy."

Howard paused. She wasn't quite ready to tell the research director about her daughter's illness and its dizzying ups and downs.

"Yes, she does," Howard said. "She's the most important thing in my life."

BEFORE HOWARD KNEW IT, they had turned off Route 6 onto the half-dirt, half-paved road that led to her house. She felt a twinge of embarrassment at how the cottage must look to Tangredi-Hannon. The roof had been patched, and the ivy, honeysuckle vines, and wild roses creeping up the sides did a good job of masking the sagging walls. But the lilies, white yarrow, and hollyhocks in the front yard looked wild and untended. One of her dogs was batting playfully with a small kitten in the sand-eroded driveway.

Tangredi-Hannon cut the engine and turned toward Howard. "Do you need a ride to work tomorrow? I'd be happy to give you one."

"Oh, that's okay. I can rent a car from the garage down the street. They give me a good rate."

Tangredi-Hannon looked appalled.

"Oh no, I can't let you do that! I enjoyed your company. I'd be happy to drive you until your car is fixed. Really."

HER FIRST FEW MONTHS at Brown, Howard had been buried beneath an avalanche of paperwork. Not only was she new to the department, but the woman she reported to, Carolyn O'Sullivan, the department administrator, had arrived only a few months before and was still trying to get a handle on things. Sometimes Howard felt as if she were on an archaeological dig, sifting through layers of reports, memos, and faxes detailing all the research Martin Keller had his hand in. There was the ongoing study of the psychobiology of depression, funded by the National Institute of Mental Health (NIMH), which Keller had landed while still at Mass General; a longitudinal study of eating disorders, also funded by the NIMH; a study of anxiety disorders, funded first by Upjohn and now NIMH; and a more recent five-year, NIMH-sponsored study of whether lithium could prevent the recurrence of manic depression in adolescents. In 1993, the pharmaceutical giant Pfizer had given Keller more than $1 million to coordinate a six-year, multicenter study of Zoloft in treating chronic depression. And then there was the clinical trial funded by another drugmaker, SmithKline Beecham, to compare the effectiveness of Paxil with placebo and an older tricyclic antidepressant in adolescents. As one of six sites, Brown had been awarded an initial $800,000 in 1993 for the Paxil study, and Keller was principal investigator for that one too.

Keller, it was clear, had jumped aboard the fast-moving juggernaut of drug companies eager to capitalize on the success of Prozac. After the FDA dismissed the Prozac-suicide link and approved Zoloft and Paxil in quick succession, other pharmaceuticals hurried to develop their own SSRI products. Meanwhile, the makers of Prozac, Zoloft, and Paxil, recognizing the potential for even greater market share, began positioning their drugs for use in other populations and disorders (besides depression). Lilly, Pfizer, and SmithKline Beecham all had their sights on the under-eighteen market, and by the mid-1990s, all three had embarked on what the FDA called "the gold standard" of drug research: comparative studies that randomly assigned young patients (without their knowledge) to one of two groups, with one group taking the new drug and the other taking a sugar pill or placebo. The clinical trials Marty Keller was leading on Paxil and Zoloft also randomly assigned patients to a third "blinded" group for comparison's sake: those taking imipramine, an older tricyclic antidepressant. For some new medicines, the FDA only required proof of efficacy over an older drug; but with most medications, and especially with psychoactive drugs like Prozac and Paxil, the FDA wanted proof of efficacy over placebo. The human mind, after all, is a tricky thing, and past research had revealed a surprisingly high rate of response to placebo among people with depression and other mental illnesses. Perhaps, some experts speculated, the symptoms of depression were alleviated just by virtue of being involved in an intensive clinical trial, with all the extra support and attention that such studies provide. To win FDA approval, the new drug had to work significantly better than placebo in two different randomized studies.

The federal agency would soon give drug companies another incentive to test these drugs on children and adolescents. In 1997, Congress would enact the FDA Modernization Act, which promised that drug companies conducting pediatric clinical trials would get an additional six months of patent protection from generic competition, whether or not the drugs they studied were found to be effective for use in children. Over the next decade, such extended patent exclusivity would earn the SSRI makers millions of dollars in additional revenue.

Doing such studies served another important purpose. If the results of the trials were positive, the drug companies would encourage researchers to present their findings at medical conferences and publish them in respected medical journals. This kind of publicity was priceless: it convinced many physicians that the drugs being studied were safe and effective enough to prescribe for non-FDA-approved uses. It was this very strategy that would permit drug companies like Pfizer, Lilly, GlaxoSmithKline, and Forest Labs (the maker of Celexa) to vastly extend their market share, as physicians flocked to prescribe the SSRIs for a host of off-label uses, ranging from depression in children to obsessive-compulsive disorder, generalized anxiety disorder, and social phobia. And indeed, as soon as the results were in on the Paxil trial that Keller had spearheaded, its pharmaceutical sponsor would hatch plans to submit the multisite study to one of the most prestigious medical journals around: the *Journal of the American Medical Association* (*JAMA*).

In 1995, however, Brown was still enrolling participants in the Paxil study, and Howard found herself spending more and more time in the department's dusty file room on the second floor of Duncan, reading closely as she sifted through documents and filed them away. Her file room explorations and conversations with co-workers convinced her that Keller was playing fast and loose with the protocols for the Paxil study and another clinical trial. She had noticed, for instance, some discrepancies in the documentation for the Paxil trial. Participants in such studies frequently develop adverse side effects from taking a new drug, some of them serious enough to require hospitalization. Such side effects could range from suicidal thoughts and hostile behaviors to dizziness, nausea, headaches, and chest pain. According to FDA research guidelines, research investigators had to document each and every one of these "serious adverse events"—known in the trade as SAEs—in memos to both the drug company and the research site's Institutional Review Board. And they had to make an educated guess as to whether that adverse event was caused by the drug under study.

Howard suspected that researchers on the Paxil trial were not accurately coding these adverse events. According to a trail of faxed memos, at least two adolescent patients enrolled in the Paxil trial had been yanked from the study after threatening or attempting suicide. Yet on several memos submitted to Brown's Institutional Review Board, Keller wrote that these teenage girls "withdrew during the acute phase for reasons of noncompliance." Howard wondered how the girls' suicidal behavior could be considered noncompliant. Wouldn't it be more accurate to describe their behavior as an adverse effect of the drug? Having read so much of the literature on depression herself, Howard knew that miscoding even a few suicidal patients in this kind of study could skew the results.

She had also stumbled across inconsistencies in yet another Keller-headed study. This one involved taking manic-depressive adolescents off lithium and then putting them back on it to see if the drug prevented the recurrence of their disorder. It seemed as if the researchers were having trouble recruiting and keeping teenagers in the study. No surprise there, Howard thought: what parents want their kids to be yanked off meds that are helping them? Yet the number of participants listed in the grant renewal proposal didn't seem to reflect the actual number of teenagers in the lithium study.

Howard had also unearthed copies of several invoices to the Massachusetts Department of Mental Health requesting payment for a study of chronically ill schizophrenic patients at the Corrigan Mental Health Center, a state-funded hospital in Fall River, Massachusetts. These invoices baffled her. She couldn't find any documentation for the Corrigan study itself—informed consent protocols or memos indicating who was involved in the study or how long it had been ongoing. Theo Manschreck, a schizophrenia researcher from McGill University, had arrived at Brown a few months after Howard, apparently to do research at Corrigan Mental Health Center. But the payment invoices to the Department of Mental Health in Massachusetts, which apparently had a contract with Brown for the research at Corrigan, indicated that the study had started three years earlier. From what Howard could divine, Keller first obtained $70,000 from the Massachusetts mental health agency in 1992 and slightly higher amounts each of the succeeding three years. The invoices indicated that Brown had received more than $200,000 thus far from the Commonwealth of Massachusetts for research at Corrigan Mental Health Center.

Whenever Howard asked Carolyn O'Sullivan about Corrigan, the harried administrator would say, "I don't know anything about it. Just send the invoices over to Peg."

Once, after a meeting of ECOR, when some of the hospital chiefs hung around to exchange the latest gossip, Howard had turned to one doctor and asked if he knew anything about Brown's involvement in a schizophrenia study at Corrigan. No, he said, Brown isn't affiliated with Corrigan. Another psychiatrist said much the same when she asked him about it a few weeks later. He had never heard of Corrigan Mental Health Center, he said.

By the time Howard's car broke down that Tuesday in September, she had become convinced that the psychiatry department at Brown was getting paid for research it wasn't doing. She also suspected that Keller had submitted falsified invoices to Massachusetts state officials. There were names of researchers on those invoices who Howard knew had nothing to do with a state hospital in Fall River.

Howard had discussed her concerns with several co-workers but had been advised not to say anything. The last time one of Keller's employees had spoken out—about his boss's apparent double-billing on travel expenses—the whistleblower had been demoted and moved against his will to another department at the university. An internal audit had confirmed the double-billing: Keller seemed to have made a practice of getting reimbursed by both Brown and his pharmaceutical company sponsor for the same trips. State police, who were also investigating Keller's billing practices at the time, acknowledged that Brown had uncovered evidence of overbilling by Keller that amounted to several thousand dollars. In the end, the state police investigation was dropped at the request of Brown officials, and Keller was required to refund the university just under one thousand dollars. But that didn't help the whistleblower's career at Brown. He left under a cloud soon afterward.

THE DAY AFTER her car broke down, Howard found herself standing stock-still in the middle of the file room, a bunch of loose papers gripped tightly in one hand. Realization struck her like lightning, clearing the dust ball of confusion in her mind. "I've got to tell someone about what's going on. It's wrong," she announced to the large, empty room. "I can't go on like this."

When Alice Tangredi-Hannon drove her home that afternoon, Howard waited until the research director had swung onto Route 195 toward

Fall River. And then she asked, "Do you know anything about the re-search Brown is doing at Corrigan Mental Health Center?" she asked.

The administrator shot her a sharp look.

"We don't have anything to do with Corrigan. Why?"

Howard proceeded to tell her about the invoices she had found and her suspicions. She also mentioned her concerns about the Paxil and lithium studies. Tangredi-Hannon's hands gripped the steering wheel tightly as she listened. When Howard was finished, the administrator shook her head, mouth drawn down into a grim line.

"Why am I not surprised? Listen, do me a favor. Photocopy some of those documents and bring them with you tomorrow. I'd like to take a look at them."

Howard nodded, her heart racing. In one corner of her mind, she felt tremendous relief that this highly respected administrator believed her and wanted to probe further. Surely, with Alice Tangredi-Hannon asking questions, Brown wouldn't be able to sweep things under the rug. But the inquiry could cost Howard her job. Could she trust Alice? Would Keller figure out where the university's director of research administration had obtained her information? Howard lay awake for a long time that night, thinking about what she had done.

# 7. Donna Howard Talks to the Press and Becomes a Pariah, January 1996

It was dark by the time Donna Howard pulled into her driveway, but she could see the black Lincoln Continental parked on the side of the road, an anomaly in her working-class neighborhood of beat-up pickup trucks. She knew the two men sitting inside the car were federal agents because one of them had called her earlier that day at the hospital. He said he was from the U.S. Postal Service, investigating the possibility of mail fraud. Howard didn't quite know what that meant, and she was afraid to ask. The man sounded friendly enough. Could he drop by this evening to talk to her?

Aghast that a law enforcement agent had called her at work—how did he know her number, anyway?—Donna tried to quell the queasiness surging up her throat. This was the last thing she needed right now. Thinking fast, Howard told him she had to take her daughter for a doctor's appointment and wouldn't be home until after 7 p.m.

"That's okay," the agent said. "We don't mind the late hour."

HOWARD'S COTTAGE WAS ISOLATED, a quarter mile from the nearest neighbor. When she first saw the Continental parked on the side of the road, she had to resist an impulse to turn around and drive madly away. Instead, she took a deep breath and told Maria in as light a tone as she could muster, "We've got visitors. I was expecting them."

As she emerged from her car, the two men got out of theirs. The older man looked to be in his fifties. He was heavyset and balding. When he introduced himself, Howard recognized his voice: he was the one who had called her. The other man, who was probably in his forties, was built like a football player, muscular, broad around the shoulders, with a crew cut. A Secret Service type, Howard thought shakily as she ushered the two men inside and invited them to sit down at her kitchen table. Her new puppy, Hudson, a spaniel-collie mix, barked excitedly and ran circles around the room. Maria, who was on a new medication and not feeling well, said she was going to bed. Howard walked her to her room and gave the puppy some food. Then she poured herself and the two agents some water and sat down at the table.

The men wanted to know all about the accusations leveled against Martin Keller and the Brown psychiatry department in a page-one story that I had written for the *Boston Globe* a few weeks earlier. Headlined STATE PAID SCHOOL $218,000 ON FALSELY BILLED DMH STUDY, the January 7, 1996, article described how the Massachusetts Department of Mental Health (DMH) had been paying Brown's psychiatry department hundreds of thousands of dollars to fund research that wasn't being conducted. Moreover, it said, the psychiatry department had submitted partially fabricated invoices to the Massachusetts agency to obtain the funding. Dr. Martin Keller denied the allegations in the article; he said that the first few years of the DMH contract had been devoted to planning for research that was to take place at Corrigan. State officials, however, said they were not in the business of awarding grants for planning, just for actual research. The story's publication prompted immediate calls for an investigation by top Massachusetts officials.

As Donna Howard wearily answered the agents' questions, she wondered, not for the first time, how she had gotten herself into this mess. She thought she had done the right thing by telling Alice Tangredi-Hannon of her concerns.

For weeks afterward, Howard heard nothing. Then one evening,

Tangredi-Hannon called her at home. She said she had gone to the dean of the medical school with the information Donna had given her. But the dean had told her to let it go. All they had here, he insisted, was a bunch of disgruntled employees. Tangredi-Hannon told Howard that she was sorry, but there was nothing more she could do.

Shortly after that conversation, Howard started looking in earnest for another job. She could already sense a freeze in Carolyn O'Sullivan's attitude toward her. Despite her fears that Keller was onto her, the memos and faxes that Howard had unearthed in the file room at Duncan ate away at her. She hated the thought that a prestigious academic institution might be benefiting at the expense of indigent people with mental illness. After Maria was diagnosed with bipolar disorder, Howard had become active with a group of patient advocates in southeastern Massachusetts that was working to raise public awareness about mental illness. At one point, Howard had even coordinated an interdisciplinary conference on depression in New Bedford. So she knew all about the deep cutbacks in mental health services that Governor William Weld had implemented in Massachusetts beginning in the early 1990s. It just didn't seem right to her that the research department of an Ivy League institution was collecting seemingly bogus research money at a time when services to the state's mentally ill were being slashed to the bone.

But that wasn't the only aspect that bothered her. Howard knew by name many of the troubled teenagers enrolled in the department's Paxil and lithium trials. They came through Duncan every week for their regular checkups, and she always made time to chat with them. A good number of them were in foster care, and they reminded her, uncomfortably, of Maria.

In mid-November, as the trees bared their limbs and the sandy beaches near her home turned cold, Howard called the Massachusetts attorney general's office. She was connected to an officer in the criminal bureau who seemed completely disinterested in what she had to say, so the day after she got word that she had been hired as a community relations coordinator by the Arbor-Fuller Hospital in Attleboro, Massachusetts, Howard steeled herself and called the city desk at the *Boston Globe*. Someone there took down her name and number, but no one called back. She tried again. This time the message was forwarded to me, and I returned her call. We agreed to meet at the Burger King on Route 24 outside Brockton (it was roughly halfway between Boston and Providence). There, Howard turned over a box full of incriminating documents from the Brown psychiatry department.

Since she was still working at Brown, Howard asked that she not be identified in the initial story. In a case of pure serendipity—Howard had no way of knowing exactly when the *Globe* piece would run—she ended up leaving Brown on Friday, January 5, and starting her new job at Arbor-Fuller the following Monday. The front-page story that I wrote on Keller and Corrigan ran that Sunday (the seventh). Even though Howard was not identified in the piece, everyone at Brown knew she had been the primary source. The day after the piece ran, Marty Keller called a meeting of the research staff and came in person to the Duncan Building for the first time in years. At the meeting, he called Donna a "very sick individual" and angrily denounced the *Globe* article. He told the assembled group that he planned to rebut the allegations and warned them not to speak to reporters. Howard wished she could have been a fly on the wall at that meeting. Fortunately, one of her co-workers was considerate enough to call and tell her all about it.

NOW IT WAS LATE JANUARY, and here she was, sitting at her own kitchen table with two formidable-looking federal agents asking her the strangest questions. She felt as if she were the suspect in a gruesome murder trial.

"So what kind of car does Dr. Keller drive?" the heavyset agent asked.

Howard stared at him in disbelief.

"I have no idea," she said. She explained that she worked across campus from Keller and very rarely saw him.

"Do you know what his wife does?"

"No."

The agent scratched his balding head and looked at his companion. The younger man, who had been occupied tossing a drool-covered ball to Hudson, shrugged.

"Um, Mrs. Howard, what possessed you to copy all these documents and give them to a reporter?" the older man finally asked.

Howard told him what she had told me: that she cared deeply about the welfare of patients with mental illness and had been outraged to learn that at a time of major cutbacks in services, all this money seemed to be disappearing into the coffers of a wealthy institution.

By the time the agents left, close to 10 p.m., they were joking about her puppy's ball-fetching skills. They thanked Howard for her time and drove away. As she watched their big black car recede into the darkness, Donna Howard hoped fervently that these were the last federal agents she would ever have the privilege of speaking to. Her wish would not be granted.

# 8. The Humiliation of Martin Teicher, October 1996

**M**artin Teicher had been testifying under oath for nearly six hours, and he was exhausted. This was his second day of being deposed by an attorney for Eli Lilly. The drug company was being sued by Joan Greer, a widow whose husband, a prominent attorney in Washington, D.C., had killed himself while taking Prozac. It was one of the dozens of wrongful death lawsuits that had been brought against the maker of Prozac in recent years. But it marked the first time that Teicher had agreed to become an expert witness. He had signed on to *Greer v. Eli Lilly* more than six years earlier, after taking a call from Allen Sandler, the deceased man's psychiatrist. Teicher had already turned down a request to testify in a case that had evolved into perhaps the most notorious Prozac trial of the 1990s: the Wesbecker writ. In 1989, a former factory worker named Joseph Wesbecker opened fire with an AK-47 in Louisville, Kentucky, killing eight people, wounding twelve, and fatally shooting himself. Wesbecker had been taking Prozac, and the families of his victims sued Eli Lilly. After reading Wesbecker's medical records, Teicher felt that there wasn't a clear enough cause-and-effect relationship between Prozac and Wesbecker's homicidal behavior for him to testify for the plaintiff. That case, which went to trial in the fall of 1994, resulted in a verdict for Lilly, which the drugmaker trumpeted as a victory "vindicating" Prozac. Only later would the judge on the case discover that Lilly, fearing it was going to lose in court, reached a secret agreement to pay the plaintiffs' attorneys and their clients a tremendous amount of money if they would throw the trial. In a 1996 book summarizing the trial and its impact, *The Power to Harm: Mind, Medicine, and Murder on Trial,* John Cornwell described the secret deal as "unprecedented in any Western court." A resulting investigation by the Kentucky attorney general's office confirmed the secret settlement and the "mind-boggling" sums Lilly paid to the plaintiffs' attorneys and their clients to deceive the court. After the Kentucky AG's report was issued in March 1997, the official record on the Wesbecker case was changed from a jury verdict in Lilly's favor to "dismissed . . . as settled." But by then the deception had achieved its intended effect: many other Prozac users were discouraged from suing Lilly. (No charges were ever brought against any of the parties to this sordid tale.)

Teicher strongly believed that Prozac *was* a factor in the death of Joan Greer's husband in 1990. The *Greer* lawsuit had been filed in 1991, and now, five years later, he was finally being deposed. Attorneys in civil actions routinely subpoena opposing witnesses to testify under oath in the hopes of catching them in a lie or factual discrepancy so that their testimony can be discredited should the case come to trial. Jonathan Cole, another of Greer's expert witnesses, had already been deposed. Now it was Teicher's turn.

His deposition was taken in the glass-enclosed conference room of one of those downtown law firms with ornate offices overlooking the Boston Harbor. The lead attorney for Eli Lilly (who had borrowed the space for the occasion) was an attractive, dark-haired woman whom Teicher judged to be in her late thirties or early forties. A partner in the Philadelphia law firm of Pepper Hamilton, Nina Gussack had built a lucrative practice representing the pharmaceutical industry. Teicher found her to be a consummate professional, well-prepared and knowledgeable not only about the medical issues involved, but about other matters as well. She had certainly done her homework when it came to him. Years later, Teicher would acknowledge that if he hadn't been on the receiving end of her rapier, he might have admired her skill in disemboweling him.

Looking back, Teicher could see that Gussack spent the first day of the deposition softening him up. She asked Teicher about his research, his private practice at McLean Hospital, and why he thought Prozac was to blame for the suicide of Michael Rosenbloom, Greer's husband. Rosenbloom had jumped off a bridge five days after starting Prozac. Gussack also wanted to know what Teicher had discussed with Andrew Greenwald over dinner at Legal Seafood the night before. Teicher was only too happy to tell her. Among the matters they talked about was his analysis of data that Lilly had submitted to the BGA (short for Bundesgesundheitsamt), the German equivalent of the FDA, when seeking approval to market fluoxetine in Germany in 1984.

Teicher could remember exactly where he had been when he first took a close look at the BGA data: sitting in his doctor's office at Harvard Community Health Plan. As he skimmed the BGA material while waiting to go in, it suddenly dawned on him that the data Lilly had submitted to the German authorities showed an almost twofold increased risk of suicide attempts among patients taking Prozac compared to those on placebo. Here was evidence that Lilly had known all along that Prozac carried a heightened risk of suicide! Not only had the drug company lied to him and his McLean coauthors about not being aware of any such risk, but a senior Lilly scientist had omitted this data from his presentation at the pivotal 1991 FDA hearing on Prozac. No wonder the BGA had initially refused to approve the drug in Germany. Teicher jumped up from his seat in the waiting area and paced around the watercooler, aware that some of the other patients were watching him curiously. But he couldn't sit still. After taking a few sips of water, he walked back to his seat and read through the papers again, shaking his head in disbelief.

Responding to Gussack's question that first day, Teicher had mentioned his epiphany while reading the BGA data. But his interlocutor didn't seem particularly interested. She moved on to another line of questioning, and the first day of the deposition ended pretty much on time at 5:40 p.m.

Driving home that evening, Teicher replayed the day's exchanges over in his mind. He'd gotten off easy, he thought. Too easy, as it turned out. He was sitting down to a late dinner when the phone rang. It was his ex-wife. Bev was now a highly regarded cancer researcher at Dana-Farber. Teicher knew that although Bev enjoyed her work at the Harvard teaching hospital, she felt somewhat hamstrung there in her desire to develop practical applications from her research.

"Hey, Bud, you're not going to believe it—I just got a call from the oncology division of Eli Lilly." Bev said. "They are calling to see if I'd be interested in a position."

"Lilly?" Teicher asked.

"Yes, I could go in as their top research scientist in oncology. Their program needs new blood—it could be a tremendous opportunity. It may be too good to refuse."

"In Indiana?" Teicher felt the beginnings of a massive headache.

"Yes, Lilly's labs and headquarters are there."

Marty was having a hard time wrapping his mind around her words. Was Bev seriously considering moving to Indiana? That meant taking their son, who was in his last year of high school, and their twelve-year-old daughter with her. Bev had physical custody of the children, but until now, that had posed no major problem. Their divorce six years earlier had been amicable, and Bev had made it clear that he was welcome at their house in Belmont anytime. He typically drove his daughter to school in the mornings, and he saw both children every other weekend and one or two times during the week as well.

"They just called today?" Teicher asked.

"Yes, out of the blue," Bev said. "They called—I didn't apply or anything."

"Do you know how weird this is? I'm going through this horrendous deposition with their attorneys, and they just called you out of the blue about a job."

Bev laughed and assured him it was just a coincidence. Lilly wanted to ramp up its cancer research, she said, and this would be a fantastic opportunity to help the pharmaceutical firm develop some very beneficial cancer products.

"Yeah, okay," Teicher finally said, even though it wasn't okay. He tried to keep things light. "Just make sure you don't mention my name in the interviews," he said, only half-joking.

DRIVING INTO BOSTON the next morning for the second day of his deposition, Teicher wondered just how coincidental Bev's job opportunity really was. But now, sitting at the polished cherry conference table as his deposition dragged into its thirteenth hour, he was too busy concentrating on not saying the wrong thing to think about the prospect of his ex-wife and children moving to Indianapolis. Gussack's next question brought him up short.

"Sir, you mentioned yesterday you have been sued for malpractice. Is that correct?" Gussack asked.

"Yes," Teicher replied, feeling a prickle of unease.

"On one occasion, the malpractice suit was brought by patient number six in your case series. Is that correct?"

Teicher's mouth felt dry. Patient number 6, a private patient of his during the 1980s, had been hospitalized numerous times with borderline personality disorder and a serious substance-abuse problem. From what this patient herself had told him, Teicher also suspected that as a child, she had been drugged and sexually abused by her father.

Teicher had included this patient as the sixth case in his now-famous

Prozac case study. It was a mistake he soon came to regret. A few years later, she sued Teicher for malpractice, alleging that he'd had sex with her on numerous occasions. She also wrote to the Massachusetts Board of Registration in Medicine, prompting an investigation. The board decided her allegations had no merit and closed the complaint against Teicher in 1993. But some months later, an investigative series in the *Boston Globe* (which I was not involved in) accused the state board of being too lax in disciplining doctors; the newspaper article included the allegations against Teicher as one example. Shortly afterward, the medical board felt compelled to reopen its investigation of the complaint against Teicher, and the case was still pending. Andrew Greenwald, Greer's attorney, had warned Teicher that Lilly's attorneys might bring up the complaint during his deposition. And now here it was.

As Teicher gathered himself to reply to Gussack's question, Greenwald spoke up.

"Objection!"

The two attorneys sparred for several minutes, leaving Teicher to wonder if this was when things got rocky.

Finally Gussack continued: "Now, patient number 6 was a patient of yours for what, six years?"

Teicher looked at Greenwald, who nodded. They had discussed what Teicher should say if the defense attorney started asking about patient number 6.

"I'm happy to discuss what's here in the case study [from the Prozac paper], what's here in these notes," Teicher said. "My attorney, Mr. William Daley, has instructed me not to discuss any details of the [board of medicine] case." Daley, who couldn't attend the deposition, said it was too risky to discuss patient 6 in much detail because Teicher's board complaint was still under review.

Gussack was having none of it. She continued to press Teicher for details that were not part of the 1990 case study he'd written up for the *American Journal of Psychiatry*. And Teicher continued to respond that he couldn't talk about it. Every now and then, the Lilly attorney would slip in a question that Teicher could answer because it pertained to his case study notes about patient number 6. But then she would interject a question that he didn't remember from the case study, and Teicher would frantically scan the notes in front of him before telling her he couldn't discuss it.

At one point, Gussack threatened to go in front of the judge and seek an order compelling Teicher to answer her questions. "And I am going to ask that [Teicher] be compelled at his own expense, paying for my costs incurred in returning for these questions," she added.

Greenwald took issue with this, concluding, "That is, I think, a kind of unfair threat."

Gussack smoothly replied that she was not threatening, simply stating her intent. She continued asking Teicher questions he couldn't answer, and as he repeated, "I am unwilling to answer that," again and again, he wondered how long this cat-and-mouse game would go on. It was after 5 p.m. and he had a pounding headache. But the Lilly attorney was far from finished.

"Now, Doctor, it is true, isn't it, that in the course of the malpractice suit . . . patient number 6 alleges that you had sexual relations with her starting in the fall of 1984. Correct?"

"I am unwilling to answer that."

"And she further testified, sir, didn't she, that you had sexual relations with her at the Battle Green Hotel. Correct?"

"I am unwilling to answer that."

"Doctor, are you denying those allegations?"

Greenwald interjected, "This is an unfair question. The man has said on advice of counsel he is not going to discuss anything except what's in the papers that he has produced."

But the Lilly attorney would not let it go.

"It is true, isn't it, that . . . patient number 6 in this lawsuit testified that sexual relations occurred between you on multiple times. Correct?"

Alison Bass

In one dim corner of his brain, Teicher realized that Gussack was trying to wear him down. Her questions were like Chinese water torture. He felt like shouting, Enough, I'll say anything you want, just stop! But he couldn't; that was precisely what she wanted him to do.

"She testified, didn't she, sir, that on three or four occasions she had sexual relations with you at your home. Correct?"

"Unwilling to answer on the advice of counsel."

"Doctor, you are aware, aren't you, that patient number 6 has alleged that she engaged in oral sex, intercourse, and anal intercourse with you on a number of occasions?"

"I am unwilling to answer on the advice of counsel."

"I still have my continuing objections, right?" Greenwald interjected.

"Sir, is it accurate that considering the office visits patient number 6 had with you between 1984 and 1990, some sixty-five to seventy percent of those visits you engaged in sexual relations with patient number 6?"

Drip, drip, drip: Teicher thought he might go out of his mind. He wanted nothing more than to set the record straight. But if he answered Gussack, even to deny his former patient's allegations, he knew it would make the whole subject admissible in court. In his response to the state board of medicine's complaint, Teicher had acknowledged that he signed birthday cards to this patient, "Love, Marty," and had given her a $3.50 pair of earrings as a birthday present, all to keep her spirits up and show her that he cared. He also acknowledged that he had allowed her to come to his home once when she was in crisis. Teicher would later admit that he made "some serious errors of judgment" in a misguided attempt to keep a suicidal patient alive. But he said he did not have sexual relations with her.

WHILE THERE IS no way to know for sure what happened between Marty Teicher and his patient, a close reading of the medical board's documents indicates that Teicher is telling the truth. At the time

Teicher's patient filed her complaint with the Massachusetts Board of Medicine in the early 1990s, the state agency was under a lot of pressure from the local media to discipline doctors charged with sexual misconduct. And many of these cases were indeed heinous, with the same doctor taking advantage of multiple female patients in a twisted exercise of power and lust.

The complaint against Teicher, however, seems more akin to another highly publicized case in which a female psychiatrist, Margaret Bean-Bayog, stood accused of having sex with a young male patient of hers. Paul Lozano, a bright but tormented young man, had come from a humble Mexican American family in Texas and had gone on to Harvard Medical School, where he killed himself while under Dr. Bean-Bayog's care. His family sued Bean-Bayog for wrongful death in 1992. From covering that story and reading hundreds of pages of medical notes and records, it became apparent to me that Lozano had been sexually abused as a young child and was deeply troubled long before he met Margaret Bean-Bayog. While Bean-Bayog may have become overly involved on an emotional level with Lozano, there is no evidence that she had sexual relations with him. Similarly, there is no evidence that Teicher had sex with his patient.

As a young psychiatrist out to make a name for himself, Martin Teicher was a risk taker, someone who cared deeply about his patients, too deeply sometimes. He may have overstepped the proper boundaries of psychiatric conduct, the rules that discourage therapists from socializing with their patients and giving them gifts. But Teicher did so for the same reason Bean-Bayog had—to try to keep a deeply troubled, suicidal patient alive.

So where did the allegations of sexual misconduct come from? you might ask. In the case of Teicher's former patient, they may have grown out of a process that occurs in psychotherapy, known as transference. In transference, patients commonly transfer the mixed-up feelings of anger, desire, hatred, and love that they have felt for important family figures to their therapist. Teicher's patient may have confounded her father with her psychiatrist in remembering the sexual abuse she had suffered as a child. Patients rarely make up allegations of sexual misconduct, but it sometimes happens. And when it does, it is most likely to occur in patients who, like Teicher's patient, are extremely troubled and have developed borderline personality disorder or multiple personalities to cope with unforgivable childhood trauma. There may also have been financial incentives involved. As the medical board documents reveal, Teicher's former patient and her husband, a carpenter, were in severe financial straits during this period and thus perfect targets for personal injury attorneys who make a handsome living from suing physicians for malpractice. Andrew Meyer, the lawyer who represented both the Lozano family and Teicher's patient, was a controversial figure in Boston media circles at the time. In 1992, Meyer was sued by another physician, an obstetrician, for defamation, libel, and malicious prosecution in connection with his handling of two malpractice suits against her. The physician accused Meyer of libeling her in a letter he sent to her employer, a medical school in Hawaii, after she refused to settle either of his malpractice suits against her. (One of the lawsuits was dismissed as "frivolous" by a Massachusetts Superior Court judge, and the other resulted in a mistrial.) There are some who say that Meyer's handling of the wrongful death suit against Bean-Bayog was also questionable. In garnering publicity for the case, Meyer provided reporters with selectively chosen salacious passages from the psychiatrist's own notes that made it appear as though she had had sex with Lozano. In August 1992, Bean-Bayog resigned her medical license rather than face what was rapidly becoming a media circus (reporters from magazines like *People* and *Vanity Fair* were planning to descend on Boston for the hearing, and the board had already agreed to allow television cameras and move the hearing from a small room in its downtown Boston offices to a huge auditorium nearby). Margaret Bean-Bayog never recovered from the ordeal and died of leukemia in 2006.

Teicher later acknowledged that the publicity surrounding Bean-Bayog's case weighed heavily in the decision to settle his own malpractice suit a few years later. But her sad fate was hardly uppermost in his mind that afternoon in October 1996, as Nina Gussack pounded him with questions about his own conduct. Teicher was simply trying to keep to the script he and his attorney had decided upon. Yet it bothered him enormously that he couldn't respond to Gussack's assault. He couldn't explain that his former patient had spun an ever bigger castle of lies out of air.

At some point, Teicher realized that Gussack probably understood this. But she kept attacking him, each question a battering ram against his weakening sense of dignity and self-respect. In a haze, he heard Greenwald saying, "Nina, I think this is really at this point getting kind of oppressive and harassing. I understand you want to put questions on the record, but you've been doing this for over an hour . . ."

But she wouldn't stop. Teicher was reduced to muttering, "Unwilling to answer." Finally, at 6:22 p.m., Gussack asked for a two-minute break to see if she had any other questions for him. When they came back, Gussack asked a few more general queries about borderline personality disorder and the effects of Prozac on the brain, and then she announced she was suspending the deposition and intended to go before Judge Penn to seek an order to compel Teicher to answer questions about the board of medicine case. As it turned out, that third round of questioning would never take place, but it didn't matter. By the time Martin Teicher walked out of the downtown law office that evening, one of the preeminent experts on SSRIs in the United States had sworn that he would never testify in a civil suit again.

# 9. Eliot Spitzer's Crusaders Win Round One against GlaxoSmithKline but Get Knocked Off Course in Round Two, July 2004

The morning of July 1, 2004, Rose Firestein dragged herself to work. Could it have been only yesterday that her boss, Tom Conway, had issued his ultimatum to GlaxoSmithKline? It seemed to Firestein as if it had been an eternity since Conway had walked out on the drug company's attorneys, his stunned colleagues having no choice but to follow suit. Firestein had not slept much that night. Lying awake under a blanket of humid air, her thoughts kept circling back to the same question: had Conway thrown away their one chance of settling with Glaxo? Even Shirley Stark, a staunch loyalist who had worked with Conway for years, confided that she too feared that their boss's brinkmanship might backfire.

Firestein certainly understood Conway's motives for abruptly ending the talks. But she feared that GlaxoSmithKline might now decide to fight fire with fire. At the very least, its attorneys might file to remove the case to federal court. And once it was in federal court, all bets were off. Not only were federal judges not as familiar with New York's inclusive statute on consumer fraud, but they might also be more likely to object to a state attorney general's delving into issues of drug safety. After all, that was an area long considered the turf of the federal Food and Drug Administration.

Having being involved in several large class action suits against state agencies, Firestein knew that the practice of medicine, which included the dispensing of drug prescriptions, was regulated by the states and was thus under each state attorney general's purview. But a federal judge might not so readily grasp that. And once the case was removed to federal court, it could be bundled together with similar actions in other states. New York's prosecutors would lose all control over it, as they had on other cases removed to federal court. In addition, such bundled cases tended to take forever. The last thing Firestein wanted was a long-drawn-out battle with GlaxoSmithKline in federal court.

AN EARLY RISER, Firestein was usually the first to arrive in the consumer bureau, by seven or eight at the latest. Stark would come in soon after. Tom Conway, who commuted by train to Manhattan from Albany two or three times a week, would lope in a little after nine. By then, the secretaries and summer law interns—Conway called them the "kids"—had shown up.

This morning, Stark was already there. Her office was two doors down, and shortly after Firestein settled down at her desk, Stark popped her head into her colleague's office.

"Any word from Wick?" Stark asked.

With his Brahmin background, the lead defense attorney for Glaxo-SmithKline hailed from a world far removed from Firestein and her Brooklyn walk-up. But she had worked with Wick before on the average wholesale pricing case and found him to be a genuinely nice guy, the kind of adversary who would not twist anything you said privately into grist for a legal attack. After twenty years of battling bureaucratic and corporate malfeasance in numerous states, Firestein knew Wick's sense of honor to be a rare attribute indeed.

She shook her head. "Nothing yet."

"Darn," Stark said, and retreated back into her office.

Two hours later, Tom Conway called from Albany. Tall, with a prominent nose, a generous mouth, and crisp white hair, Conway had been with the AG's office for eighteen years. That made him and Stark, who had been there twenty years, "career" attorneys, as opposed to the newcomers brought in by Spitzer when he entered office in 1999. But Spitzer had been good to Conway—the new AG had promoted him to bureau chief of the twenty-attorney consumer bureau shortly after his arrival—and Conway admired his boss's derring-do. Spitzer may have started out as the scion of a wealthy New York real estate developer, but the Harvard Law School graduate had substantially expanded the mandate of the attorney general's office to take on corporate behemoths in the name of the little guy. To longtime public servants like Conway and Stark, it was clear that although Spitzer may have come to the AG's office by a different route, their leader had gone into law for much the same reasons they had.

Like Rose Firestein, Conway and Stark had both landed at 120 Broadway after stints with the Legal Aid Society of New York. During Firestein's interview for the job, Conway asked Firestein about her work for Legal Aid, and Firestein mentioned her part in the mammoth lawsuit against New York City and its Department of Social Services. Legal Aid had prevailed in the *Doe* case—at least for the moment. The judge hearing the case had issued a contempt order, holding the city's Social Services Department liable for huge fines until it improved conditions in its field offices and did a better job of providing permanent placements for the foster children in its custody. From the vantage point of hindsight, however, Firestein wasn't sure that *Doe* had really succeeded in improving the lives of New York City's abandoned children. The needs of New York's poor were so vast, their problems so insurmountable, that Firestein felt that she and all the other overworked attorneys for Legal Aid who came before and after her were like that little Dutch boy holding his finger in the dike in a vain attempt to hold back the deluge.

Conway, however, had seemed impressed. Firestein left 120 Broadway the day of her interview thinking she might just have an inside track on the job. She was right.

Now a bona fide member of Spitzer's team, Firestein liked to refer to herself and the two other Legal Aid alumni on the third floor as "professional do-gooders." She was only half-joking. Conway and Stark, she felt, were genuinely caring people. Shirley Stark would give you the shirt off her back if she thought it would help. And despite his sometimes brusque tone, Conway had an uncanny knack for knowing when to break the ice with a funny story or a joke. When he laughed, his grin stretched wide across his face, wrinkling up the sides of his eyes. True, the head of the consumer protection bureau could be a hard sell at times. He was a stickler for legal facts and seemed to delight in the Socratic method of debate. Nothing escaped his notice, no detail or nuance was too small to be pounced upon. Yet once Conway bought into your legal argument, he was a rock of support.

When he called Firestein from Albany that day, Conway wasted no time on chitchat.

"Hi, Rose. Heard anything from Wick?" he asked.

"No. I think they're going to stonewall," Firestein said.

Conway laughed. To Firestein, the bureau chief seemed annoyingly cheerful.

"Nah, they'll call," he said. "Just watch."

Sitting at her desk, surrounded by piles of papers that only she could find, Firestein smiled wryly through her anxiety. Conway hadn't always been so supportive. When she had first concocted the idea of going after GlaxoSmithKline for consumer fraud, Conway and others in the AG's office had been openly skeptical, if not dismissive. It had taken her weeks of persistent arguing, backed up by reams of documentation, to bring first Stark and then Conway around. And now all those months of hard work, browsing through the fine print of scientific papers, FDA transcripts, and internal GlaxoSmithKline documents until her eyes stung, might have been for naught. All because Tom Conway wanted to see if the other guy blinked first.

That afternoon, Firestein had trouble concentrating. She was tired of waiting for the phone to ring, only to have her hopes dashed every time it turned out not to be Wick. She had just begun work on another consumer fraud case, this time against Guidant, the makers of a defective heart valve stent that was alleged to have caused patients' deaths. Firestein and her colleagues were hoping to build their case against Guidant around the same theory that had guided the Glaxo action: if they were able to prove that the stent maker had known about defects in the heart valve stents (which would later be recalled) but hadn't disclosed them quickly enough, they could show that the medical device company had defrauded consumers. But although she had plenty to do on the Guidant investigation, her heart wasn't in it. Late in the afternoon, her sister Janice called. Would Rose still be able to take Ellie to ballet class that evening? Ellie loved strutting around their Brooklyn apartment in her tutu. She had a mischievous side too. Sometimes she'd sneak up on Firestein's left side, where she had no vision, and shout, "Boo," startling her. But Firestein didn't mind. She much preferred Ellie's playfulness to the pity of strangers who saw her walking with her cane in downtown Manhattan. She found it ironic that many people assumed that she couldn't function without their help. They never seemed to stop and consider how she had made it to that particular intersection in the first place. One woman had even grabbed Firestein by the elbow, and when she wrenched her arm away—she hated being grabbed unawares—the woman had gotten testy and called Firestein an ungrateful bitch. Those were the times when Firestein wanted to throw her cane into the Hudson. Yet she knew it gave her a sense of independence that she wouldn't otherwise have. Essentially, it boiled down to pride versus mobility, and for Firestein, mobility almost always won.

. . .

AROUND NOON THE NEXT DAY, Wick called. He told Firestein that GlaxoSmithKline would delay launching its online registry, since that seemed to be such a big sticking point. He added that Glaxo was still interested in talking about settlement and said he would be in touch. Firestein carefully hung up the phone, stood up, and brought her fist down on the desk in jubilation. Yes! Conway's all-or-nothing ploy had worked. She had been wrong to doubt him. Rounding her desk with care—she was always bumping into sharp edges—Firestein walked off to tell him and Stark the good news.

IN BUILDING THE CASE against GlaxoSmithKline, Firestein had sought advice from a number of medical experts, including several who had studied the link between antidepressants and suicidal behavior. One of them was Dr. David Healy, a British psychiatrist and director of the North Wales Department of Psychological Medicine at the University of Wales. Healy was intimately familiar with the research literature on the SSRIs, having reviewed clinical trial studies that the drug companies had submitted to the FDA to gain approval of these drugs. By the late 1990s, the FDA had collected a wealth of clinical trial data about the SSRIs and similar antidepressants like Effexor and Serzone, which were also known to boost serotonin levels. There was only one problem: the data wasn't available to the public. For the most part, these "proprietary" research results could only be pried from the pharmaceutical companies under subpoena in civil or criminal lawsuits. Even then, the information was often sealed from public disclosure.

Healy was one of the few medical experts to have gained access to this data, while working as an expert witness in several lawsuits against the drug companies. What he uncovered was alarming. The drugmakers' own clinical trial data showed that adults and children taking the newer antidepressants were at least twice as likely to attempt or commit suicide as those taking a placebo. And the FDA knew this. In the late 1990s, the agency had come under considerable pressure from drugmakers to scrap placebos in antidepressant trials. The drug researchers argued that the use of these sugar pills exposed depressed patients to a higher risk of suicide. In an effort to defend the placebo standard, Dr. Thomas Laughren, an official in the FDA's Psychiatric Drug Products Group Division, had examined the available clinical trial data for eight of the newer antidepressants (Prozac, Zoloft, Paxil, Wellbutrin, Serzone, Effexor, Remeron, and Celexa). In his analysis published in the November 2001 issue of the journal *European Psychiatry,* Laughren reported that there were no excess suicides in the placebo groups—therefore using placebos as a point of comparison was not dangerous to patients.

In fact, the data from these trials showed that the active drug or antidepressant was twice as likely as placebo to be associated with suicides in adults. While Laughren did not discuss these results in his paper, they were listed in two tables in the text. When asked about this outcome years later, Laughren, who is still with the FDA as director of the Division of Psychiatry Products, became testy. "That was not the intent of my paper," he said. "I'm quite sure I didn't include a statistical analysis [of suicidality] in my paper. It's really disingenuous of you to present that to me when I don't have the paper in front of me."

Intentional or not, Laughren's 2001 paper is not the only evidence that the FDA knew years ago that there was an increased risk of suicide in the SSRI trial data. In toxicity studies of Zoloft performed by Pfizer on healthy volunteers and submitted to the FDA in the late 1980s, some of the patients randomized to Zoloft developed severe anxiety or agitation, a state known as akathisia. Patients with akathisia became so agitated that they often felt like jumping out of their own skin. Teicher and his colleagues at McLean had found the same phenomenon occurring in some of their suicidal Prozac patients. At the 1991 FDA hearing on Prozac and in a follow-up paper to his first case report on Prozac, Teicher had hypothesized that akathisia could make some patients so miserable that they wanted to kill themselves. Yet while the clinical trial data linking the SSRIs to akathisia and higher rates of suicidal behavior was known to the FDA, it had not been reported in mainstream medical journals or to the general public. Healy was eager to publish his findings, but his paper was rejected by a number of journals, including the prestigious *Archives of General Psychiatry.* The *Archives* may have rejected his paper, Healy said, because it contained a negative conclusion, and most medical journals were (and still are) not particularly interested in publishing negative findings. Although many journals derive a lucrative income from the drug ads they publish, their desire for clear-cut results that will attract readership and publicity probably plays a bigger role in their bias against negative findings.

Dr. Mark Helfand, a professor of medicine at Oregon Health and Science University, has studied this issue as head of the Evidence-Based Practice Center there. Journals "want to publish results that get them the top headlines," he told me. "They are not interested in publishing the subtle clues that might reflect a mixed message, a more balanced view."

Many prominent physicians agree. Dr. Joseph M. Heyman, a trustee of the American Medical Association, was quoted in a press release as saying, "Studies with positive findings are more likely to be published than studies with negative or null results."

Finally, in 2003, a little-known periodical called *Psychotherapy and Psychosomatics* published Healy's paper linking the SSRIs to akathisia and suicidal behavior. Healy's outspokenness did not endear him to the SSRI makers. They routinely tried to discredit him as a biased gadfly out to enrich himself at their expense. Pfizer, for instance, called Healy a practitioner of "junk science" in an attempt to have him disqualified as an expert witness in a lawsuit brought by the parents of a thirteen-year-old boy who hanged himself while taking Zoloft. Lilly also tried (and failed) to have Healy disqualified from another case involving a man who had killed himself and his wife while taking Prozac.

While the pharmaceutical companies were unable to discredit Healy in court, they did succeed in muddying his reputation to the point where many psychiatrists and journalists in the United States viewed him as "controversial." In fact, in 2001, the University of Toronto rescinded Healy's appointment as a professor of psychiatry at its Centre for Addiction and Mental Health (CAMH) after Healy gave a speech at the university in which he talked about the link between SSRIs and suicidal behavior. At the end of his lecture, Healy showed a slide of the British serial killer Harold Shipman—a doctor who killed his patients by giving them lethal injections of painkillers—to make the point that patients should not always put their trust in the medical profession. In rescinding its job offer, CAMH wrote a letter to Healy saying that it was alarmed at the "extremity" of his views. Healy and his supporters countered that there might be another reason why CAMH had revoked its job offer: Eli Lilly, the maker of Prozac, was then CAMH's largest sponsor, having donated more than $645,000 to the institute.

In other circles, however, Healy was considered a modern-day Sinclair Lewis. The BBC, in large part because of Healy's prodding, had aired several *Panorama* programs about the SSRIs, which eventually caught the eye of the Medicines and Healthcare Products Regulatory Agency (MHPRA), Britain's equivalent of the FDA. By the summer of 2003, when Rose Firestein caught up with Healy, his biography listed him as the author of 120 scientific articles and twelve books on psychiatry and the history of medicine. Firestein, for her part, found the British psychiatrist extremely knowledgeable, his opinions about the SSRIs grounded in scientific research. "David is the person who really brought this to the MHPRA. He has been cast in a bad light, but he's as far from a crackpot as anyone in the field, she said."

Now, LITTLE MORE than a month after the AG's lawsuit had made front-page news, Healy was in New York to do research for his latest book, a history of electroshock therapy. He called Firestein to let her know he was in town, and the assistant attorney general said she'd love to meet him for coffee.

Which they did, on July 8, in the newly refurbished art deco lobby of the Metropolitan Hotel in Midtown Manhattan, where Healy was staying. Even though Firestein had told him she would be toting a cane, Healy, a tall, lanky Irishman with a Beatles haircut, had to mask his surprise at seeing a small, slightly stooped woman walk haltingly into the lobby with the trademark white cane.

"She was a bit different from what you'd expect," he recalled with typical British understatement. Healy had been on the lookout for someone taller and, well, more formidable-looking. "You don't expect a person who is five foot zero and has to struggle with blindness to cause such problems for a major pharmaceutical company."

Over coffee at a shop next door, Firestein pressed Healy for his thoughts on other pharmaceutical companies her office should look into. She didn't mention any names, but Healy got the distinct impression that the AG was already hot on the trail of another drugmaker. Firestein made no mention of how the AG's lawsuit against GlaxoSmithKline was progressing, and Healy knew better than to ask. Having been an expert witness, Healy understood how delicate and unpredictable the negotiations could be. He also knew that plaintiffs' attorneys, whether they worked for private firms or for the government, were extremely tight with information before their cases had settled and sometimes afterward as well. That was fine with Healy. It was enough for him to know that a government agency in the United States had finally put consumer safety ahead of pharmaceutical company profits.

LATER THAT AFTERNOON, Firestein, back at 120 Broadway, was reading a brief on her large-print computer screen when the phone rang. It was Wick. He was calling to let her know that his office had just filed a motion to remove the Glaxo case to federal court.

"You'll probably get notice tomorrow," he said.

"Oh, hell," Firestein muttered under her breath. This was bad. It meant that the pharmaceutical giant was going to fight the complaint. It also meant that she and her colleagues now had to prepare the papers necessary to get the case remanded to state court. And even if they won, that battle wouldn't be decided for six months or more. With the case being removed to federal court, they were looking at a long-drawn-out war.

"Thanks for letting me know," Firestein said, her voice drained of emotion. She hung up and sat back in her chair, suddenly too tired for words.

# 10. A Tale of Two Psychiatrists Named Martin, Spring 1998

**M**artin Teicher stood back and studied his creation with pride. It was magnificent! He had built the cherrywood rolltop desk from scratch in the basement workshop of his home. It was almost an exact replica of a desk he had coveted at Crate and Barrel. The salesman at the Chestnut Hill furniture store had been good enough to take a Polaroid of the desk for him, and Teicher had measured its dimensions and scanned them into a computer program that gave him the exact measurements he needed. Building the desk had been a labor of love. Now all he had to do was figure out how to get it up the stairs.

Teicher had taken up woodworking in the dark days after the Massachusetts Board of Medicine decided to reopen its complaint against him. The news had devastated Teicher, and he found that working with wood—designing the pieces, planing the edges, applying the stain—was therapeutic. It calmed his nerves and took his mind off his troubles. Matters had gone from bad to worse. First came the decision by the state board to reopen its investigation into the sexual misconduct charges his former patient had levied against him. Then the drug company Lilly—in the guise of its avenging attorney—had ripped his dignity to shreds on the stand. Finally, his ex-wife had actually gone and taken the job with Lilly, moving to Indiana with their children. She had purchased a house in a suburb of Indianapolis and made it clear that Teicher was welcome to visit at any time. But he only saw his children on holidays now. One of the things he missed most were those early morning chats with his daughter when he would drive her to school in Belmont.

After his family moved away, Teicher turned to woodworking with a vengeance. He bought thousands of dollars in woodworking tools and read every how-to book and magazine on furniture construction he could lay his hands on. He spent a lot of time in his basement work-shop, making one piece after another, each more complicated than the last. First he made a nightstand. Then he constructed a coffee table and an ornately carved bookcase.

IN AUGUST 1997, Teicher was summoned to the state medi-cal board's headquarters in downtown Boston and compelled to tes-tify before the administrative judge assigned to review his case. It was an incredibly painful ordeal, with the board's prosecutor, an attorney named Muriel Finnegan, dredging up every sordid detail of the sexual misconduct allegations against him. It was clear that Finnegan saw Teicher as public enemy number one. To her, Teicher was just the lat-est in a long line of psychiatrists she fervently believed were guilty of sexual misconduct. By the time Teicher's case came before the state agency's administrative judge in the summer of 1997, at least thirty-six psychiatrists had lost or resigned their medical licenses after hav-ing been charged by the disciplinary board with making inappropriate sexual advances to patients.

Yet in the end, the administrative judge for the state board found for Teicher. He ruled that the woman who had accused Teicher of having sex with her was not a reliable witness. Her testimony at the hearings conflicted with previous sworn testimony she had given in depositions and was, in some cases, contradicted by written records. The judge ruled that although Teicher had violated ethical boundaries by sending the woman cards and giving her a cheap pair of earrings, he had done so out of concern for her well-being, with the intent of helping a severely depressed and suicidal patient. The judge found him not guilty of any sexual misconduct. On November 19, 1997, over Muriel Finnegan's vehement objections, the board of medicine agreed with the judge's ruling and dismissed its complaint against Teicher, for the second and last time. By then, however, Teicher had taken his attorney's advice and settled the separate malpractice suit his former patient had brought against him. The settlement of the private malpractice case cost $450,000, most of it paid by Teicher's insurance.

BY THE TIME the state board of medicine absolved Teicher once and for all, he had already resolved to replicate the elegant rolltop desk from Crate and Barrel. And he had succeeded, devoting every spare minute to the task over the next few months. There was just one problem. He couldn't get it out of the basement. He enlisted the help of a friend, but neither of them could figure out how to get the huge desk up the stairs and out the basement door without damaging it. As he stared at the piece sitting on its rollers at the bottom of the stairs, it suddenly came to him: he would have to dismantle the roll top from the desk and rebuild the mechanism so he could remove the top and slide it back in place on a dovetail assembly. Teicher spent much of his spare time painstakingly reconstructing the desk. His solution worked. In less than a month, the desk claimed its rightful place in his home office on the first floor.

The other piece of good news for Teicher that spring was the signing of the contract between McLean Hospital and Sepracor for a percentage of the royalties from the Prozac alternative he was helping the biotech company to develop. He had convinced Sepracor executives that the compound in fluoxetine they should be developing was different from the one they had initially settled on. Both compounds, labeled R– and

S+, were isomers (mirror images of each other) of the main chemical found in Prozac. Teicher had steered Sepracor to R– because it had a shorter duration of action than S+ and might therefore be less toxic to patients. Teicher's lab had already completed animal studies to determine that R– was not toxic in rats. In January 1998, the U.S. Patent and Trademark Office granted a patent on R– fluoxetine to Teicher and two executives at Sepracor: James Young and Timothy Barberich. The patent states that the three inventors intend to develop R– as an antidepressant. It notes that fluoxetine, or Prozac, as a mixture of both isomers and a chloride salt, had certain disadvantages. According to the patent, Prozac "produces a state of inner restlessness (akathisia)" and "in some patients . . . is associated with severe anxiety leading to intense violent suicidal thoughts and self-mutilation." The patent concludes that it would be "desirable to find a compound with the advantages of fluoxetine which would not have the above-described disadvantages."

In April 1998, McLean and Sepracor completed the contract, which called for McLean to receive $1 million up front and then 10 percent from sales of the new drug. The Harvard teaching hospital collected 50 percent of the up-front money, or $500,000; Teicher's lab received 25 percent, or $250,000, according to the terms of the contract; and Teicher, as one of the co-inventors of R–, walked away with $250,000 for himself. He invested most of it in the stock market, which was soaring on the wings of an innovation known as the Internet.

LITTLE MORE THAN a month later, Marty Teicher found himself staring out the window of a shuttle bus that was taking him from his hotel to Toronto's sleek-looking convention center several blocks away. He had come to Toronto to attend two conferences: the annual meetings of the American Psychiatric Association (APA) and the Society of Biological Psychiatry. This year, the two back-to-back meetings had drawn more than twenty thousand psychiatrists and psychiatric researchers to a bustling four-block destination in Canada's largest metropolis.

Teicher, who saw himself foremost as a researcher with a few private patients on the side, liked to spend much of his time at the biological psychiatry conference because most of its sessions were devoted to new research. By contrast, the APA meeting was intended for the general practitioner—the non-research-oriented psychiatrist who needed to catch up on new developments in clinical practice. The APA relegated its new research findings mostly to poster sessions, in which an abstract and some charts were slapped on a poster and hung in a large exhibit room. The lead author usually made a brief scheduled appearance to discuss his results with whoever happened by. Teicher found the poster sessions less satisfying than the research presentations at the biological society and the lively question-and-answer sessions that followed. Moreover, in recent years, he had noticed that the pharmaceutical industry dominated the APA conference, bankrolling huge, well-attended symposia in the convention's biggest ballrooms. Many of these industry-supported symposia pretended to be about new developments in one mental illness or another, but to Teicher's way of thinking, they were really about promoting the drugmakers' newest products.

Just the previous day, he himself had attended an industry-supported symposium in the Grand Ballroom of the Sheraton Centre Hotel titled "Chronic Depression: Optimizing Long-Term Treatment." Teicher had decided to sit in on the three-hour session because it was being chaired by an old friend of his, Dr. Alan Schatzberg, a prominent psychiatrist who had mentored him at McLean. Schatzberg was now head of the Massachusetts Mental Health Center in Boston but still kept a research lab at McLean.

It just so happened that the symposium chaired by Schatzberg was being funded by Bristol-Myers Squibb (BMS), a pharmaceutical company with a hot new antidepressant on the market called Serzone. Unbeknownst to Teicher and the hundreds of other doctors in attendance, all three of the speakers at the symposium moderated by Schatzberg were principal investigators in a newly finished study of Serzone, also funded by Bristol-Myers Squibb. The study, which concluded that Serzone was spectacularly effective in treating chronic depression when prescribed in conjunction with psychotherapy, would be published with much fanfare in the *New England Journal of Medicine* two years later, in May 2000. Its publication would precipitate an unusual editorial by the journal's editor, titled "Is Academic Medicine for Sale?" In her editorial, then-editor Marcia Angell would decry the fact that all but one of the twelve principal authors of the Serzone study had "extensive financial associations" with Bristol-Myers Squibb and other pharmaceutical companies. Indeed, the list of their financial ties to the drug industry was so long that the journal could not fit the full text in its print version of the article. (In 2003, a number of countries would ban the sale of Serzone after it caused liver failure and the deaths of at least twenty patients. Bristol-Myers Squibb would pull its once-promising antidepressant from the U.S. market in May 2004.)

At the 1998 APA meeting in Toronto, however, the buzz about Serzone was all positive. The first speaker at the Bristol-Myers Squibb symposium that morning was none other than Dr. Martin Keller, chief of psychiatry at Brown University. As it turned out, Keller was also the principal investigator of the newly finished Serzone study, but no mention of that was made to the five-hundred-odd doctors attending his talk, which focused on the clinical course of chronic depression. Nor did Keller disclose that he was not there on his own dime. According to testimony in a later lawsuit, Brown's psychiatry chief had been paid $1,500, plus $2,000 in travel expenses, to be one of the featured speakers that day. The other speakers, along with the moderator, were similarly well reimbursed for their time.

Teicher had never actually met Keller, though he had been one seat away from the Brown psychiatrist on a plane heading toward San Juan for the annual meeting of the American College for Neuropsychiatry (ACNP) the previous December. Engrossed in sorting through his slides, Teicher had not paid much attention to the woman sitting next to him or to the elegantly dressed man in the aisle seat. Then the couple, who Teicher felt were obviously married, began arguing, and he couldn't help looking up from his slides. Only later, when he saw Martin Keller give a presentation at the ACNP meeting, did he realize who his flying companions had been.

Keller, he knew, was a very successful guy. Mutual colleagues had described him as smart, funny, and well connected to the circle of psychiatrists appointed to top positions in the National Institute of Mental Health, the nation's premier funding agency for mental health research. Keller indeed seemed to have a golden touch when it came to winning research grants from the NIMH.

Keller was also a sought-after speaker on the psychiatry circuit, and his schedule for the 1998 APA conference in Toronto reflected this status. According to the APA program, he was participating that year in two industry-supported symposia. One was the Bristol-Myers Squibb symposium that Schatzberg chaired; the other was sponsored by Pfizer, on the topic of managing depression among baby boomers. Keller himself was chairing that session. And as it turned out, he had just put the finishing touches on a paper for *JAMA* that contained great news about Zoloft, Pfizer's SSRI product. The *JAMA* paper, which would be published in a few months' time with Keller as the lead author, concluded that Zoloft was significantly more effective than placebo in preventing the recurrence of major depression in chronically depressed patients.

Keller was also on the APA program in 1998 as the lead presenter of a poster session on "Paroxetine and Imipramine in the Treatment of Adolescent Depression." This was the newly finished multicenter trial sponsored by SmithKline Beecham that Keller had been principal investigator of; it compared paroxetine (Paxil) to placebo and an older antidepressant known as imipramine. According to the program's abstract, the study's results showed that "paroxetine is an effective treatment for major depression in an adolescent outpatient population." It was the first public announcement of a study that would receive much scrutiny in the coming years.

IT SEEMED TO TAKE Teicher's shuttle bus forever to travel the few blocks to the convention center. He should have walked. The bus finally pulled up to the curb. Teicher hopped out and saw Alan Schatzberg in the group milling about outside the entrance. Schatzberg was some years older than Teicher, a gregarious, backslapping type of guy whom Marty fondly referred to as "one of the world's greatest schmoozers." They shook hands, and Schatzberg clapped Teicher on the back.

"It's great to see you, Marty," Schatzberg said. "Hey, do you have time for a quick walk? It's such a nice day!"

As the two men ambled along Lakeshore Boulevard, enjoying the crisp late spring breeze off Lake Ontario, Schatzberg wanted to know all about what Teicher was working on, how things were going at McLean. Teicher was flattered by the older man's attention.

"Things are going pretty well," Teicher replied. He was working on some promising research about the long-term consequences of childhood abuse. His lab, in fact, was in the midst of a five-year, $1.5 million grant from the National Institute of Mental Health to study the impact of childhood abuse on changes in the brain. Teicher knew that a few of his colleagues privately suspected that his pummeling by Lilly—both inside and outside the courtroom—may have been one reason why he had shifted his research focus away from Prozac. But Teicher later offered a different explanation for his change in focus: "Once I became involved in this patent for Sepracor and felt there was potential for profiting from it [an alternative for Prozac], I felt it would be a conflict to continue studying and speaking out about Prozac," he said.

During their stroll around downtown Toronto, Teicher did not get into any of this with his friend. And Schatzberg did not mention the symposium on chronic depression he had chaired, or its speakers' close ties to Bristol-Myers Squibb. Looking back, Teicher doubted that

Schatzberg even knew the extent to which Martin Keller and some of the other speakers that day were profiting from their involvement with pharmaceutical companies.

It would be another sixteen months before Keller's colleagues, along with the general public, learned the full extent of Keller's pharmaceutical winnings. In a front-page story for the *Boston Globe* on October 4, 1999, I reported that the Brown psychiatry chief was earning hundreds of thousands of dollars (above and beyond his salary from Brown) in personal consulting and speaking fees from the pharmaceutical industry.

Even before the *Globe* published that story, though, it had been no secret in psychiatric circles that Keller was a friend of Big Pharma. His six-page résumé from the mid-1990s openly lists him as a consultant to seven of the largest pharmaceutical companies then in existence: Upjohn, Bristol-Myers Squibb, Eli Lilly, Johnson and Johnson, Pfizer, Sandoz, and SmithKline Beecham. And on the disclosure form for the 1998 APA meeting, in which participants were required to note "any significant financial interests or affiliations" that might conflict with commercial products discussed in the scientific program, Keller's list included just about every drug company then marketing antidepressants in the United States: Wyeth-Ayerst (Effexor), SmithKline Beecham (Paxil), Pfizer (Zoloft), Pharmacia and Upjohn (Vestra), Bristol-Myers Squibb (Serzone), and Eli Lilly (Prozac).

Even so, some of his colleagues were startled to discover just how extensive the Brown chief's conflicts of interest were. Two of the drug companies providing Keller with especially generous stipends in 1998 — Pfizer (which paid him $218,000) and Bristol-Myers Squibb (which gave him $77,400) — stood to benefit handsomely from the positive findings that Keller and his colleagues would soon publish (about Zoloft and Serzone) in prestigious medical journals.

In 1998, according to his own tax returns, Keller also earned $62,500 in personal income from Forest Labs, the distributor of Celexa, a relatively new entry to the SSRI market; $19,669 from Merck, the maker of Roxindole, a promising new antidepressant at the time; $8,785 from Wyeth-Ayerst, producer of the antidepressant Effexor; and $8,625 from Organon, which made Remeron, yet another antidepressant just coming onto the market. And that was only a partial list of the money he collected from the pharmaceutical industry. According to his tax returns Keller pulled in a total of $444,000 in 1997 and $556,000 in 1998 from firms either making drugs or promoting them.

Keller declined to comment for the *Boston Globe* article in 1999. But several ethicists I quoted in the article said that such unusually large consulting fees constituted the most serious potential conflict they'd ever heard of in academic medicine. They also expressed dismay that Keller had not fully disclosed his financial conflicts to the medical journals that published his research, or to the American Psychiatric Association.

"If I were this person's supervisor, I would have major concerns that such a large sum of money would bias his thinking and judgment," said Dr. Arnold Relman, a former editor of the *New England Journal of Medicine* and professor emeritus of medicine at Harvard Medical School.

In the 1990s, academic medicine was just beginning to sort through the ethical conundrums posed by the enormous sums companies were pouring into drug development and testing. Until the advent of managed care in the late 1980s, drugmakers had been able to raise their prices at will and were not under much pressure to bring new products to market. But when managed care plans began to squeeze their profits, drug companies felt compelled to increase the number of drugs they sold and speed up development times. Faculty at many medical schools joined the stampede, finding clinical trials to be a particularly lucrative source of income. According to a survey conducted by the *New York Times* in 1999, drugmakers were paying doctors between $1,600 and $4,581 per patient for clinical trials. Between 1990 and 1998, according to his résumé and his department's annual report, Martin Keller brought in nearly $8.7 million in research funding from pharmaceutical companies, many of which were also paying him thousands of dollars in personal consulting income.

By then, a few of the more prestigious medical journals, such as the *New England Journal of Medicine* and the *Journal of the American Medical Association,* had begun requiring that authors disclose if they had "substantial" financial ties (more than $10,000) to companies whose products they were studying—either from consulting income or from equity in the companies. But none of the journals required authors to reveal the exact amount of their earnings. And while a handful of top medical schools, such as Harvard and Georgetown, began actively discouraging faculty from doing research for companies who were paying them more than $10,000 or $20,000 a year in consulting fees, most universities merely required faculty to complete pro forma disclosure forms, again without revealing the exact dollars going into their bank accounts. Federal funding agencies like NIH and NIMH had similar requirements, as did professional organizations like the American Psychiatric Association. But these policies were rarely enforced. When my *Boston Globe* article revealed that Martin Keller had failed to fully disclose the extent of his financial ties to the drug industry, Brown University leaped to their star rainmaker's defense, saying it had no problem with Keller's consulting arrangements. Likewise, top officials at the APA and at NIMH, which had given Keller millions of dollars in research grants over the years, took no punitive action against him. "Alas, knowing there is impropriety and proving there is impropriety are vastly different issues," said Dr. Stephen Goldfinger, chair of the Department of Psychiatry at SUNY Downstate Medical School and chair of the APA Committee on Commercial Support.

As a scientist himself, Teicher had no problem with academics' making money from research. After all, he stood to benefit handsomely from the contract he had signed with Sepracor for inventing R−.

Teicher, in fact, would make out very well when Lilly bought the rights to R– from Sepracor for $20 million in December 1998. The Indianapolis-based company was hoping to have the R– ready for market as an antidepressant by the time its patent for Prozac expired in 2001. Of the $20 million the drug company paid to Sepracor for the rights to R–, $2 million went directly to McLean Hospital, with Teicher's lab and Teicher himself each netting $500,000.

Despite this windfall, Teicher held a rather conservative view of research conflicts. Like many of his colleagues at Harvard, he took the medical school's strict conflict-of-interest policy to heart. Years later he would note that there is a distinct difference between getting royalties for a drug one helped develop and earning thousands of dollars in personal income from the very companies whose drugs you were touting in medical journals and at conferences.

"When you do that, you've become a shill for the company," Teicher said. "You want to continue getting those payments, so you're biased toward saying favorable things about their drug product. By contrast, most institutions consider getting royalties from a company that has licensed your work as not posing a conflict, as long as you're not sitting on its board of directors and getting consulting income from the company."

Teicher is far from alone in drawing that distinction. In 2004, researchers at the Social Policy Research Institute in Illinois would publish a study showing that authors with self-admitted conflicts of interest were ten to twenty times *less* likely to present negative findings than those without such financial conflicts. This inverse relationship was strongest among researchers studying drug treatments. In their study, published in the *Journal of General Internal Medicine,* the authors concluded, "Conflict of interest is widespread among the authors of published manuscripts and these authors are more likely to present positive findings."

By then, Sheldon Krimsky, a Tufts University professor and author of the book *Science in the Private Interest,* had also found that the amount of money consultants receive makes a difference. "If you're only getting a thousand dollars for a year, you would have a different response than if you're getting two hundred thousand a year," Krimsky said. "At some point the quantity of money produces a qualitative change in people, and the integrity of the scientific endeavor is tarnished."

But in 1998, such findings had yet to be drawn, and the overweening influence of the pharmaceutical industry on medical research was not part of the public debate. The notion that science was pure—that money and prestige couldn't possibly influence a scientist's judgment—held sway. Even journalists, by and large, believed this party line. In reporting on the latest health findings, most medical writers took what they read in press releases and journals at face value and did not dig much further.

As TEICHER AND SCHATZBERG continued their jaunt around Toronto that late spring morning in 1998, conflicts in medicine were the last thing on their minds. They were far more interested in catching up with each other. Back at the convention center, the two men promised to keep in touch and parted ways. Schatzberg dashed off to a previously scheduled luncheon, and Teicher made his way inside the 104,000-square-foot convention center to prepare for a poster session. The poster was titled "A Strong Association between Suicidal Ideation and Ratings of Limbic System Irritability in Children with a History of Early Abuse." Despite the grim topic, Teicher was in a good mood. The walk had put some color in his cheeks, and for the first time in years, Marty Teicher was feeling upbeat about the direction of his career.

# 11. Tonya Brooks Becomes a Nomad, and Rose Firestein Fights to Protect Florida's Foster Children, 2000–2001

When Tonya Brooks was eleven, she and her parents moved into a campground in Lockhart, Texas. Her mother and father were trying to save money to build a new home. All three of them lived in a camper-trailer with just enough space for a tiny kitchen, a couch, and two twin beds. There was no such thing as privacy. Halfway through her sixth-grade year at Burnett Junior High, Tonya was sent to live with her grandmother in Granbury, 240 miles away. But she hated being away from her mother and father. So a month or two later, she moved back to the trailer to live with her parents. In such a cramped space, tempers flared. Tonya remembers her parents quarreling a lot. She finished out the school term in Lockhart Intermediate—her third school in one year.

That fall, her parents separated, and Tonya and her mother went to live with her mother's sister, Aunt Meme, in Clyde, Texas. There, Tonya attended Clyde Junior High. On her first day at school, she sat down at a mostly empty table in the cafeteria to eat her lunch. One of the girls at the other end of the table said, "You can't sit here."

This kind of thing happened over and over again. Tonya stopped eating in the cafeteria. She stopped trying to make new friends at school.

It almost got to the point where she would run and hide if another kid so much as looked at her.

That winter, Tonya and her mother moved to Georgetown, Texas, to live with other relatives. There, Tonya attended Benold Middle School and hated it—the kids were so cruel. In the spring of that year, she and her mother moved again, this time to Baird, Texas, to live with her mother's brother. In May 2000, her parents finally got back together, and they moved with Tonya into a new home in Pflugerville. Tonya's father walked her to school on her first day of eighth grade at Pfluger-ville Middle School. But she didn't want to be there; after he left, she sat and cried for ten minutes straight. She was thirteen years old, and all she wanted to do was disappear.

HAD ROSE FIRESTEIN known Tonya Brooks at the time, she would have empathized. Before joining the New York AG's office, Firestein had spent a lot of time on the road herself. For five years she had crisscrossed the country as senior litigation counsel for Children's Rights, a nonprofit organization that defended the rights of vulnerable children nationwide. In 2001, Florida was Firestein's latest battleground, and she seemed to be on a plane heading south every few weeks. On each trip, she bought a present for Ellie: a pink beaded shoulder bag, bubble bath, little cutters for the cookies Ellie loved to help bake. The five-year-old accepted the gifts as her due, as the least Rosie could do after going away so many times. Ellie did not understand why her aunt had to keep taking that big bird in the sky to a faraway place called the Sunshine State. How come she never came back with any sun on her face?

"I don't want you to go! Why?" Ellie would wail when Rosie announced she had to leave yet again. Firestein would gather the little girl onto her lap and explain that she had to go and help some other children who didn't have a mommy or a Rosie to hold them tight.

"You know I always come back to you," Firestein told her. "You are my sweet potatoes! How about I make another cake when I get back?"

Firestein baked a gourmet cake for Ellie's birthday every year. For her niece's third birthday, Rose created what her sister Janice dubbed the Eiffel Tower cake—a delicious concoction of butter and cream and flour that was eighteen inches tall and almost a foot wide. Eiffel Tower cookies decorated the top of the cake, and buttercream flowers and trees adorned the sides. And every year for the Chinese New Year, Firestein whipped up an orange and black cake in the form of a fire-breathing dragon—in honor of Ellie's Chinese ancestry.

Firestein didn't tell Ellie this, but she was just as sick of the constant travel as her niece was. Yet she had no choice. This was a crucial phase in the class action suit that Children's Rights was helping several local attorneys bring against the Florida Department of Children and Families. The *Bonnie L.* complaint, filed in federal court, was just the latest in a string of lawsuits targeting Florida's decades-old habit of foisting foster care onto private agencies that warehoused children in large, poorly supervised residential facilities.

Firestein spent much of her time in Florida taking affidavits and depositions in an attempt to show that many of the state's foster children were being overmedicated with drugs like Prozac, Paxil, and Risperdal, an antipsychotic. At times she felt as if she were reliving her Legal Aid days. The abuses were the same; only the names of the drugs had changed.

In one affidavit, a teenage girl named Karina testified that the drugs she had been given in foster care made her tremble and drool.

"When I was on the medication, I couldn't function," Karina later told Carol Marbin Miller, a reporter for the *Miami Herald* who wrote a series on the problem. "I was a zombie . . . I was always sleeping. I didn't know what was going on. Everything was a blur."

Another teenager named Leslie F. described how as a young child in foster care she had been forced to take Prozac. Leslie had been in foster care from the age of five, ever since her mother died. She had cycled in and out of shelters, locked residential treatment facilities, and countless foster homes. In an affidavit, Leslie said, "When I was younger, DCF [Department of Children and Families] made me take Prozac, which made me very drowsy. I had a very difficult time staying awake in school, and I couldn't concentrate on my schoolwork." Leslie dropped out of school and gave birth to a child out of wedlock when she was eighteen. The *Miami Herald* series revealed that as many as 45 to 46 percent of foster children, some as young as five, were on psychotropic drugs.

For *Bonnie L.*, as the class action suit was known, Firestein had to travel all over Florida—to Tampa, Miami, Fort Lauderdale, Palm Beach, Tallahassee. At times, Firestein felt as if she had stepped back into a time warp, to the months she had spent traversing rural Georgia, talking to African American families whose children had been labeled mentally retarded and dumped into warehouselike classes where no real teaching was going on. This time, of course, she wasn't camping by the side of the road ("I'm too old for that," she told her boss at Children's Rights), but it seemed as if she were spending nights in the same forgettable motel room in every town she passed through.

As if the constant travel weren't bad enough, Firestein was having continuing problems with her eyes. She had undergone several laser procedures in her eye surgeon's office to no avail, but Firestein felt that she couldn't just stop working: the *Bonnie L.* case was heating up. So a few weeks after the emergency surgery to reattach her retinas, Firestein flew back to Florida for a previously scheduled round of depositions. On this trip, she flew directly into Tampa. Her cocounsel, a Florida trial lawyer named Karen Gievers, met her at the Holiday Inn Express where they were staying. Gievers, who had raised two children while practicing law, made a decent living litigating commercial and personal injury suits in Tallahassee. But in the past several years, Gievers had taken on the thankless and considerably less remunerative task of advocating for Florida's foster children. Gievers first sued the Department of Children and Families in 1995 and won a settlement in which state officials promised to improve the care of children in their custody. But by 2000 it was clear that the new state administration under Governor Jeb Bush was not going to live up to those promises. So Gievers decided it was time for another class action suit. This time, she brought in Children's Rights to help with the heavy lifting.

Gievers could tell that Firestein was having problems with her eyesight. It seemed as if her cocounsel's vision had gotten progressively worse since they'd begun working together. But Firestein had been quick to adapt, figuring out a few ingenious work-arounds: She enlarged the font size of the computer so that she could read the documents she needed for her work. And during the depositions, which were taped and then transcribed electronically, she memorized the key questions so that she didn't need to look at her notes. Firestein always seemed to know exactly what she wanted to ask and in what order. Her mastery of the subject matter for each deposition never failed to amaze Gievers.

Over dinner that night in Tampa, Firestein told Gievers and her husband, a paralegal in the same law firm, about her detached retinas and how she was hoping that surgery might eventually restore some of her sight. The most recent procedure hadn't done the trick, she said.

"She didn't complain or ask that somebody else do the work," Gievers recalled. "She just kept trucking."

Gievers and her husband offered to help in any way they could. And later that evening, they did get a call from Firestein, who was staying in a nearby room at the Holiday Inn. Could Gievers and her husband help her find a document that had gone missing?

The couple walked over to her room. To their astonishment, Firestein showed them to the bathroom, where legal documents lay strewn all over the countertop, bathtub, and floor. The litigator chuckled at their surprise and explained that the bathroom had the best light in the entire room. With her limited eyesight, the lamps around the bed and desk just didn't cut it.

Gievers found the document Firestein was looking for, and they chatted briefly. It was getting late, and Gievers almost offered to stay and help her cocounsel prepare for the next day's deposition. But she sensed that Firestein didn't want or need any further assistance. So Gievers said good night and left. She remembered thinking it was going to be a late night for the New York litigator. But when she and her husband came down for breakfast the next morning, Firestein was already there, dressed and ready to go.

FIRESTEIN WOULD LATER confess that she didn't know how she kept going during this period. She was desperately afraid she would not be able to work again. She and her sister Janice talked late into the night about what they were going to do. Even if by some miracle her vision was partially restored, she had a feeling that her days at Children's Rights were numbered. The nonprofit ran on a shoestring budget, and it needed litigators who could hop on a plane at a moment's notice and travel anywhere in the fifty states. With her failing eyesight, she knew she couldn't sustain that pace. Yet who else would hire a female attorney who was legally blind and approaching fifty? Already she had learned that blindness carried with it a stigma and the lingering suspicion among people with sight that people without it couldn't possibly be as smart or as capable as they were.

WHAT SCARED FIRESTEIN most of all was the thought of becoming dependent on others. When she and her siblings were growing up in Indiana, their proud and distinguished father would sometimes fall ill from complications of diabetes, occasionally for months at a time. Nursed by his wife with endless devotion, he would eventually recover and resume his medical duties. But finally he had a stroke and just seemed to give up. Not long afterward, he died of a heart attack.

Rose wasn't about to give up. She had seen the toll her father's health problems took on the family: during the periods when her father lay ill, her mother was too preoccupied to pay much attention to her children. So his third daughter—the one with the self-professed "biggest mouth in the group"—was determined not to let *her* health problems interfere with the lives of her sister and the little girl they were raising together.

She was especially upbeat around Ellie. As much as possible, Firestein tried to make her eye problems into a source of amusement for the little girl. At home in Brooklyn, they ate off china with a decorative flower pattern, and there were times when Firestein would mistake the flowers for food.

"The sight of me chasing those flowers around the plate made Ellie laugh her head off," Firestein recalled. "She was five then and she thought that was really funny."

In 2001, Rosie could no longer see well enough to create her extravagant cake productions or take Ellie on day-long treks to Coney Island. But when the two of them were walking somewhere and had to cross the street, Ellie would take Rosie's hand and gently, unobtrusively, guide her across. Firestein was touched by her niece's tenderness, but it was all she could do not to pull her arm away. She had always had a hard time accepting help from others. She prided herself on her independence. And now here she was being squired around in public by a five-year-old. For the first time in her life, Rose Firestein felt helpless and dependent on the goodwill of others. And she hated that feeling.

## 12. Donna Howard Discovers That in the Nonprofit World of Patient Advocacy, Money Shouts, Fall 2002

The storefront office of the Rhode Island chapter of the National Alliance for the Mentally Ill (NAMI) was built into the side of a hill in a run-down neighborhood of North Providence. Even in broad daylight you felt as if you were working underground in a dank hovel. And because the office was one big room split into small, cluttered cubicles, there wasn't much privacy. But Donna Howard didn't mind. As assistant director of NAMI Rhode Island, she had found her calling. She loved working directly on behalf of people with mental illness, and she was not about to let the gloomy environment or lack of privacy bother her. True, the other employees of NAMI Rhode Island could hear every word of her phone conversations, but she could hear theirs too.

So when Jim McNulty, president of the board of directors for the parent NAMI, called one morning in October 2002 to speak to Nicki Sahlin, executive director of the Rhode Island chapter, everyone in the office knew it. McNulty was calling about a lecture NAMI Rhode Island was planning for families who had children with bipolar disorder. Howard herself had organized the event as part of a community education series for that fall. This particular lecture was scheduled to be held on November 13, 2002, at Butler Hospital on the outskirts of Providence, where Brown University's psychiatry department was located. Howard was not thrilled at the thought of visiting her old stomping grounds, but Butler was a convenient location for NAMI members, and as Sahlin was always reminding her, the hospital *was* a generous supporter of NAMI Rhode Island.

Even so, the November 13 lecture had been a bone of contention between Howard and Sahlin for weeks now. Researchers from Brown's psychiatry department had asked permission to pass out flyers at the lecture advertising for a new study to follow adolescents with bipolar disorder. The National Institute of Mental Health was funding the study under the direction of Brown's chief of psychiatry, Martin Keller. But as the Butler clinician who had first called Howard explained, the researchers were having trouble recruiting teenagers for the study. A public lecture on child-onset bipolar disorder, they figured, would be the perfect place to find participants.

"We thought there might be some families at your lecture who would be interested," he said. "That okay with you?"

Howard froze. It was most definitely *not* okay. She had heard about COBY (an acronym for the study's official title, "Course and Outcome for Bipolar Disorder in Youth"), and she wanted no part of it. Having worked in Keller's research department at Brown, she had seen what could happen to troubled adolescents enrolled in research studies there. In two of the trials under way during Howard's tenure at Brown in the mid-1990s, many of the participants had been teenagers who had no idea what they were getting into. Some had been recruited from foster homes; a few, right off the street. And among patients who did have parents in the picture, there seemed to be little understanding of the risks involved. As it turned out, Howard was not the only Brown employee who had complained to authorities about the way these adolescent studies were being conducted. Around the time that Howard called the *Globe,* another Brown employee contacted the inspector general's office of the federal Department of Health and Human Services (HHS) about problems with one of the studies, a trial of lithium in bipolar adolescents. Keller and his researchers were having trouble recruiting for the lithium study, whose purpose was to determine the efficacy of lithium in preventing the recurrence of manic depression. That meant taking vulnerable teenagers off lithium, waiting until they became manic again, and then putting them back on the drug. The study design had risks, one of which was a heightened chance of suicide. It was not the kind of research that most parents would rush to sign their children up for.

In a June 1995 progress report to the National Institute of Mental Health, which was funding the study, Keller wrote that he had amended the original study design to include other mood stabilizers in addition to lithium. He acknowledged that there were not enough participants in the lithium-only study to allow valid statistical comparisons.

Yet despite the redesigned study's broader net, the Brown researchers continued to have problems recruiting for it. Sometime in the fall of 1995, when Howard was still working there, a social worker in the Brown psychiatry department found a computer disk lying in the hallway. The social worker, who was working part-time on another of Keller's studies, popped the disk into her computer to find out to whom she should return it. What she saw there alarmed her. On the disk, researchers in the bipolar study were "saying they had X number of youngsters enrolled in the study, but it was clear they didn't have these adolescents in the study at the time," recalled the social worker, who is no longer working at Brown. Since she is still practicing in Rhode Island, she asked me not to use her name.

"These people had either dropped out of the study or they weren't in the study in the first place," the social worker added. "It looked as if [the researchers] were making up data to say they had these adolescents in the study."

The social worker shared what she had found on the disk with several co-workers. A few weeks later, she received a call from the inspector general's office of the Health and Human Services Department: they wanted to talk to her about the disk she had discovered. Shortly after that, the social worker transferred to another department at Brown, and Howard lost touch with her. In January 1996, Keller acknowledged in an interview with me that the National Institute of Mental Health was investigating the lithium bipolar study. The NIMH inquiry was in response to a letter from a Brown employee (not Howard) alleging the falsification of data in Keller's application to the federal institute for the renewal of his department's $188,000 annual contract for the lithium study. (A NIMH spokeswoman later confirmed that the institute had indeed sent an auditor to Brown. The auditor found the department's "books" on the lithium grant and two other NIMH-funded studies were in order, she said.)

Three years later, in the summer of 1999, Howard herself was contacted by an agent from the HHS inspector general's office. He wasn't as nice as the two agents who had visited her home in January 1996. "He implied that I could come and talk friendly-like or he would subpoena me," she recalled. Howard met the man, whom she would describe as "a sixtyish professional bureaucrat," at a Providence hotel and spent an anxious hour in the hotel café answering his questions. She never heard from him again, and no federal charges were filed against Brown or its chief of psychiatry, according to a spokeswoman for HHS.

At the time, what bothered Howard most about the lithium study was her sense that participants were not being adequately informed about the risks involved. She had also come across what she considered blatant conflicts of interest in the recruitment process. One homeless, manic eighteen-year-old girl had been recruited for the study by the same psychiatrist who was treating her at a public clinic in Fall River, Massachusetts. According to Howard and the psychiatrist who treated and recruited the girl, Keller had hired him as a paid consultant to do "subject recruitment" for the lithium study. Who, Howard wondered, was looking out for this girl's best interest?

Sheldon Krimsky, the Tufts University medical ethicist, expressed the same concern. "There's a general, widely accepted agreement you shouldn't get paid for recruiting your own patients," he said. "That would be a deep conflict of interest." Receiving financial remuneration (to the tune of $25,000, in this particular case) for recruiting a vulnerable teenager could easily clash with the best interests of the patient, Krimsky said. (When interviewed for this book, the psychiatrist who was paid for recruiting the girl said he saw no such conflict.)

Years later, Donna Howard would point to such issues as one reason she never enrolled her own daughter in a clinical trial at Brown or its affiliate hospitals. Fortunately, by the fall of 2002, Howard's daughter was doing much better. Maria had recently earned a general equivalency diploma (GED) and was now enrolled in Bristol Community College in Fall River, about twenty-two miles away. She continued to live at home, and Howard drove her to campus on her way to work every morning. When classes were finished for the day, Maria would wait for her mother to pick her up. Howard felt as if all those years of struggle, of trying to keep Maria safe and sane within the confines of her illness, were finally paying off. She was intensely proud of her daughter for having the courage to insist on a normal life.

In the COBY study Keller was recruiting for that autumn, the aim was to follow adolescents with bipolar disorder over the long term and see how they did on various medications and measures of psychosocial functioning. The COBY study was not a randomized clinical trial, where patients were blindly assigned to either a group taking the active drug or a group taking a placebo. No matter. Howard felt strongly that she couldn't allow teenagers already in deep trouble to be recruited for a study run by researchers she didn't trust. She was also still upset over what had happened at an earlier lecture, when another Brown-affiliated hospital had distributed literature without authorization, disrupting the discussion. So she politely but firmly told the Butler emissary that it was against NAMI's policy to allow advertising or recruitment at a lecture intended for educational purposes only.

Within a few days, someone from Butler called Howard's boss to ask for clarification of NAMI Rhode Island's policy on recruiting at educational events. To Howard's relief, Nicki Sahlin backed her up. As the executive director herself recalled, she agreed that it was not a good idea to allow recruiting among vulnerable families who had come to an educational event desperate for information on how to deal with a bipolar child.

Howard had hoped that would be the end of it. But now, listening in on Sahlin's conversation with Jim McNulty, she could tell it wasn't over, not by a long shot. As president of the National Alliance's board of directors, McNulty was a powerful presence in Rhode Island. He himself had been treated for bipolar disorder and was now a patient advocate. He sat on key advisory committees to the National Institute of Mental Health that made important decisions about what kind of research the institute should fund. At the same time, McNulty was also, to use Howard's term, a "professional patient spokesman" for the drug industry. According to Howard, Sahlin, and McNulty himself, he received money from GlaxoSmithKline, Eli Lilly, Pfizer, and other pharmaceutical companies to travel to and speak at various company-sponsored events. In an arrangement that medical ethicists say is highly questionable, McNulty would process the "grants" through NAMI Rhode Island.

The scheme worked like this: McNulty's pharmaceutical sponsors would give NAMI Rhode Island a check—usually several thousand dollars—and then Sahlin would write a check to McNulty as compensation for his speaking engagements on behalf of whichever drug company was paying him. In interviews with me, both Sahlin and McNulty acknowledged this arrangement.

"Jim didn't have a job for many years, and he was singing for his supper," Sahlin said. "He didn't have an employer; he was not a non-profit unto himself, so it would go through NAMI Rhode Island." When I asked McNulty why he had been paid that way, he said, "Paperwork: it was simpler that way."

Sahlin knew the check-processing scheme was improper, according to Howard. But Sahlin couldn't bring herself to speak out against McNulty; he was, after all, her überboss.

Several ethicists say this kind of arrangement is patently unethical because, as McNulty acknowledged, he did not disclose to the audiences at his various speaking engagements, or to NAMI's membership, that he was being paid by the pharmaceutical industry. "Here is someone who's acting like a citizen advocate, and he's getting paid by the pharmaceutical companies and not disclosing it," said Sheldon Krimsky. "Most people would question whether he's truly a citizen advocate after that."

McNulty said that if he had similar speaking engagements today, he would disclose who was paying his way. "Where people are today is very different from where they were in 2002," he said.

Over the years, the National Alliance for the Mentally Ill has itself accepted millions of dollars in corporate donations from the pharmaceutical industry. In 2002 and 2003, the years that McNulty served as president of the national organization's board of directors, corporate contributions to the national nonprofit totaled more than $4 million each year, almost half of the nonprofit's annual revenues, according to NAMI's posted annual reports. And that didn't include the millions of dollars in corporate donations to the organization's Anti-Stigma Foundation. The list of NAMI's corporate "partners" on its annual report for 2002 and 2003 includes every major pharmaceutical company in the world, including Abbott Labs, AstraZeneca, Bristol-Myers Squibb, Eli Lilly, Forest Labs, GlaxoSmithKline, Novartis, Pfizer, and Wyeth. (NAMI continues to receive millions of dollars from drugmakers, but its annual reports no longer break out the amount of money given by corporations as opposed to individual donors. The organization merely provides a list of its corporate partners—which continues to be a roll call of every company making psychoactive drugs.)

On this particular day in October 2002, it was clear from the strain in Nicki Sahlin's voice that McNulty was insisting that she allow Brown recruiters into the November 13 lecture. Listening in the next cubicle, Howard frowned. This wasn't the first time she had run afoul of the NAMI board president. In December 1999, a year after she was hired by NAMI, the news broke that Brown University had agreed to repay the Commonwealth of Massachusetts for the thousands of dollars in research funding it had received from the state's Department of Mental Health. After a long investigation, the Massachusetts attorney general's office had determined that Brown had "improperly collected" a total of $300,170—a sum even greater than the amount Howard had dug up. As part of the settlement with Brown, Massachusetts officials agreed to drop the lawsuit they had filed against the Ivy League institution in Suffolk Superior Court. At the time, I quoted Howard in the *Boston Globe* having said, "I'm glad the Commonwealth stuck in there against Brown's formidable efforts to deny and cover the matter up."

Upon seeing that article, McNulty had thrown a fit. Sahlin, of course, knew all about Howard's whistleblowing at Brown and had hired her in spite of it (or, as Howard liked to think, because of it). In time, Sahlin managed to calm McNulty down.

But now, as Howard listened in on her boss's conversation with McNulty, she feared that Sahlin would cave and allow the Brown recruiters to come to the lecture. Howard was fond of Sahlin, a well-meaning woman in her fifties, but she knew the former executive director was an emotionally fragile woman who often wilted under pressure. How long would it be before she buckled under this time?

Much to Howard's surprise, she heard Sahlin say, "We're going to support Donna on this."

Her joy proved premature, however. Within the hour, Sahlin received another call, this time from someone high up at Butler. As Howard was later to learn, the Butler official was offering to expedite the hospital's annual donation to NAMI Rhode Island's yearly conference in exchange for the opportunity to pass out COBY literature at the November 13 lecture.

Howard didn't hear that particular conversation, but from that day forward, she felt as if her boss was trying to change her mind about the recruitment drive.

"I really think it wouldn't be a bad idea to allow the Brown researchers to pass out these flyers," Sahlin said one afternoon a few days before the November 13 lecture. Brown was doing an important study to find out what the course of bipolar disorder looked like in adolescents, she added. "This is research."

At this point, Howard had already printed up and distributed flyers for the event. She herself was the guest speaker, and she was especially proud of the title for her lecture: "Injured Bird in the Cat Cage: Understanding the Family Impact of Childhood Onset Bipolar Disorder." The words had come from an essay written by Maria.

"If you allow this, I'm not going to do the lecture," Howard said flatly. "I'll just cancel it."

Nicki's face folded up into itself.

"Okay, Donna, this is your show," she said, and walked away.

THE NIGHT OF THE lecture was overcast with the kind of brisk November wind that chills right through to the bones. The leafless limbs of the trees surrounding the Butler campus looked stark and lonely in the reflected lights of the cars driving up to park. In the brightly lit Ray Conference Center, seats were rapidly filling with people. Howard and Sahlin were busy greeting parents and guests and preparing the podium. The plan was for Sahlin to introduce Howard as the guest speaker. As Howard passed by the table near the entrance where NAMI placed its education literature, she noticed a stack of lime green brochures that hadn't been there before. She looked closer: they were the COBY brochures.

Howard couldn't breathe. It felt as if someone had just punched her in the gut. In the shock of that moment, she realized that Sahlin had taken the money from Butler as a quid pro quo after all and hadn't had the courage to admit it. After a few seconds, Howard straightened up and grabbed the stack of brochures from the table. She looked around. Someone from Brown was also passing out the flyers to families as they entered the auditorium. Howard strode over to two NAMI volunteers setting up floor microphones nearby.

"Would you do me a favor?" she asked them in a casual voice. "These flyers aren't supposed to be distributed tonight; someone made a mistake. Would you go around and scoop up as many of them as you can?"

"Sure." The women were happy to be of assistance. "What do you want us to do with them?"

"Just give them to me," she said.

IN A TELEPHONE interview with me, Nicki Sahlin, by then retired from NAMI, acknowledged that the Rhode Island chapter had received "something like one thousand dollars" from Butler toward its annual educational conference. Sahlin admitted that the check had been contingent on her allowing Brown researchers to pass out flyers advertising the COBY study.

"We wouldn't have gotten the money unless we cooperated with them fully. What do you think?" Sahlin said with exasperation in her voice. But then she immediately became defensive, insisting, "That wasn't a sufficient payoff to corrupt anyone."

During our phone conversation, Sahlin tried several times to warn me off doing a book about the drug industry and detailing what happened that night at Butler, even if the account was "factually accurate." "This is not a book you should be writing," she cautioned. "The reaction—it could ruin you."

As DONNA HOWARD remembers it, the rest of the evening went remarkably well. In the end, more than 150 people showed up and listened intently as she spoke about the difficult family dynamics of living with a child with bipolar disorder—the loneliness, the stress of dealing with an unpredictable roller coaster of mood swings, reckless mania one minute, abject depression the next. She had culled case examples from her own experience and from the stories that many people had shared with her over the years. When she finished, the audience applauded warmly.

Afterward, one of Howard's friends, a mental health professional who had come to give her moral support, offered to walk her out to her car.

"That's not necessary," she said. "This is Butler—I know my way around."

"That's precisely why I should," he said, and then grinned. "You never know: Marty could be hiding in the bushes."

Howard laughed uneasily. Marty Keller and his unwelcome presence in her life was an inside joke between the two of them. But after that night's escapade, it didn't seem so funny anymore. NAMI Rhode Island needed the money that Brown and Butler could shovel its way, and Howard knew that her boss had been caught in the middle. The fact that Sahlin had caved in and allowed Brown researchers to pass out flyers over her assistant director's objections made it clear to Howard that her days at NAMI were numbered.

# 13. Rose Firestein Begins Probing the Paxil Puzzle, Summer 2003

When Rose Firestein found out that she had landed a job with the New York State attorney general's office in June 2002, she couldn't believe her luck. Eliot Spitzer was just beginning to grab national attention for his investigation of the financial conflicts between Wall Street analysts and the huge investment banks they worked for. The month before, Merrill Lynch had agreed to settle for $100 million Spitzer's charges that it had pressured its own stock analysts into misleading investors about start-up companies that were clients of its banking arm. This was the first time a state prosecutor had taken on Wall Street—traditionally the preserve of the federal Securities and Exchange Commission—and New York's powerful business community was furious. The conservative editorial pages of the *Wall Street Journal* attacked Spitzer as a deluded publicity seeker. The incoming flak only intensified Rose Firestein's desire to join his team.

Even though her eyesight had stabilized—she had no vision in her left eye but could still see things up close with her right—she knew it was time to find a job with a more forgiving travel schedule than she had at Children's Rights. So when she heard about the opening at 120 Broadway, she jumped at it. At this particular juncture in her life, Firestein wanted nothing more than to be part of a large, high-powered team, all rowing in the same direction under the orders of a granite-jawed coxswain who seemed to know exactly where he was going.

Had Firestein known what lay in store for her those first few months, she might have felt differently. Almost as soon as she walked in the door at 120 Broadway, she found herself buried in an enormously complicated case involving the way the pharmaceutical industry priced its products for sale.

"I won't pretend this is a simple case," Joe Baker said when he sketched the assignment for Firestein her very first week on the job. Baker had come to the AG's office by way of the Medicare Rights Center, a national patient rights consumer advocacy group, and the Gay Men's Health Crisis. The forty-two-year-old Philadelphia native favored pink shirts and was open about the fact that he was gay. Although Baker was head of the Health Care Bureau and had an imposing corner office on the twenty-fifth floor (near Eliot Spitzer's), he had developed a good working relationship with Tom Conway and his consumer team on the third floor.

"In fact, this case is incredibly complicated. I don't really understand all the ins and outs myself," said Baker, sitting around the conference table with Firestein, Conway, and Stark. "It's going to involve a lot of research and drilling down into the facts." At the core, however, was a simple premise: that the drug companies were wildly inflating the average wholesale price (AWP) of their drugs so that Medicare, Medicaid, and private insurers would reimburse doctors for the drugs at a higher price than they actually paid. Drugmakers employed the AWP scheme, Baker explained, as a way of essentially bribing doctors and pharmacies to use their products.

"That's what we think is going on here, anyway," Baker said. "Rose, we need you to pull together enough evidence to build a case with. This is a good way to get your feet wet. You up for it?"

Firestein nodded with a lot more confidence than she felt.

"You're really putting me to work here, aren't you?" she said in a joking tone of voice. Everyone around the table laughed with relief. This was a huge undertaking, particularly for someone so new to the AG's office. Baker, for one, appreciated Firestein's can-do attitude.

There were times those first few months, however, when Firestein didn't feel so confident. She knew next to nothing about the byzantine world of health care reimbursements. It took her months to understand the mechanisms by which pharmaceutical companies were inflating their prices. Prosecutors for several other states and the U.S. Department of Justice had already sued a number of pharmaceutical firms for inflating the average wholesale prices of their products. In fact, in 2001, TAP Pharmaceutical Products Inc. paid a record-breaking $875 million to settle civil and criminal charges of Medicaid and Medicare fraud in the marketing and pricing of its prostate cancer drug, Lupron.

But this was new territory for the New York AG's office, and Firestein spent hours reading up on New York case law, working late into the night to understand why and how the whole scheme worked in her state. The AWP case, she would later recall, was "ridiculously complicated, with so many permutations that there were times you just wanted to put your head in the oven."

Tom Conway sensed her frustration. When she accepted the job, Conway had told her that they were going to have lots of fun together, "a great time." Now, every few weeks, he would stop by and ask her with deadpan earnestness, "Is this the way I promised you it would be? Did we tell you the truth in advertising?"

Firestein would reply in a tone of mock gruffness, "No! Where's the fun?" And Conway would laugh heartily, delighted that Firestein had a sense of humor about it all.

FIRESTEIN WAS SO preoccupied with figuring out the complexities of the drug reimbursement system that she didn't have much time to dwell on the unhappy fate of *Bonnie L. v. Jeb Bush et al.* A few months before she had left Children's Rights for the AG's office, U.S. District

Court judge Federico Moreno in Miami had dismissed the class action suit on grounds that it was a case that should be heard in the Florida state courts. In doing so, Moreno had ignored years of legal precedent, other judges having consistently found that the federal court had a right, indeed an obligation, to intervene on behalf of abused and neglected foster children. Firestein was disappointed by Moreno's decision, but she tried to comfort herself with the knowledge that other jurists were continuing the fight. Karen Gievers had already launched an appeal of Moreno's decision, and other activist lawyers in Florida were initiating similar actions in the state courts. Firestein hoped the plight of Florida's foster children would not be forgotten, but she knew how stacked the system could be against a handful of well-meaning litigators who were trying to bring about large-scale change through the courts. She had learned from hard experience not to let such legal defeats haunt her. "You can't take it personally," she said. "It's a function of the adversarial system: sometimes you lose. You say some nasty words and then you get on with it."

FIRESTEIN HAD BEEN toiling on the AWP case for eight or nine months when Conway informed her that Eliot Spitzer was keen on investigating the profit-driven labyrinth of drug research. As Spitzer himself told me, he and Joe Baker, as his health care czar, had been discussing whether some of the financial conflicts his investment division had uncovered on Wall Street existed to some degree in the pharmaceutical industry as well.

"It began with our being tempted and intrigued by the notion that there was cross-ownership here," Spitzer said, citing news articles about the pharmaceutical companies' having equity in some of the private companies that tested the drugs they had in development. "So we wondered: Is there something that goes amiss here? Do they play games with the numbers?"

Spitzer's desire to probe the unexamined corners of drug research coincided with a conversation Firestein herself had had with Shirley Stark, her immediate supervisor. Firestein had mentioned her desire to look into the off-label use of psychoactive medications in children. From her work with Children's Rights, Firestein knew that the FDA had not approved such drugs for use in children and adolescents; Prozac was the only antidepressant drug okayed for pediatric use, and that green light had come only a few months earlier—in January 2003. Yet potent medications like Paxil, Zoloft, Celexa, Effexor, and Risperdal were widely prescribed off-label for the under-eighteen age group. In many cases the drugs were helpful in treating symptoms of depression, anxiety, and (in the case of Risperdal) bipolar disorder and psychosis. But in many situations, they were dispensed too readily. Busy primary care doctors and pediatricians were sending pediatric patients home with samples from the drug companies and failing to monitor their reactions to the drugs. Serious side effects were common, as Firestein had discovered in *Bonnie L*. While she understood that it was legal for doctors to prescribe such off-label use, it seemed to her as though medical professionals were making judgments based on very little information about the drugs' impact on children.

To Firestein, the FDA's general attitude toward off-label drug usage seemed disturbingly laissez-faire. Why this was so, Firestein couldn't really say. She knew, of course, that some consumer groups believed that the FDA had become beholden to the very industry it was supposed to regulate. Consumer advocates, including Dr. Sidney Wolfe and his colleagues at the Public Citizen in Washington, D.C., contended that the agency's increasing reliance on hundreds of millions of dollars in user fees from the drug industry had exerted a corrosive effect on the FDA's ability to monitor the safety of already approved drugs and to review new drugs objectively. FDA medical officers surveyed by the Public Citizen in 1998 cited growing pressure on them to approve new drugs, and they identified twenty-seven new drugs that they believed should not have been approved but were anyway. "Inappropriate pressure from

Congress, the drug companies and senior FDA employees create an atmosphere in which the likelihood of drug approval is maximized," concluded the Public Citizen survey.

The FDA, of course, was not the only beneficiary of the pharmaceutical industry's largesse. Its tentacles reached deep into the corridors of power in Washington. Between 1998 and 2006, the drug companies spent a total of $1.2 billion on lobbying and political contributions in the United States, according to the Center for Responsive Politics, a nonprofit, nonpartisan research group that tracks money in politics. In 2002, the pharmaceutical industry ranked tenth among the top industries in political contributions and seventh in the amount of money it spent on lobbying members of Congress and others.

From her cramped third-floor office in Lower Manhattan, there wasn't much Firestein could do about the pharmaceutical industry's favored status in Washington. What concerned her, as an assistant attorney general, was whether the companies selling drugs in the state of New York were leveling with physicians who were writing all those off-label prescriptions for children and adolescents.

"Mind if I look into this once I get my head above water with AWP?" Firestein asked Stark. Stark was only too glad to see her take the initiative. In working with Firestein on the AWP case, Stark had found her to be very bright and creative in her approach to the law. The two women had a lot in common. They were both Jewish and committed to social change, having come of age in the antiestablishment 1960s. Yet both dressed conservatively, favoring suits and pearls. Stark, then forty-nine, was slender, with large green eyes, and teeth that protruded slightly when she smiled. She had dark brown hair cut in a pageboy style similar to the cut of Firestein's more unruly, platinum blond locks. But Stark was more reserved than Firestein, who had strong opinions and was not afraid to get into a verbal dustup with their boss, Tom Conway. On several occasions, Stark, more conciliatory by nature, found herself having to mediate between her two equally stubborn colleagues.

Stark, of course, had noticed Firestein's vision difficulties from the outset but hadn't said anything about them. A few months after Firestein joined the AG's office, Stark herself had to undergo eye surgery for a weak muscle in one eye. When she returned to work, Firestein confided in her about her own eye problems, and the two women found one more reason to bond.

In early 2003, Shirley Stark was in the midst of a massive, multistate case against Pfizer for illegally marketing an epilepsy drug called Neurontin for treating conditions for which it had not been approved by the FDA. Neurontin had been approved in 1994 to treat epilepsy for a relatively narrow usage: as an add-on when other drugs failed to control seizures. But there wasn't much money in that, and Parke-Davis, which produced Neurontin, wanted to expand the drug's market. (Parke-Davis was a subsidiary of Warner-Lambert, which itself would later be swallowed up by Pfizer.) Since Neurontin's patent was due to expire in 1998 (it was eventually extended to 2000), the company didn't feel it had time to do the kind of extensive clinical trials that might win FDA approval for additional uses. So Parke-Davis, according to a whistleblower's lawsuit filed in 1996, devised a plan to promote the drug for off-label uses, primarily by paying academic experts to put their names on research papers prepared by the drug company. The papers were written with the express purpose of showing that Neurontin worked for common conditions such as pain and anxiety. Although the research was less than authentic, the marketing strategy worked: Neurontin emerged a blockbuster, with sales of $2.7 billion in 2003 alone. But federal prosecutors in Boston eventually filed a brief in support of the whistleblower's suit, and by 2003, forty-eight states, including New York, had launched parallel actions against Pfizer (which by then owned Parke-Davis and Warner-Lambert).

Swamped by the Neurontin case, Stark was only too happy to have Firestein look into other cases of off-label marketing. Eliot Spitzer's conversation with Joe Baker sealed the deal, and by the spring of 2003, the newest member of the AG's consumer protection bureau had turned her attention to the drug industry's widespread practice of making billions of dollars from the off-label marketing of psychotropic drugs.

SOME MONTHS LATER, in July 2003, Rose Firestein was browsing the official Web site of the Food and Drug Administration when she suddenly reared back in surprise. She blinked and looked again. Buried in the third paragraph of an FDA press release, dated June 19, 2003, was this sentence: "Three well-controlled trials in pediatric patients with MDD [major depressive disorder] failed to show that [Paxil] was more effective than placebo." The reference to these negative findings about Paxil mystified Firestein. Why would doctors so readily prescribe Paxil (making it by 2003 the second most widely prescribed antidepressant for those under eighteen years old) if the results of drug tests were uniformly negative? What was going on here? Was there something that America's physicians weren't being told?

Up to that point, Firestein had been stuck on the idea that the companies selling psychoactive drugs were somehow misleading doctors with their marketing material. That's what Parke-Davis/Warner-Lambert had been caught doing with Neurontin, and Firestein thought that perhaps a similar phenomenon could explain the widespread prescribing of SSRI antidepressants for children. At one point she believed she had found evidence that GlaxoSmithKline, in its advertisements for Paxil in professional medical journals, omitted the required boilerplate language acknowledging that Paxil had not been approved for use in children and adolescents. She also noticed that a number of drug companies, including Glaxo, claimed on their Web sites that the SSRIs were safe and effective in "people," making no distinction between adults (for whom the antidepressants had been approved) and children (for whom they had not). Firestein knew from her years of working with psychiatrists at Legal Aid and Children's Rights that children and adolescents reacted differently than adults to psychotropic medication. Research had shown, for instance, that children aged ten to fourteen years had a much higher rate than adults of becoming manic after being treated with an SSRI antidepressant. And a review of data from the drug trials would soon reveal that children and adolescents who were treated with SSRIs were two to three times more likely than adults to experience the kind of agitation or hostility that frequently accompany suicidal behavior. Researchers weren't exactly sure why pediatric patients were more sensitive to drugs like Prozac, Zoloft, and Paxil; all they knew was that they were.

Firestein would later discover that she was wrong about Glaxo's pediatric warning. The required fine print had been folded into the warning for pregnant women on Paxil advertisements, and she had simply missed it. But by then she had stumbled upon the June 2003 FDA press release and was starting to wonder if the drug giant was engaged in something more than marketing shenanigans.

Reading the FDA Talk Paper on her computer, Firestein learned some surprising news: nine days before the FDA made its own public announcement, the British health authorities had issued a warning that Seroxat (the brand name for Paxil in the United Kingdom) should not be used to treat children and adolescents for depression. The regulatory agency based this advisory on the startling conclusion that "there is an increase in the rate of self harm and potentially suicidal behavior in this age group when paroxetine [the generic name for Paxil] is used for depressive illness." In its Talk Paper, the FDA announced that it too was reviewing reports of a possible increased risk of suicidal thinking and suicide attempts in minors treated with Paxil. "Although [the agency] has not completed its evaluation of the new safety data," the release said, "FDA is recommending that Paxil not be used in children and adolescents for the treatment of major depressive disorder."

This was news to Firestein—and, she suspected, to many doctors and consumers as well. Although the FDA had posted the release on its public Web site, the fact that the agency in charge of regulating

America's health was taking a second look at a widely prescribed antidepressant had not yet been reported in the mainstream press or in any medical journals. Most physicians on this side of the Atlantic knew nothing about the British advisory against using Paxil in children and adolescents.

But what really startled Firestein was the FDA's conclusion that there was currently no evidence that Paxil was effective for children and adolescents with depression. This was very strange. According to what had been reported in the medical literature and at conferences, Paxil not only reduced symptoms of depression and anxiety but was a safe and well-tolerated medication in children and adolescents, and many primary care physicians and psychiatrists swore by the drug. The medical community's confidence in prescribing the SSRI had made it into a blockbuster: in 2002, GlaxoSmithKline earned $55 million in Paxil sales to children and adolescents alone.

So why was the FDA now challenging the conventional wisdom? Was it possible that the maker of Paxil had in some way misled physicians and consumers about the drug's safety and effectiveness?

Firestein sensed she was onto something. Feverish with excitement, she began searching the medical Web site PubMed for published studies about Paxil in minors. She soon came across a study titled "Efficacy of Paroxetine in the Treatment of Adolescent Major Depression: A Randomized, Clinical Trial." The study had been published in July 2001 in the respected *Journal of the American Academy of Child and Adolescent Psychiatry* (*JAACAP*). It was the only published randomized clinical trial she could find on Paxil in this age group, and its abstract concluded: "Paroxetine is generally well tolerated and effective for major depression in adolescents."

Its lead author was Martin B. Keller, MD.

Downloading the study onto her computer, Firestein read the full text of the report and then read it again. And again. She grew increasingly baffled. It appeared as if the positive conclusion in the abstract simply did not correspond to the actual data. The study, for instance, said that there were two primary outcome measures by which the researchers planned to gauge the effectiveness of the drug in treating depression. First, patients in the study had to have a 50 percent reduction in their symptoms on the Hamilton depression (HAM-D) scale or a score of 8 or less on the HAM-D scale for the drug to be considered effective. Second, participants had to show a significant change in their total HAM-D score between the beginning of the study and the end. The protocol for the study also included five other secondary end points against which to measure whether the patients' depression had improved. But according to Firestein's reading of the results, Paxil had not performed significantly better than the sugar pill on either of the two primary measures. Nor had it "separated significantly from placebo" (in scientific parlance) on two out of the five secondary measures listed in the original protocol. How, then, could the authors have concluded that Paxil was significantly more effective than placebo in treating depression in adolescents?

Firestein was stumped by yet another inconsistency: The abstract and the paper itself had concluded that Paxil was generally safe and well tolerated in adolescents. Yet according to Firestein's reading of the data, Paxil was significantly more likely to cause serious adverse events (SAEs) than the placebo or the older antidepressant it was being compared with. In the guidelines for the study, an SAE was defined as "any event that is fatal, life-threatening, disabling, incapacitating, or results in hospitalization." Eleven of the ninety-three patients taking Paxil developed SAEs. That contrasted with only two SAEs in the eighty-seven patients taking placebo and five in the ninety-five patients taking imipramine, a tricylic antidepressant that had been around for decades. Very weird, Firestein thought. If anything, there should be more serious adverse events among patients taking the older tricyclic than among those taking the newer SSRI. After all, the drug companies had based their highly successful marketing campaigns on the argument that

[147]

SSRIs had fewer serious side effects than the older antidepressants. What was going on here?

Reading further, Firestein discovered that of the eleven patients with serious adverse events in the Paxil group, six were listed as having had "emotional lability (e.g. suicidal ideation/gestures)"; two, as having had "conduct problems or hostility"; two, "worsening of depression"; and one, a bad headache. In all, 10 percent of the ninety-three patients taking Paxil had to be prematurely withdrawn from the study because their reactions seemed to have been so severe. Yet the study itself concluded that "the findings of this study provide evidence of the efficacy and safety of the SSRI paroxetine in the treatment of adolescent depression."

How could a prestigious journal like the *JAACAP* have published a study with such glaring discrepancies between the actual data and its conclusions? At the very least, Firestein thought, there were some serious methodological issues with this study.

The next thing Firestein did was google Martin Keller, the lead author of the Paxil study. What she found shocked her to her core. Up popped the series of articles published a few years back in the *Boston Globe* that essentially cast doubt on Keller's integrity as a scientist. As a doctor's daughter, Firestein had up to this point pretty much believed in the purity of science, the tenet that its practitioners were honorable scholars laboring away in the isolation of their ivy-covered labs, impervious to the siren song of big money. But here was the chief of psychiatry at Brown essentially accused in the pages of a respected newspaper of being beholden to the drug industry. And that was not all. Firestein found an earlier article in the same newspaper charging Keller's department with falsifying invoices to obtain money from a financially strapped state agency for research that didn't appear to have happened. Still another clip noted that Brown had repaid the Commonwealth of Massachusetts more than $300,000 for the contract dollars that Keller's department had obtained under these dubious circumstances.

"When I read the pieces about Keller, it made me look at psychiatry

in a whole different light, with new cynicism," Firestein later acknowledged. "I had not realized the depth of the connection between academic researchers and the pharmaceutical industry."

A FEW WEEKS LATER, Firestein went to see an economist who
worked for the antitrust division of the AG's office. She wanted to know
what he thought of the methodological problems with the 2001 Keller
study.

"Does this look right to you?" she asked him, after showing him the
journal paper and explaining her concerns. "Could it be that they are
claiming statistical significance where there is none?"

"Yeah, I think you're onto something here," the economist said,
squinting at the tables of data Firestein had laid on his desk. "But don't
take my word for it."

Firestein realized she would have to find an outside expert who understood data analysis and was familiar with the Paxil study. But who?
During her searches online, she had come across a muckraking Web
site — www.socialaudit.org.uk — that regularly posted articles critical
of the SSRI antidepressants. It was run by Charles Medawar, a Brit
who billed himself as a specialist on medical policy and drug safety.
Firestein picked up the phone and called Medawar. He in turn referred
her to a British psychiatrist by the name of David Healy.

Near the end of August, after a round of e-mails with Healy, Firestein
finally spoke with him by phone at a hotel in Philadelphia. Healy had
told her he would be visiting the United States on a fact-finding mission
for Baum Hedlund, a Los Angeles–based law firm then suing Glaxo-
SmithKline on behalf of three thousand families whose children had
allegedly become addicted to Paxil. (Most of these lawsuits would not
be settled for years, but in 2002, GlaxoSmithKline agreed to stop airing
television commercials and distributing literature claiming that Paxil
was not habit-forming.) When Firestein called that late summer evening in 2003, Healy had just returned from an exhausting day of poring

through documents in the corporate archives of SmithKline Beecham, now a subsidiary of GlaxoSmithKline.

Healy gave Firestein a quick overview. He explained that the British authorities, after reexamining the pediatric data on Paxil (which included the Keller study), had found that among eleven hundred children enrolled in those trials, children taking the drug were nearly three times as likely to consider or attempt suicide as those taking placebos. It was that reanalysis that had led the British regulators to issue their advisory against Paxil in June, compelling the FDA to begin its own reexamination of the SSRIs.

Firestein then asked the British psychiatrist about the inconsistencies she had noticed in Keller's Paxil paper. Healy confirmed that she was correct in her analysis: the primary outcome measures had indeed failed to show that Paxil was significantly better than placebo. He told Firestein that several medical professionals had leveled the same accusation in letters to the journal's editor after the Keller et al. study was published in 2001.

"You might be able to find those letters online," Healy said. "And when I get back to Wales, I'll look around to see if I saved any copies."

Firestein also mentioned her confusion with the term "emotional lability." According to the medical dictionary, it meant emotional instability. Healy said that based on data he had seen of clinical trials of Paxil in both adults and children, GlaxoSmithKline commonly coded participants as being emotionally labile when in fact they had expressed suicidal thoughts or made a suicide attempt.

"It's a bit of a trick," he said. "People just reading the tables of the [published paper] might not be aware that they should look behind the term." Even FDA officials might not have understood that the term "emotional lability" was a code word for suicidal behavior when Glaxo first presented the clinical trial data on adults and children to the federal agency, he said.

As Healy would later recall, Firestein didn't say much during that phone conversation. She asked him to go through some of the statistics again, and he had the impression that she was taking notes. "She didn't give too much away and I didn't know where she was going with this," he said. "She played things fairly deadpan."

But back in her cluttered office at 120 Broadway, Firestein could barely contain her joy. Her reading of the data had been accurate. She still hadn't found the other pediatric studies the FDA Talk Paper alluded to, and she wasn't even sure whether the Keller study was one of the three negative studies the Talk Paper mentioned. But after talking to Healy, Firestein knew that she had sufficient ammunition to convince her colleagues that this was a case worth exploring.

She was right. In the fall of 2003, after going over the information she had, first with Shirley Stark and then with Tom Conway and Joe Baker, Rose Firestein received the go-ahead to write an official letter to GlaxoSmithKline demanding all internal corporate documents relating to the testing and marketing of Paxil in the under-eighteen age group. Upon receiving such an official demand letter from the AG's office, corporations doing business in New York were required by law to cough up all documents, although the process could take months. Firestein was prepared to be patient. She had a feeling GlaxoSmithKline's internal documents would give her the keys she needed to unlock the mystery of why a study published in a prestigious medical journal could purport to conclude one thing when it actually showed the exact opposite.

# 14. Rose Firestein's Epiphany, Winter 2004

O n Christmas Day, 2003, Rose Firestein accompanied Janice and Ellie to the corporate offices of Merrill Lynch in Midtown Manhattan (where her sister worked) to help out with an annual holiday ritual. Every Christmas, Merrill Lynch invited in seniors who lived in the New York area to use the brokerage firm's phones to call their families all over the world. Merrill Lynch employees served the visitors coffee and cookies while they waited to use the phones. Firestein had baked some cookies, and she was eager to see what her eight-year-old niece would make of it all. It was important to Rose and Janice that Ellie, growing up in privilege, far from her place of birth, understood the importance of sharing with others less fortunate than she.

The afternoon didn't turn out the way Firestein had expected. At one point, one of her sister's colleagues asked her where she worked. Without thinking, Firestein told him. The man reared back in surprise and looked at her as if to say, What the hell are you doing here! The rest of the afternoon, Firestein could feel the stares following her around the room. It didn't matter that she personally had not been involved in Spitzer's high-profile case accusing Merrill Lynch stock analysts of misleading investors. For those who worked at the Wall Street firm, the wounds were still fresh. Firestein realized she would have to be more discreet about her place of employment: to many people in New York's insular business community, the New York State attorney general and his staff were public enemy number one.

A FEW WEEKS LATER, Firestein was sitting in Shirley Stark's office nursing a Diet Coke, one of many she would down in the course of the day. Stark's caffeine of choice was a Starbucks Venti, and she liked to tease Firestein about her predilection for Diet Coke. "How can you drink that stuff?" she'd say. "It's disgusting!" But today it was clear that Stark was in no mood for banter. Even though her face was a blur, Firestein could hear the distress in her supervisor's voice.

"I just got off the phone with a child psychiatrist who is a friend of mine," Stark said. "I told him in general terms what we were doing. And he was very opposed to it."

Stark's friend believed that if the AG's office went after a drug company for its marketing of an SSRI antidepressant, the ensuing publicity would make many doctors reluctant to prescribe the drugs at all.

"He felt that we might be taking away the tools he needs to treat children with," she said.

The conversation jolted Stark, making her question whether they were in fact doing the right thing in pursuing legal action against GlaxoSmithKline. After all, almost everything the AG's office had heard from the medical community seemed to indicate that SSRI antidepressants worked in the treatment of depression and other disorders like anxiety. Who were they—a bunch of attorneys—to tell physicians differently?

Firestein listened patiently to her supervisor's concerns. The conversation helped both women understand that if they were going to pursue action against GlaxoSmithKline, they would have to do it in such a way as not to pass judgment on whether Paxil was safe and effective as a medication for children or adults. As far as Firestein was concerned, that wasn't the issue anyway. In her mind the crux was whether the drug company had somehow misled doctors and consumers in its research and marketing of Paxil.

At this point, of course, she couldn't even prove that. True, the FDA had issued another public health advisory in October, alerting physicians to "reports of suicidal thinking (and suicide attempts) in clinical studies of various antidepressant drugs in pediatric patients." But Firestein found the FDA advisory frustratingly equivocal. On one hand, the FDA announced completion of a preliminary review of eight antidepressants, concluding that "the data do not clearly establish an association between the use of these drugs and increased suicidal thoughts or actions." But in an accompanying letter to physicians, the FDA said it could not "rule out an increased risk of suicidality in any of these drugs." Concluding that additional data were needed, the FDA Talk Paper announced that on February 2, 2004, the FDA would convene a meeting of its Psychopharmacological Drugs Advisory Committee to discuss the issue. This was the same advisory group that had brushed aside similar concerns about Prozac thirteen years earlier.

Then in mid-December, the British health authorities issued a much stronger advisory, recommending against the use of all the SSRI antidepressants, except for Prozac, in treating depression among children and adolescents.

In reading the press coverage, Firestein was surprised to see that among the data the FDA and British regulators had reanalyzed were nine pediatric studies on Paxil, including three randomized clinical trials. Wow, she thought. In her exhaustive search of the medical literature, she had found only one published study: the Keller report. Where were the other eight?

As 2003 drew to a close, Firestein was still waiting for the documents she had requested from Glaxo. She wished there were some way she could quickly get her hands on the data that the British and American authorities were privy to. But the FDA had a long-standing policy of not releasing even completed clinical trial data without the consent of the company that sponsored the research.

Firestein had no choice but to be patient. She had plenty of other work to keep her busy, having been drafted to help with several other pressing complaints. The Paxil investigation would have to wait.

NOT FOR LONG, as it turned out. By late January, with the date of the FDA's long-awaited advisory meeting looming, press coverage of the SSRI controversy heated up. Firestein found herself drawn back to the Paxil investigation as a cat to the sound of skittering mice. Joe Baker had passed along an intriguing article published in the *New York Times* a few months earlier. The piece written by Gardiner Harris, confirmed Firestein's suspicions that GlaxoSmithKline had selectively published the one Paxil trial by Keller et al. and suppressed other clinical trials that found Paxil was no more effective than placebo in treating pediatric depression. In the *Times* article, Harris quoted Dr. Graham Emslie, chief of child and adolescent psychiatry at the University of Texas Southwestern Medical Center in Dallas and one of Keller's coauthors on the published Paxil study. Emslie, who had been involved in four of the pediatric Paxil studies, said he suspected that the other studies had gone unpublished in part because their results were unfavorable. Harris also reported that while most of the clinical studies done on the SSRI antidepressants had found them to be no more effective in fighting pediatric depression than sugar pills, much of this data had not been made public. He quoted Emslie as saying, "I know of at least a half-dozen other studies of antidepressant treatments in children and adolescents that have been completed but as yet have not been published."

Firestein was astounded. A prominent psychiatric researcher was publicly admitting the practice of not publishing negative results. This admission would help bolster the AG's case against GlaxoSmithKline. Firestein was further heartened by what she read in the next paragraph of the article; it quoted Dr. Marcia Angell, the former editor of the

Side Effects

*New England Journal of Medicine,* as saying that drug companies, by not disclosing negative research results, can actually "change the way medicine is practiced."

Yes! She had finally found an expert who was willing to say that the drug companies, by publishing only the positive results and suppressing the negative, were actually interfering with the practice of medicine.

A few days later, Firestein stumbled across another news story, from the *Washington Post,* headlined ANTIDEPRESSANT MAKERS WITHHOLD DATA ON CHILDREN. In that article, a growing chorus of critics took aim at the industry's practice of suppressing data unfavorable to their drugs. Even the director of the American Psychiatric Association's Division of Research chimed in, saying, "We need a journal of negative findings. The probability of those negative findings being published is far less than the chances of positive studies."

Firestein began perusing the news coverage on a daily basis now. On February 1, she was appalled to read that the FDA intended to gag one of its own scientists, Dr. Andrew Mosholder, preventing him from testifying about his findings at its public hearing the next day. According to the exclusive in the *San Francisco Chronicle,* Mosholder, the FDA's longtime specialist in antidepressants and pediatrics, had reached a conclusion similar to that of the British: that a number of these antidepressants were indeed linked to an increase in suicidal thoughts and behavior among children and teens. But top FDA officials had decided that Mosholder couldn't present those preliminary findings at the agency's own public hearing. This was crazy, Firestein thought. "Here was someone who had been asked to do the analysis, and no one was saying it was wrong, and yet they prevented him from testifying before the very committee that was considering what to do about the SSRIs," she said.

At the same time, the psychiatric community was mounting a vigorous defense of the SSRI antidepressants. Many prominent psychiatrists felt, as Shirley Stark's friend did, that a stronger warning on the labels

[157]

for these drugs, or any restrictions on their usage, would scare physicians away from using them. And without the availability of these drugs, key practitioners believed that the suicide rate among minors would go up, not down. National statistics, in fact, showed that the suicide rate among American adolescents and adults had dropped in the 1990s, and some researchers attributed that decline to the rising use of SSRI antidepressants. Other psychiatric researchers, however, countered that there was little evidence that the two trends were connected. Dr. Ross Baldessarini, director of the Neuropharmacology Laboratory at McLean Hospital, was among those who believed there was a far stronger correlation between reduced suicide rates and environmental factors, such as better access to mental health care.

While the epidemiological picture on long-term suicide trends remained unclear, many psychiatrists and primary care physicians, Baldessarini included, were convinced that the SSRI antidepressants helped depressed patients, particularly adults. They had seen the beneficial results in their own practices. By early 2004, most doctors had still not heard about the data linking the drugs to suicidal behaviors in some children and adolescents.

On January 21, just two weeks before the FDA hearing, a task force of the American College of Neuropsychopharmacology (ACNP) issued a reassuring report. It concluded that SSRIs did not appear to increase the risk of suicide in teens and children. Only later would Firestein learn that of the ten members on the ACNP task force, nine (including three coauthors on the 2001 Paxil study) had been paid consultants to companies selling SSRIs, including GlaxoSmithKline, Pfizer, and Eli Lilly. Hardly an impartial jury of experts, she thought.

IT WASN'T UNTIL February 6, four days after the FDA hearing, that Firestein found time to open the package of background information for the hearing. The twenty-four-page memo from the FDA's

Thomas Laughren was an eye-opener. Laughren was the same FDA official who had written the 2001 paper that noted (in passing) a heightened suicide risk from SSRI antidepressants. Now a team leader with the FDA's Neuropharmacological Drug Products Division, Laughren reported that out of the fifteen clinical trials done to examine the effectiveness of these drugs in treating *pediatric* depression, only three studies had positive results. Among the twelve studies the FDA deemed negative were all three of the randomized clinical trials done on Paxil, including the Keller study on adolescents published in 2001.

Aha! Firestein thought. Here was the FDA reaching the same conclusion she had reached about the Keller study. Yet this particular trial had been presented to doctors as a glowing endorsement of Paxil for use in the pediatric population. In his background memo, Laughren took note of that fact, writing with dry understatement, "The published literature gives a somewhat different perspective" than the FDA's analysis. He went on to conclude, "The failure of most of these [studies] to show a benefit in major depressive disorder does heighten the concern about the possibility of certain risks that may be associated with these drugs, in particular the concern about induction of suicidality." In other words, if these drugs have not even been shown to be effective in children, that makes it all the more difficult to accept the risks of their generating suicidal behaviors in some patients.

Laughren's memo also confirmed what David Healy had told Firestein: that in the fall of 2002, it was the FDA (and specifically Andrew Mosholder) who pressed GlaxoSmithKline to clarify what it meant by the term "emotional lability." Glaxo had applied for an extension of its Paxil patent on the basis of having done the requisite pediatric trials—studies 329 (the Keller study), 377, and 701. The FDA used that opportunity to demand that Glaxo separate out the possible suicidal events it had originally subsumed under the umbrella of emotional lability. It was this demand that finally prompted GlaxoSmithKline to acknowledge that there did appear to be a heightened risk of suicide in its pediatric data, prompting British and American regulators to begin investigating all the SSRIs.

The pieces were beginning to fall into place. Consumed by a sense of urgency, Firestein scanned the press coverage of the February 2 hearing. During the all-day event, held at a Holiday Inn in Bethesda, Maryland, members of the public had once again unleashed a torrent of grief and anger, sharing stories of beloved family members who had killed themselves after taking the antidepressants. The cast of witnesses with tragic stories far outnumbered the patients and physicians who spoke up on behalf of the drugs. Patient advocacy groups entered the fray, a few — like NAMI — arguing that the benefits of the antidepressants outweighed their risks. But other advocacy groups expressed concern about the risks of the SSRIs, pointing out that the drug companies had hidden clinical trial results showing that the antidepressants were ineffective and dangerous in children. Vera H. Sharav, president of the Alliance for Human Research Protection, testified that the FDA had known for years that these antidepressants did not demonstrate a benefit in children and had failed to warn physicians and consumers that they increased the risk of suicide and hostility in the pediatric population. "The FDA is foot dragging, equivocating and tinkering with definitions while children are dying," Sharav charged.

Near the end of the February 2 hearing, several members of the FDA's advisory panel called on the agency to immediately alert physicians about the possible link between SSRIs and suicidal behavior. FDA officials, however, stalled again. They announced that any definitive action would have to wait until after they had reclassified all the clinical trial data on thousands of patients according to a new definition of what constituted suicidal behavior. They promised to have the results of their reanalysis by late that summer.

. . .

ROSE FIRESTEIN WAS not about to wait for the FDA's reclassification of the data. She began writing a preliminary memo outlining the facts of what she knew about the case against GlaxoSmithKline. She found that writing memos helped her pull her thoughts together, allowing her to step back from the details so that she could see the larger picture. While she had uncovered some damning facts indicating that Glaxo had misled doctors and consumers by not publishing negative results on Paxil, she still didn't have a working hypothesis or a hook on which to hang the facts. She didn't have the basic raison d'être for the lawsuit, the theory explaining how and why GlaxoSmithKline had incontrovertibly violated New York law.

On the evening of February 10, Firestein left the office feeling tired and dispirited. It was cold and depressingly dark outside, and the streets were wet and slippery. Piles of dirty slush littered the curb. As Firestein made her way to the subway, tapping the ground in front of her, she felt grateful she had her cane. It was a relatively recent acquisition, something Firestein had resisted for a long time. A few months earlier, however, she had walked right into a metal barrier, smashing her foot into the bottom bar. No bones were broken, fortunately, but the foot took a long time to heal. Before then, Firestein had done her level best to ignore the fact that she had no peripheral vision and couldn't really see more than a few inches in front of her face. She had clung to an illusion of normalcy despite the impediments that clogged the streets and sidewalks of Lower Manhattan—speeding cabs, people rushing by, sidewalk vendors, dogs on leashes, newspaper stands and construction fencing on almost every block. Her collision with the metal barrier finally broke through her denial. A few days later, she called a state hotline, which referred her to a nonprofit service for the blind. The agency not only promised to set her up with a cane for free but said one of its representatives would provide training in its usage at a location of her choosing. Firestein chose Lincoln Center, where a very complicated grid of streets intersected. She figured if she could negotiate Lincoln

Center without getting run over, she could go anywhere in New York with some modicum of safety.

That evening, after putting Ellie to bed, Firestein couldn't stop thinking about the GlaxoSmithKline investigation. Bits and pieces of facts from the case kept swimming in and out of her consciousness all night.

The next morning, she was taking a shower when suddenly it hit her. This was a case of consumer fraud! The negative study results on Paxil were material to a doctor's judgment in treating patients, and they had been concealed. Yet at the same time, GlaxoSmithKline had touted the positive results from Keller's Paxil study. According to the New York statute, you didn't have to show there had been deliberate intent to conceal relevant material in proving consumer fraud, only that it had been hidden from consumers. The AG's office could charge GlaxoSmith-Kline with fraud because it had provided only part of the story, giving doctors and their patients a misleading picture of Paxil.

At work that morning, Firestein waited impatiently for Shirley Stark to come in and settle down at her desk. Then she rushed into her office.

"Got a minute?" she asked, trying to contain her excitement.

"Sure," Stark said.

"I reread New York's consumer fraud statute and I think I've found the hook we need for the Paxil case," Firestein said. "We know Glaxo withheld important information about Paxil from doctors, right? So wouldn't that be considered fraud? I think we can argue that by not fully disclosing all of its research results, Glaxo is guilty of fraud under the New York statute!"

Stark slowly sipped her Starbucks Venti.

"That's not the kind of case we normally bring under that statute," she said. The AG's office usually invoked New York's consumer fraud statute in going after loan companies who tried to bilk customers, or contractors who built defective homes. The law had never before been used to sue a company selling medical products.

Firestein persisted, outlining just how Glaxo's refusal to publish negative study results might fit New York's definition of consumer fraud. But Stark didn't sound convinced.

"It might be worth looking into this," she said. "I don't know. Why don't you think about it some more?"

Firestein's throat constricted. Stark didn't seem to get how innovative, how truly powerful, this legal approach might be. Firestein knew in her gut that the consumer fraud statute would give the AG's office the perfect hammer with which to curb the marketing of off-label drugs to vulnerable children. But she had learned from long experience not to argue when she was upset. Instead, she walked back to her office, closed the door, and let loose a few words more suited to a dockyard than a law office.

# 15. How Rose Firestein Found the Smoking Gun Memo and Converted the Skeptics, Spring 2004

Within a week, Firestein had convinced Shirley Stark that the consumer fraud angle was the way to go. The next step was bringing Tom Conway on board. In Conway's eyes, Firestein was still a newcomer to the AG's office, a relatively unknown, untested presence. So Stark suggested that she go to Conway first and give him the bare bones of the idea. Then the three of them could sit down and hash it out.

"Rose has a really good idea," Stark remembers telling her boss. But at their very first meeting in his office, Conway seemed dubious. He had a lot of questions. First, he wanted to know how GlaxoSmithKline's decision not to publish its negative study results could be considered consumer fraud if the concealment was primarily directed at doctors who were running a business.

Firestein had anticipated this question. She'd run into it before — in the drug-pricing case. In thinking through the average wholesale pricing lawsuit, she and her colleagues had concluded that because a doctor has a fiduciary relationship to his or her patient, the doctor is not really acting as a business; he or she is acting as an agent of the patient's. Based on that interpretation, they had included a bribery claim in the AWP complaint. As Firestein recalled, "If you're arguing that the AWP is essentially a kickback to the doctor, then because of the doctor's fiduciary relationship with his patient, it amounts to bribery."

The same fiduciary relationship would be operative in a doctor's prescribing of antidepressants to a patient, she told Conway. "So a fraud directed at a doctor is in fact a fraud directed at a consumer," she said.

Conway pursed his lips. "You may be right. But I think you need to think this through some more."

Firestein nodded, trying not to look chagrined. Here she had come up with her most creative idea in years, and the guy who counted—her boss—was not impressed. Nor was he finished.

"Isn't this the FDA's bailiwick?" Conway pressed. Firestein explained that since state government regulates the practice of medicine, this kind of legal action was entirely within the state's purview.

Conway wasn't convinced.

"Are you sure we're not treading on the FDA's authority?" he persisted. "Are you sure there's nothing that says the FDA has exclusive jurisdiction here?"

"Yes, I'm sure," Firestein snapped. Her voice sounded loud and shrill to her own ears. She flushed, and added, "But I'll check it out again and get back to you."

Over the next weeks, Firestein and Stark worked hard to satisfy their chief's concerns. Joe Baker also had some questions. But it became progressively clearer that the man they had to win over was the tough-minded czar of the third floor, Tom Conway. As both Firestein and Stark would later recall, he seemed to relish the role of devil's advocate and would home in on any weakness in their arguments like a mosquito zooming toward exposed human flesh. "He seemed to do it more with Rose, and sometimes it got to the point of pickiness," Stark recalled.

By the beginning of March, Firestein still hadn't received the documents from GlaxoSmithKline. She was getting antsy. Conway and

Baker were on her back to flesh out the facts in the case. On an impulse, Firestein decided to see if anything new had been posted on the Web. She typed "Paxil" into the Google search engine, and to her surprise, up popped a newly published article in the *Canadian Medical Association Journal* titled, "Drug Company Experts Advised Staff to Withhold Data about SSRI Use in Children."

The article told of a confidential internal memo written in 1998 by the Medical Affairs team at SmithKline Beecham (which subsequently merged with Glaxo Wellcome to become GlaxoSmithKline). The document, marked "SB Confidential—for Internal Use Only," discussed the results of two recently finished clinical trials on Paxil. It concluded that these two trials were "insufficiently robust" to support the FDA's approval of the drug for the treatment of pediatric depression. (While some physicians were already prescribing the drug off-label to children, FDA approval would have allowed SmithKline to substantially increase Paxil's market share.) One of the two studies mentioned in this confidential memo was the Keller Paxil trial (study 329); the other one was referred to as study 377. The memo acknowledged that study 329 had "failed to demonstrate a statistically significant difference from placebo on the primary efficacy measures." Even so, "a full manuscript will be progressed," the memo's authors wrote. "It would be commercially unacceptable," they added, "to include a statement that efficacy had not been demonstrated, as this would undermine the profile of paroxetine."

Firestein sat back in astonishment. This memo, if it was for real, would explain why Keller and his coauthors had published an abstract and conclusion that contrasted so starkly with the actual data. The drug company had insisted on it!

According to the *CMAJ* article, the confidential memo also acknowledged that study 377 "failed to demonstrate any separation" of Paxil from placebo. "There are no plans to publish data from study 377," the memo authors wrote. They recommended that SmithKline Beecham "effectively manage the dissemination of these data in order to minimize any potential negative commercial impact."

"Holy shit!" Firestein exclaimed. "This is unbelievable!"

Stark's eyes widened with amazement when Firestein showed her the journal article. "Gotcha," she said, grinning. As Stark would later recall, "We finally had something we could point to and say, Look at this, they really intended to suppress these results. It was the kind of evidence you look for in a case."

There was just one problem: Firestein had to get ahold of the actual memo without revealing much, if anything, about her investigation. The AG's office didn't want to tip its hand before it was ready to. In addition, she had to get permission from her superiors before even making the attempt. Even though the attorneys in each division of the AG's office worked in a collaborative, mostly collegial way, there was an unwritten set of rules and a strict hierarchy by which the attorney general governed his 630-attorney staff. Spitzer himself stood at the top of this pyramid, insulated by several top lieutenants. Although he would often pick up the phone and check in with the heads of his various divisions (such as Baker and Conway), if they wanted access to him, they usually had to go through his lieutenants. Likewise, attorneys such as Firestein and Stark, who worked in the "trenches," had to check in with their superiors on any unusual developments in their investigations.

Once again, Stark acted as go-between, asking Conway if it would be okay for Rose to call the Canadian medical journal. He said sure, go ahead. The next day, Firestein picked up the phone. After identifying herself, she was referred to an editor at the *CMAJ*. Without much preamble, she asked him if she could get a copy of this internal corporate document and then held her breath.

"Sure," the editor said without a moment's hesitation. "What's your fax number?"

THE NEXT DAY, Firestein called a meeting. Once she and her three colleagues were seated around the conference table in Conway's office, she plunked down the fax she had received. Baker and Conway were impressed.

"I remember we all rubbed our hands together and said this is great," Baker said. "This memo showed that [SmithKline] knew they were holding back information and that what they were doing was wrong."

As the AG team later discovered, the incriminating memo had been passed along to the Canadian medical journal by none other than David Healy. Healy, in turn, had received a copy from the BBC, which had obtained it from an anonymous whistleblower after the British broadcaster aired its second program on paroxetine and suicide.

But while the consumer attorneys now had their "smoking gun," they still didn't have the raw data from study 377 or any of the other pediatric studies on Paxil. "We didn't know the lay of the land," Firestein said. "The [British authorities] and the FDA were saying slightly different things, so there was no way we could go forward without seeing the documents."

Finally, on March 19, the long-awaited package from Glaxo arrived. It contained thousands of pages of documents, including data on the three randomized clinical pediatric studies for Paxil and a number of internal corporate memos. Also enclosed were the medical information letters that the company routinely sent out to doctors about new developments relating to Paxil.

It took Firestein weeks to pore over all the documents. What she found was a "gold mine" of duplicity. GlaxoSmithKline knew back in the 1990s that the first two of its three randomized clinical trials on Paxil in children (studies 329 and 377) failed to statistically show the drug's effectiveness in children and adolescents. (A third randomized trial, 701, finished in 2000, also failed to show efficacy in minors.) Yet here was evidence that the drug company had gone ahead anyway and paid a medical consulting company to ghostwrite a manuscript for publication of study 329. A draft of the manuscript was prepared by a woman named Sally Laden at Scientific Therapeutics Information (STI), in Springfield, New Jersey, and sent to Marty Keller and the other researchers who conducted the study. Despite data showing that Paxil did no better than placebo on the study's primary outcome measures and that patients in the Paxil group had an unusually high number of serious adverse events, the manuscript concluded that Paxil was well tolerated in adolescents and effective in treating depression in that age group. It would later be revealed that Keller and his coauthors made some minor changes in Sally Laden's manuscript but did not object to the wording.

The manuscript, however, did not fool everyone. Back in November 1997, during a meeting at SmithKline Beecham's headquarters in Philadelphia, officials from the drug company and several authors of the study (including its principal investigator, Marty Keller) had decided to submit the paper first to *JAMA,* because that journal reached beyond psychiatry to many primary care physicians and pediatricians. But *JAMA* rejected the manuscript. Several of the doctors who read the paper as peer reviewers for *JAMA* had flagged the Paxil study's inconsistencies and given it a decided thumbs-down.

Finally, in January 2001, the *Journal of the American Academy of Child and Adolescent Psychiatry* accepted the paper, even though several of its reviewers had also flagged problems. One reviewer noted, "Overall results do not clearly indicate efficacy. Authors need to clearly note this." Another pointed out, "A relatively high rate of serious adverse effects was not addressed in the discussion." Why the journal published the Paxil study despite such criticism from its own reviewers remains unknown. The editor of the journal, Dr. Mina Dulcan, declined to be interviewed for this book. It's worth noting, however, that one of the paper's coauthors, Dr. Graham Emslie, had been on the journal's editorial board since 1996 and thus wielded tremendous clout with the journal's editors. Emslie was also the lead author on two of the primary pediatric Prozac trials sponsored by Eli Lilly, and like Keller, he had extensive ties to drugmakers. According to a 2004 task force report by the American College of Neuropsychopharmacology, Emslie was a paid consultant to GlaxoSmithKline, Eli Lilly, Pfizer, Forest Labs, Bristol-Myers Squibb, and Wyeth, among other drug companies.

Shortly after the Paxil paper was accepted, Martin Keller contacted Sally Laden, the paper's ghostwriter, to request that GlaxoSmithKline pick up the cost of sending him five hundred reprints of the published study. (In an e-mail to Glaxo officials, Laden estimated the cost of the reprints to be about fifteen hundred dollars). In a telling response to Laden on April 25, 2001, a Glaxo official wrote, "Because Dr. Keller is a member of our advisory board and an influential KOL, we will support his request to purchase 500 reprints." KOL is an industry acronym for *key opinion leader,* and it refers to doctors who, as prominent members of their profession, command the attention of their colleagues when they publish articles in medical journals or speak at conferences about new drugs or devices. Keller was a KOL in good standing with GlaxoSmithKline, as were Graham Emslie and two other coauthors on the Paxil paper: Neal Ryan, a professor of child psychiatry at the University of Pittsburgh School of Medicine, and Karen Wagner, a professor of psychiatry at the University of Texas Medical Branch at Galveston. (Like Keller and Emslie, Ryan and Wagner also had close ties to the drug companies that sold antidepressants. According to the ACNP report, Wagner was a consultant for GlaxoSmithKline, Lilly, Pfizer, Abbott, Forest Labs, and Bristol-Myers Squibb, among other drugmakers. Ryan consulted for GlaxoSmithKline, Pfizer, Wyeth, and Abbott.)

Their Paxil paper finally saw the light of print in the July 2001 issue of the *JAACAP.* A few weeks later, a Paxil product manager at Glaxo-SmithKline sent a memo to all the sales representatives charged with selling Paxil to doctors in the United States. In the memo, the product manager, a man named Zachary Hawkins, wrote, "This 'cutting edge' landmark study is the first to compare efficacy of an SSRI and a [tricyclic antidepressant] with placebo in the treatment of major depression in adolescents. Paxil demonstrates REMARKABLE efficacy and safety in the treatment of adolescent depression." (Hawkins himself capitalized the word "remarkable" in his memo.)

Firestein couldn't believe her eyes. This was further evidence that GlaxoSmithKline was deliberately trying to mislead doctors about Paxil. And that was not all. In the medical information letters that the company sent out to American doctors, the company not only spoke glowingly of study 329 but made no reference to the negative results from the two other randomized trials, studies 377 and 701. Nor, she discovered, were studies 377 and 701 ever published. Although a Canadian psychiatrist and one of the coauthors of study 377 did present some findings from the multisite trial at a sparsely attended session of the American Academy of Child and Adolescent Psychiatry meeting in 1999, he later said his purpose was not to cast light on whether Paxil was an effective treatment for pediatric depression, but rather to review some of the study's methodological flaws. Dr. Robert Milin made his presentation without any financial support from GlaxoSmithKline.

Firestein also discovered that while the drugmaker had acknowledged in letters to British and Canadian physicians that its clinical trials failed to demonstrate the efficacy of Paxil in the pediatric population, it withheld that information from American physicians. For example, in one medical letter to U.S. doctors sent shortly after the FDA's advisory in October 2003, GlaxoSmithKline omitted any reference to Paxil's lack of efficacy in children and adolescents or to the increased risk of suicidal behaviors in its own pediatric trials (even though the company acknowledged that risk in its letter to British and Canadian physicians). Instead, the company wrote, "GlaxoSmithKline stands firmly behind Paxil as a safe and effective medication that continues to help millions of patients suffering from mood and anxiety disorders."

On March 22, while Firestein was still digging through company documents, the FDA issued yet another public health advisory warning physicians and families to closely monitor both adults and children with depression, especially at the beginning of treatment with antidepressants. In this Talk Paper, the FDA continued to insist that "it is not yet clear whether antidepressants contribute to the emergence of suicidal thinking and behavior." The agency did say, however, that it was asking drug companies to change the labels of ten antidepressants to include stronger cautions about the need to monitor patients "for the worsening of depression and the emergence of suicidal ideation." It also reminded the public that it was still in the process of reviewing data from studies on Prozac, Paxil, Zoloft, Celexa, Effexor, Wellbutrin, Serzone, Luvox, and Remeron. All but one of these drugs (Luvox) was approved for use in adult depression, but not all of them were SSRIs. Drugs such as Effexor, Remeron, and Serzone were thought to operate on both the serotonin and norepinephrine systems of the brain, and Wellbutrin was believed to inhibit the uptake of serotonin and dopamine.

The day after the FDA's advisory, the American Psychiatric Association weighed in on the debate. "We are concerned that publicity around the advisory may cause some successfully treated patients to stop taking antidepressants," the APA news release said. "We believe it would be tragic if publicity around the FDA advisory kept people with depression from getting the help they deserve."

On March 24, the *New York Times* published an article citing a number of psychiatrists who said they needed these antidepressants in their medicinal black bag to treat children and adolescents. Dr. Harold Koplewicz, director of New York University's Child Study Center, was quoted as saying, "The fear I have about this [FDA] warning is that many teenagers will not get the medicine . . . and that's a really tragic outcome." The article again gave Firestein and her colleagues pause.

"If the entire medical community was arrayed against us, saying [our lawsuit] was a terrible thing, that would have made it difficult for us to proceed," she said. So the assistant AGs decided to talk to a number of prominent physicians and opinion leaders to gauge what the reaction of the medical community might be to a legal action against GlaxoSmithKline.

Joe Baker picked up the phone and called the editor of the prestigious *New England Journal of Medicine*. Rose Firestein and Shirley Stark spoke to other experts, including the head of the New York State Psychiatric Institute and top officials at the American Psychiatric Association. Firestein also talked to two former editors of the *New England Journal of Medicine,* Arnold Relman and Marcia Angell. The assistant attorneys general made it clear that their case was not about whether the SSRIs were bad for kids, but whether doctors were getting enough information from the drug companies to make a good clinical judgment.

"Nobody said, Oh, that's a stupid idea," Firestein said. "A lot of people said, You won't be able to force Glaxo to publish all their data; the drug companies are never going to do that. But once these physicians understood that our case was about access to information and not a judgment by the New York attorney general's office on whether the drugs were good, bad, or indifferent, they thought it was a great idea. They all agreed that doctors should have this information."

Encouraged by what she heard, Firestein began drafting the official complaint against GlaxoSmithKline. The seminal paragraph accused the company of engaging in "repeated and persistent fraud by misrepresenting, concealing and otherwise failing to disclose to physicians information" about the safety and effectiveness of Paxil in treating pediatric depression.

As part of the complaint, Firestein wanted to spell out the results of all three randomized clinical trials, including the mixed results in 329. She wrote a memo to her colleagues carefully explaining the methodology and outcomes for all three studies.

At their next meeting, held in Tom Conway's crowded corner office on the third floor, the head of the consumer bureau jabbed at the memo in front of him.

"What does this mean?" Conway said. "Are you telling me that all three of these studies were negative?"

"Yes," Firestein said. Sitting in her usual place at the head of the table, which Conway jokingly referred to as the hot seat, she carefully explained what the primary outcome measures in studies 377 and 701 showed. And then she talked about the mixed results in study 329 and noted that the authors had actually changed an outcome measure late in the game, after the study blind had already been broken.

"When they didn't achieve statistical significance with the primary measures, it looks like they changed one of the primary end points to try to show statistical significance," she said, absentmindedly clicking the button on the end of her pen. "That doesn't look kosher to me."

"But how do you know?" Conway pressed. "Is this just your interpretation of the study or is this fact?"

Exasperated, Firestein picked up the copy of the memo she had written and waved it at him. "It's all right here!" she yelled.

Conway didn't blink an eye. He was used to her outbursts.

"It probably is, Rose. But we don't know this material as well as you do, and we have to be absolutely solid on the facts. Is there any way you can back up some of these allegations?"

Firestein sank back into her chair. It was clear that Conway wasn't going to take her word for it, even though she had carefully spelled it all out in her memo. So be it. She'd get him the backup he wanted.

"Well, I remember there were some letters to the editor talking about some of the same discrepancies I found," she said. "I wasn't able to get them online, but maybe there's a way I can get them from the journal. I'll try to do that. Okay?"

. . .

A FEW DAYS LATER, Firestein called Dr. Mina Dulcan, the editor of the *Journal of the American Academy of Child and Adolescent Psychiatry*. Could Dr. Dulcan help her understand how the process of peer review worked? The journal editor was happy to help.

"She [Dulcan] explained that the peer reviewers do this on a voluntary basis; it's not their day job," Firestein recalled. Dulcan went on to explain that her reviewers are generally committed to doing the right thing, but they may miss things. They don't see the raw data, so it would be difficult to pick up deliberate errors. The purpose of the peer review, Dulcan said, was to see whether the researchers had taken a reasonable methodological approach to the study and whether the results matched the conclusion.

"If there is a disconnect between the data and the text, isn't that something the peer reviewers would pick up?" Firestein asked.

"Oh yes," the editor replied.

Firestein mentioned that there appeared to be just such a discrepancy in a 2001 Paxil study published in the child and adolescent psychiatry journal. The editor's voice turned cold. She replied that she doubted that very much.

"That's not the kind of thing our reviewers would miss," she said. Firestein didn't press the point, and the conversation ended on a cordial note, with Dulcan promising to send Firestein the letters that pertained to the 2001 Paxil study.

Firestein found the conversation quite revealing. She now understood for the first time that peer review was not a guarantee of good science. It was an imperfect process at best. At its worst, it was a system rife with bias.

On April 15, Firestein received the journal's letters to the editor, and they confirmed her interpretation of study 329. Several of the correspondents, all psychiatric researchers, had picked up on the fact that Paxil did not show significant improvement over placebo on either of the two primary outcomes. Two of the letter writers pointed out that

Keller and his coauthors had indeed changed a primary measure disturbingly late in the game.

A Canadian physician also expressed concern over the large number of patients in the Paxil group who suffered serious adverse effects, when compared with the two other groups in the study. "This finding would appear to be statistically significant, although this was not specifically addressed in the study," wrote Dr. Mitch Parsons of the University of Alberta in Canada. Parsons also wanted to know why the investigators had so readily dismissed the possibility that Paxil could have caused some of the serious side effects that emerged among patients in the study, such as suicidal thoughts or behaviors, hostility, and other conduct problems. "A degree of emotional lability and increased defiance is so common, in fact, that I routinely warn parents that this is likely to happen during the first few weeks on medication," Parsons wrote.

Raising similar objections in another letter to the editor, two researchers from universities in Adelaide, Australia, went so far as to accuse the Keller study of "distorted and unbalanced reporting." "Given that the research was paid for by GlaxoSmithKline, the makers of paroxetine, it is tempting to explain the mode of reporting as an attempt to show the drug in the most favorable light," Jon Jureidini and Anne Tonkin wrote in a letter published in the *Journal of the American Academy of Child and Adolescent Psychiatry* in May 2003.

Firestein sat down and typed up another memo to Conway, Baker, and Stark, quoting liberally from these letters to the editor. Over the next month, the four attorneys held several more meetings to discuss what Baker described as the "large issues" that needed to be covered in their legal complaint against GlaxoSmithKline. They also met to go over their markups of subsequent drafts of the complaint. But there were no more questions about primary and secondary outcome measures. By the time the complaint was ready for review by Eliot Spitzer and his top lieutenants, Baker and Conway had come to trust that if Rose Firestein said something was so, it was so. They had accepted her as a critical thinker who could process reams of complicated material and boil it down to a few accurate bullet points.

"There was hardly a question we asked that Rose didn't know the answer to," Baker recalled. "I don't know that we ever had our mind around [the details] the way Rose did, but at a certain point, we relented and trusted that she had it right."

They were about to find out if she did.

# 16. The New York AG v. GlaxoSmithKline, June 2004

On the morning of June 2, 2004, a clerk from the New York State attorney general's office hand-delivered the eighteen-page complaint against GlaxoSmithKline to Foley Square and filed it with the Supreme Court of the State of New York. The document carried Rose Firestein's signature. Later that morning, Eliot Spitzer fielded press calls about the lawsuit. Conway, Baker, Stark, and Firestein joined Spitzer in his office on the twenty-fifth floor for the impromptu press conference. Dr. Barry Perlman, the president of the New York State Psychiatric Institute, also participated in several of the press calls. The institute, which represented psychiatrists throughout New York State, had issued a statement that day supporting the attorney general's lawsuit.

Spitzer was in his element. Talking to one reporter after another, the attorney general emphasized that his office wasn't making any pronouncement on whether Paxil was a safe or effective drug. This lawsuit, he said, focused solely on the failure of GlaxoSmithKline to disclose negative information. "Their effort to suppress [these] studies was harmful and improper to the doctors who were making prescribing decisions and it violated the law," he told the *Wall Street Journal* reporter Barbara Martinez.

"Similar suits are likely," he told Gardiner Harris, a reporter for the *New York Times.*

For their part, GlaxoSmithKline officials declined to comment on the specifics of the case. The company issued a statement saying that it "had acted responsibly in conducting clinical studies in pediatric patients and disseminating data from those studies." The day the lawsuit was filed, GlaxoSmithKline's stock price dropped 3.2 percent. (Publicity over Paxil's link to suicidal behaviors had already dampened the drug's sales. In late July, Glaxo would announce that its earnings for the second quarter of 2004 had taken a dive, falling 13 percent over the previous year's earnings.)

OVER THE NEXT few days, news of the AG's legal action appeared not only in the *New York Times,* the *Wall Street Journal,* and the *Washington Post* but also in the *Financial Times* of London and in newspapers as far away as Asia and Australia. It did not go unnoticed that the lawsuit against GlaxoSmithKline came less than a month after Pfizer had settled the multistate legal actions over the marketing of Neurontin for a whopping $430 million. (As part of the settlement, Pfizer pleaded guilty to charges that its Parke-Davis/Warner-Lambert unit had illegally marketed Neurontin to doctors for the treatment of off-label conditions.) Several news reports cast Spitzer's lawsuit as part of a broad assault on the pharmaceutical industry's practices by government prosecutors throughout the nation. A few journalists also noted that it appeared to break new ground, relying on a legal argument never used before. "The new wrinkle in Mr. Spitzer's suit is his argument that a drug maker is committing fraud if it does not tell doctors about trials of a medication that raise safety concerns," Gardiner Harris wrote in his front-page *New York Times* story on June 3.

On the third floor of the Equitable, Firestein and Stark were amazed at all the publicity the case was receiving. As was their boss. Conway kept going around with a wide grin on his face, saying, "Look what we did from our smelly little offices!"

The euphoria didn't last long. A few days later, Jean-Pierre Garnier, the chief executive of GlaxoSmithKline, came out swinging. In an interview with the *Wall Street Journal,* Garnier attacked Spitzer's lawsuit and others like it as "an outrageous cost of doing business." "The legal system is getting out of control," he told the *Journal*'s Jeanne Whalen on June 3. A few days later, Garnier upped the ante, accusing Spitzer of bullying and extortion. "The big picture here is that it's becoming too easy for many people to attack the pharma industry and hold it to standards that are higher than anywhere else. I don't have a problem with the standards but I do have a problem with extortion," he told the *Sunday Telegraph* of London in an interview published on June 6. In that interview, Garnier charged that Glaxo had fully cooperated with the AG's request for information, yet had been given no advance warning about the lawsuit. "We are not getting a fair chance to rebut because this is the almighty attorney office from mid-Manhattan," he fumed. "There is a certain amount of bullying in these tactics."

Garnier also dismissed the "smoking gun" memo from 1998, which laid out SmithKline's plans not to disclose the negative results about Paxil. He said the memo was contrary to company policy. "Can a company control the millions of memoranda that are written by, in our case, 110,000 people?" the CEO was quoted as saying. "What are the odds that stupid memos were written? What are the odds that memos asking the company to do things against company policy will be written? The odds are 100 percent."

Garnier's combative comments alarmed Firestein. They signaled that the London-based pharmaceutical company meant to fight the case in court, which could drag it out for years. And while the New York State Psychiatric Institute had joined forces with Spitzer the day the lawsuit was filed, the silence from other medical groups and federal regulators was conspicuous. Firestein couldn't help asking herself, had she and her colleagues so badly misjudged the willingness of the medical community to take a stand for full disclosure?

THE SAME WEEK, almost two thousand miles away in Pflugerville, Texas, seventeen-year-old Tonya Brooks was rushed into a hospital emergency room, bleeding from that huge, gaping hole in her leg. The self-inflicted wound would require three layers of stitches to suture it shut, and while Tonya lay splayed on the gurney, a parade of people kept coming in and asking her, "Did your father abuse you? Did he beat you up?" No, she kept telling them. No.

Later that day, she was admitted to Seton Shoal Creek, a mental hospital for children and adolescents in Austin. The doctor diagnosed her as bipolar; according to Tonya, he labeled everyone bipolar. "Ninety percent of the kids I met there, there's nothing wrong with them," she later told me. "They just wanted attention. They act out to get attention." Tonya agreed with everything the doctor said just so she could get out of there. But she liked the nurses; they were very kind. She confided in one nurse that she liked to color, so the nurse gave her a coloring book and told her that whenever she started to feel bad, she could color in pictures to take her mind off things. Tonya Brooks stayed at Shoal Creek for four days, and on June 7, 2004, she went home.

FOUR DAYS LATER, the Food and Drug Administration reacted to the news of the New York AG's lawsuit in its usual oblique fashion. On Friday, June 11, the federal agency sent an "untitled" reprimand (one step below an official warning) to GlaxoSmithKline, rebuking the company for running "false and misleading" television commercials about Paxil. The FDA letter said that the sixty-second TV ad "broadens the indication for Paxil CR beyond the . . . more serious condition of social anxiety disorder to people experiencing more ordinary degrees of anxiety, fear and self-consciousness in social or work situations, while also minimizing the serious risks associated with the drug." The federal agency asked the company to stop showing the ads. The press reports implied that the FDA's action had been prompted by the New York State attorney general's lawsuit, especially since the ads in question had first aired months earlier. It was that same series of TV commercials that had compelled Tonya Brooks in Texas to ask her doctor to prescribe Paxil.

LATE IN THE AFTERNOON on June 14, 2004, in a clear attempt at damage control, GlaxoSmithKline posted all nine of the pediatric Paxil studies (including the three randomized clinical trials and other research results) on its Web site. The company was doing this "in the interest of transparency," a Glaxo spokesperson told the *Wall Street Journal.* Spitzer pronounced the posting "a positive first step toward changing a dangerous industry practice." But the AG's office wanted more than the quick posting of a few studies related to one drug; Spitzer and his team had decided early on that as a condition of any settlement, Glaxo would have to launch a comprehensive, publicly available registry that contained the results of all its clinical trials after a certain date, negative as well as positive.

"They had to understand that we wouldn't settle absent their changing the behavior, their refusal to disclose," Spitzer later explained. He was eager to expand his action against Glaxo into a wake-up call for other drug companies. GlaxoSmithKline, after all, was not the only SSRI maker who was guilty of selective data disclosure. At the end of 2003, British regulators had made it clear that while the published results of randomized trials on several commonly prescribed antidepressants such as Paxil, Zoloft, Effexor, Luvox, and Remeron described these drugs as safe and effective in children, the actual data from their clinical trials showed quite the opposite.

"There is probably no other area of medicine in which the academic literature is so at odds with the raw data," declared David Healy in an open letter to Mr. Peter J. Pitts, the FDA's associate commissioner for external relations, earlier that year. The AG's office had arrived at much the same conclusion during its year-long investigation. Much as Spitzer's investment bureau had parlayed a big win against Merrill Lynch into broad-reaching changes on Wall Street, his consumer team now hoped to use the fulcrum of a lawsuit aimed at one drugmaker to reform the behavior of the entire industry.

That was the game plan, anyway.

Finally, on June 15, the American Medical Association, the powerful trade organization for U.S. doctors, jumped into the fray. At its annual meeting in Chicago, the AMA declared its support for full disclosure of medical studies and voted to ask the U.S. Department of Health and Human Services to create a public registry of all clinical trials and their outcomes.

In response to the AMA's declaration, Dr. Jeffrey Drazen, editor of the *New England Journal of Medicine,* told the *Boston Globe* that journal editors were considering a similar proposal. By a fortunate coincidence, twelve editors of the most prestigious medical journals in the world had been meeting in Croatia the week the AG's office filed its lawsuit against GlaxoSmithKline. This group, officially known as the International Committee of Medical Journal Editors (ICMJE), had been trying for years to achieve full disclosure of medical research results. These editors were coming at the issue from a slightly different vantage point than Firestein and her colleagues, but with the same end in mind. They wanted scientists to more fully disclose the original objectives and design of their research before they began the actual studies and submitted them for publication. That way, journal editors would know what exactly the original intent and focus of the research was.

In all too many cases, medical researchers were making last-minute changes in the outcome measures of their studies—changes that could significantly skew the results. A survey published just the previous month in the *Journal of the American Medical Association* found that at least one primary outcome measure was changed in 62 percent of all clinical trials surveyed, leading to "biased and inconsistent" study outcomes. The *JAMA* survey also found that 86 percent of respondents didn't report the changes they'd made, making it extremely difficult for journal editors to catch such manipulations.

"Of the twelve editors sitting around the table in Croatia, we'd all had the experience of someone pulling a fast one on us," said *NEJM*'s Dr. Jeffrey Drazen, one of the ICMJE members leading this effort. "All the editors had to play this hide-and-seek game about what was really being studied."

Emboldened by the New York lawsuit, Drazen and the other editors meeting in Croatia decided to get tough. There and then, they agreed to require that medical researchers register the key elements of their study protocols, including outcome measures and the size of the study groups, on one of several public research Web sites. If researchers (or their pharmaceutical sponsors) didn't register up front, they couldn't expect to be published by a prestigious medical journal. In three months' time, all twelve journals whose editors belonged to the ICMJE would publish identical editorials laying out their specific demands.

Back at the AG's office, however, Firestein and her colleagues were beginning to despair of a quick settlement with GlaxoSmithKline. They had been rattled by an editorial in the *Wall Street Journal* that viciously attacked Spitzer as a lawmaker run amok. The June 21 editorial went so far as to accuse the AG's lawsuit of threatening to damage public health. "All in all, there's something dangerous about a prosecutor making health-policy decisions for which he can't be held responsible," the *Journal*'s editorial writers declaimed. "Mr. Spitzer has to face the voters every four years, but will he take the blame for depressed kids who suffer because their doctors are scared out of prescribing Paxil?"

The editorial concluded that, "Whatever good Mr. Spitzer has done by drawing attention to Wall Street's sins, it's clear his good press has gone to his head. He's now firing press releases and lawsuits in so many directions that he's hitting and harming innocent bystanders."

For months afterward, Spitzer would carry that editorial around with him, showing it at speeches he gave to health care groups. "It says in here that the system is fine the way it is," he would say, and shake his head. "How can you defend a status quo that is so clearly broken?"

But Firestein couldn't help wondering how much the *Wall Street Journal*'s salvo had shaken Spitzer privately. The *Journal,* after all, was the most prestigious business newspaper in the country, perhaps the world. Such an ad hominem attack would certainly have stung her. While the attorney general got the lion's share of credit for his staff's victories, he was also taking all the hits—first from Wall Street and now from the pharmaceutical industry. Firestein had to admit she was kind of relieved that she wasn't the one on the firing line. She had a feeling her skin would not be as thick as Eliot Spitzer's.

# 17. Wherein Rose Firestein Goes to Court and Annoys a Federal Judge, July 2004

**R**ose Firestein was perspiring as she waited to pass through security. It was a humid, overcast day in late July and she was wearing one of the two tissue-wool suits she owned. She needed to dress in layers at work even in the summer because her office was freezing. Cold enough to make ice cream, she often said. But the weather outside was a different story. By the time Firestein walked the eleven blocks to the new Daniel Patrick Moynihan United States Courthouse on Pearl Street, she felt as if she had been baked in a 350-degree oven.

This was Firestein's first visit to the new courthouse, which had been built directly behind the old New York State Supreme Court building on Foley Square. Although the white-marbled interior of the Moynihan courthouse was airy and filled with light, Firestein couldn't help thinking that the new edifice, as costly as it must have been to build, did not have the moral majesty of the old courthouse, with its coffered ceiling beautifully sculpted with plaster rosettes.

Firestein was here because the attorneys for GlaxoSmithKline had preemptively removed the attorney general's consumer fraud case against the drug giant to federal court. One day, Joseph Sedwick Sollers (Wick) had told her the company was interested in talking about settlement; then he and his cocounsel had gone ahead and moved the case out of the New

York State courts. The case was now slated to be heard by Judge Miriam Goldman Cedarbaum of the Southern District Court of New York. The judge had called a preliminary conference for this afternoon.

Firestein and the two GlaxoSmithKline attorneys—Wick and Dwight Davis—arrived early and cooled their heels outside the courtroom until the lunch recess was over and the chamber was unlocked. While they waited, Wick mentioned that Glaxo might be ready to talk again about settling the case. But Firestein had heard that song before. She wasn't about to get her hopes up. This was not the first time she had tangled with GlaxoSmithKline—they were one of the litigants in the wholesale drug pricing case—and she knew the company, which had annual earnings of $9.32 billion, could be a formidable opponent. In the pricing case, the AG's office had accused three pharmaceuticals of wildly inflating the average wholesale price of their drugs. Millions of dollars in restitution and fines were on the table, and Glaxo and the two other defendants—Pharmacia (later acquired by Pfizer) and Aventis (which later merged with Sanofi)—were aggressively contesting the complaint. It was now in its second year, with no end in sight.

JUDGE MIRIAM CEDARBAUM presided over a wood-paneled courtroom on the fourteenth floor of the new courthouse, its royal blue window drapes decorated in stars and wreaths. The carpeting was also blue, with a matching pattern of stars and wreaths. Behind the judge's chair hung a black metallic etching of the great seal, the familiar bald eagle holding the olive branch in one talon and spears in the other. The black-robed judge herself wore an expressive face and long salt-and-pepper hair parted in the middle. When listening to an oral argument, she would rest her right hand under her chin with an index finger extended just below her lip. Her eyes were stern, and one eyebrow seemed to be in a perpetual upside-down V.

The first thing the judge wanted to know was how the AG's office planned to prove intent. How did Ms. Firestein know that Glaxo-SmithKline *intended* to deceive consumers when it withheld two studies showing that Paxil was no more effective than placebo in pediatric depression?

Firestein had spent considerable time studying New York's consumer fraud statute, and not just for this case. A few weeks after her office filed the lawsuit against GlaxoSmithKline, the *New York Times* and the *Wall Street Journal* reported that another large pharmaceutical company, Forest Labs, had also neglected to publish two negative studies about its SSRI, Celexa. Yet the same month—June 2004—the *American Journal of Psychiatry* had published a study concluding that Celexa did reduce symptoms of depression in children. Was this another example of selective disclosure? Firestein's sources seemed to think so. She had wasted no time firing off a letter to Forest Labs requesting "any information that may exist with respect to off-label clinical trials or promotion" of Celexa, which was then the fourth most commonly prescribed antidepressant for children and adolescents.

"We don't have to prove intent," Firestein told the judge, feeling very much on the hot seat as she stood alone behind the long plaintiff's table. "As you're well aware, under common law, you do have to show intent to defraud. But under the State of New York's consumer fraud statute, you don't. You might want to look at *People v. General Electric*—it has a very clean explanation of the statute."

Judge Cedarbaum looked over at the two Glaxo attorneys. They nodded in agreement. This was clearly not the issue on which they planned to stake their ground today. The judge then turned to the question they did care about: why had they removed the case to federal court?

Standing behind the defendant's table, Dwight Davis, an elegantly suited Wick by his side, explained that the AG's complaint was in fact preempted by federal law, indeed by Congress, when it had established the U.S. Food and Drug Administration as the nation's regulatory agency in charge of drug safety and approval. Under federal law, he said, only the FDA could determine whether the antidepressant Paxil was safe and effective for use in children.

"Congress has fully occupied the field here, and there's nothing left for the state legislature to do," Davis said.

Judge Cedarbaum quirked an eyebrow at Firestein, who had remained standing.

"We have a number of responses to that, Your Honor, among them being the fact that the FDA does not regulate the practice of medicine," Firestein began. "Within New York, as in other states, the regulation of the practice of medicine is solely the responsibility of the state."

Firestein argued that by selectively publishing only one study purporting to show Paxil's efficacy and concealing two other studies that showed no efficacy, GlaxoSmithKline had prevented the state's physicians from "properly and independently exercising their professional judgment on behalf of their child and adolescent patients."

She drew a quick breath and continued.

"But Your Honor, the main point I'd like to argue here is that the defendant seems to be asserting preemption as a defense," she said. The Glaxo attorneys were essentially claiming that the FDA's jurisdiction in regulating drugs preempted any regulatory role by New York State. Firestein argued that they were using this preemptive argument as a defense against the AG's lawsuit. If so, they had made a procedural mistake. There were many reasons a case could be removed to federal court, but a defense wasn't one of them.

"As Your Honor knows, a defense based on federal law is not a basis for removal," Firestein said. She cited a recent Supreme Court case affirming that a defense could not be used as a basis to remove a case from state to federal court.

Judge Cedarbaum nodded.

"You're right," she said. "A defense is not the basis for a change in jurisdiction."

The judge turned to the Glaxo attorneys. Firestein could hear the two men exchange words; they did not sound happy. Dwight began to argue that he was not using a defense as the basis for removing the AG's lawsuit to federal court, but Judge Cedarbaum waved her hand as if to say it didn't matter.

"Nobody's filed a remand yet," she said. She meant that since the AG's office hadn't yet filed a motion to return the case to state court, the attorneys on both sides would have plenty of time to argue the grounds for removing the case to federal court.

A LITTLE LATER, it was Firestein's turn to squirm. She had already made it clear to the judge that she intended to file a motion to remand the case to state court. But under the court's regulations, she had only thirty days from the date GlaxoSmithKline had removed the case in which to file the motion, and she wasn't sure she could meet that deadline, especially if Glaxo decided they wanted to talk about settling the case.

"Will I waive my objections to removal if I don't file within thirty days?" she asked the judge.

"No, of course not," Judge Cedarbaum said impatiently. "You never waive objection to the lack of federal jurisdiction."

"But sometimes you can waive your objection to procedural defects in the notice," Firestein persisted. "I just want to make sure I'm not waiving my position."

Judge Cedarbaum narrowed her eyes and frowned.

"That's ridiculous!" she said. "If I tell you you can file your papers beyond a certain date, then that's when you can file your papers!"

Firestein flushed and looked down at the table. This was not the first time she had incurred a magistrate's wrath. She knew that she came across as overly aggressive sometimes, but she couldn't help herself. Even before she lost much of her sight, a handicap that prevented her from reading other people's body language, she'd had this tendency to push people's buttons. It came, she thought, from being the third child in a family of four children with two very busy parents. If she hadn't been persistent, no one in that tumultuous household would ever have heard her. But sometimes, she knew, she went too far.

Firestein sighed. The case of the *People of New York v. GlaxoSmith-Kline,* Docket Number 04 CV 5304, would hinge in large part on the rulings made by Judge Miriam Cedarbaum. Firestein prayed that she had not alienated this all-powerful woman on her very first appearance in her courtroom.

A FEW DAYS LATER, Firestein finally made contact with a source she'd been told might be helpful in the case against Glaxo-SmithKline. The source was a woman by the name of Donna Howard, and all Firestein knew was that she had once worked for the psychiatry department at Brown University and might have some useful information about the Paxil study Keller and his coauthor published in 2001. By this time, Howard was no longer working for NAMI Rhode Island; she had been fired in May 2004. She was now on unemployment and looking for another job. In the meantime, she was volunteering at Taunton State Hospital. When Firestein finally reached Howard at her home, the two women talked for more than an hour.

One particular fact stood out in Firestein's memory of their conversation: Howard told her that a few weeks after entering the Paxil study at Brown, one of the participants, a fourteen-year-old boy, had what she called a "psychotic break" on Thanksgiving weekend, 1994. He punched some pictures, broke the glass, and cut himself badly. He was taken to the emergency room of a Fall River hospital, where he received six stitches. Because he seemed acutely suicidal, the boy was then transferred to Bradley Hospital, a psychiatric hospital for children and adolescents in East Providence. The treating psychiatrists at Bradley had been told the boy was part of the Brown Paxil study, but they didn't know what, if any, drugs he was on. (He could have been taking Paxil, Tofranil [imipramine], or the placebo.) They needed more information; how could they help their patient if they didn't have his basic medical history? Over the weekend, one of the treating psychiatrists finally reached a researcher who was involved with the Paxil study and asked him to break the blind so they could find out what medicine their patient was on. The researcher refused.

"The doctors at Bradley were beside themselves," Howard recalled. "Here was a kid in an obviously bad state, and they had no way of finding out what, if anything, the kid was on."

Firestein was appalled at what she was hearing. From the little she knew about medicine, it was an accepted principle that the needs of the patient came before the needs of a drug study or anything else. Otherwise, the doctor supervising the clinical trial could be seen as violating the basic tenet of medicine, the Hippocratic oath. According to the protocol itself for the Paxil study, "the blind was to be broken . . . in the event of a serious adverse experience that the investigator felt could not be adequately treated without knowing the identity of the study medication."

Ronald Seifer, director of research at Bradley Hospital and a member of Brown University's Institutional Review Board at the time, fired off an angry memo to Martin Keller, saying that the psychiatrists at Bradley had to have this kind of information in order to treat their patient. Shortly afterward, the blind was broken, according to the GlaxoSmith-Kline final report of this incident. It was discovered that the boy had been taking Paxil during the clinical trial. The Bradley doctors began to phase him off the drug, and on Tuesday, November 30, the fourteen-year-old was withdrawn from the Brown study.

But despite the fact that this boy was clearly suicidal and required hospitalization, he was not included among the patients listed as having developed serious adverse effects in the published 2001 Paxil study. Other patients were similarly miscoded. One was a fifteen-year-old girl who had been withdrawn from the Brown study site in 1995 after becoming combative with her mother. According to internal university documents that Howard gave me, Brown researchers knew that this girl had become suicidal after taking Paxil. In a memo to the Institutional Review Board dated October 30, 1995, Martin Keller wrote that this teenager, who had been enrolled in the study in June 1995, "was hospitalized on 9/15/95 due to becoming very combative with her mother and threatening suicide." Yet instead of coding her behavior as an adverse effect related to Paxil, Keller in his memo says she was "terminated from the study for non-compliance." The Brown investigators may have coded her as noncompliant because she had stopped taking Paxil before having her meltdown. But they shouldn't have, according to several clinicians familiar with the study. The Brown researchers should have included all adverse effects experienced by their patients, regardless of what may have caused the problems. As a Harvard Medical School biostatistician later told me, "You shouldn't try to make these subjective attributions and exclude patients who don't fit into your thesis." As research has shown, the SSRI antidepressants can cause serious side effects, including suicidal behaviors and hostility, weeks after people stop taking them.

The underreporting didn't stop there. In their 2001 paper, Keller and his coauthors reported that "serious adverse effects occurred in 11 patients in the paroxetine group, 5 in the imipramine group and 2 in the placebo group." After comparing internal Brown documents with the final report of study 329 that GlaxoSmithKline posted on its Web site, it becomes apparent that the researchers had not included among the patients with serious adverse effects yet another teenage girl who had left the study after trying to kill herself. According to a memo that Keller himself wrote to the Brown Institutional Review Board on January 30, 1995, this patient (number 70) ingested eighty-two Tylenol pills in an apparent overdose attempt on January 19. Patient 70 was admitted to a hospital and terminated from the study shortly afterward, according to Keller's memo to Brown IRB. Yet this teenage girl was not included in the group reported to have experienced serious adverse events while in the study. Instead, in another memo that Keller had written to the Brown IRB in 1995, she was described as having been terminated from the study for being "noncompliant."

In an even more mysterious turn, patient 70 was described in Glaxo-SmithKline's final report of the study as being a twelve-year-old boy. This boy was enrolled in the clinical trial a month after the teenage girl identified in Keller's memos as patient 70 overdosed on Tylenol and withdrew from the study. The boy with the same patient number was removed from the study on March 22, 1995, after developing tachycardia (rapid heartbeat) while taking the tricyclic antidepressant known as imipramine, according to the company's final report. There was no mention in the company's posted final report or the 2001 journal paper that the original patient 70 was a young girl who had ingested eighty-two Tylenol pills in a clear bid to kill herself.

During her phone conversation with Firestein, Howard alleged that the data in the Paxil study had been changed to satisfy the study's sponsor, SmithKline Beecham. "Everybody knew we had to keep Smith-Kline happy and give them the results they wanted," she said.

Howard told Firestein that she still had in her possession from her time at Brown a number of internal Brown memos showing how researchers may have miscoded the data in the Paxil study. Would Firestein like copies of them?

Sure, Firestein replied.

Before hanging up, the litigator had one more question: would Howard would be willing to testify in court if it came to that? Her heart in her throat, Howard said yes. She then asked, "Do I have to fly? Can I take a train?" Firestein laughed and said how Howard got down to New York was up to her.

# 18. GlaxoSmithKline Comes to the Table, August 2004

On August 3, 2004, Charles "Chuck" Grassley, the Republican senator from Iowa and chairman of the Senate Finance Committee, sent a sternly worded letter to Christopher Viehbacher, president of the U.S. Pharmaceuticals division of GlaxoSmithKline. In his four-page dispatch, the senator wrote that he was troubled by the New York attorney's allegations that Glaxo had concealed important information about Paxil. He said he had heard similar accusations from Dr. Andrew Mosholder.

Mosholder was the FDA official who had been prevented from testifying about his findings at the agency's February 2 hearing. Grassley's Finance Committee was investigating that gagging incident, and in the course of its probe, Mosholder had told the senators that "GlaxoSmithKline, in his opinion, was attempting to 'sugar-coat' the adverse effects of Paxil on children by 'miscoding' suicidal ideations and/or suicidal behavior."

In his letter to Viehbacher, Grassley said that he was concerned that "some drug companies" may not have provided the FDA with all the information at their disposal. He concluded by demanding that GlaxoSmithKline hand over information about all of the clinical trials on antidepressants and other drugs it had initiated between 1990 and the present. Glaxo had until August 27 to comply.

Glaxo officials would decline to comment on whether there was any connection between Senator Grassley's letter and their decision to pursue a settlement with the New York State attorney general's lawsuit. But a few days after Grassley faxed his letter to Viehbacher, Rose Firestein received a call from Wick. The drug company was ready to resume talks.

Looking back, Firestein thought the constant drumbeat of publicity might also have played a role in Glaxo's willingness to come to the table. Reporters from the *New York Times* and the *Wall Street Journal,* among other major papers, repeatedly cited the AG's lawsuit as a catalyst for the "expanding debate over the incomplete disclosure" of drug test results. And the AG's office continued to widen its net. The day after Senator Grassley dropped his letter bomb, the pharmaceutical giant Johnson and Johnson publicly acknowledged that Spitzer's office had asked for detailed information about six of its drugs, including Risperdal and Procrit, an antianemia medication. And on August 5, the *Wall Street Journal,* having somehow obtained a draft FDA document, reported that the federal agency had finally found evidence of a link between antidepressant drugs and suicidal tendencies in young people. The FDA's latest reanalysis appeared to be consistent with earlier conclusions reached by Mosholder.

In an e-mail to me, Mary Anne Rhyne, a spokeswoman for Glaxo-SmithKline, said she couldn't comment on whether any or all of these high-profile events contributed to the company's decision to resume talks. Whatever the reason, on August 11, Wick and Dwight Davis, along with Frank Rockhold and an in-house attorney for Glaxo, took a cab downtown to meet with Firestein and her colleagues at 120 Broadway. This time the Glaxo lawyers were escorted to a different conference room, a little bigger than their previous gathering place, but just as drab and airless. It too had half-empty metal bookcases lined up on one side of the room, boxes stacked in the corners, and no windows. No one seemed to mind.

"I'm glad we're not in the bad karma room," Wick joked. Everyone around the table laughed.

GlaxoSmithKline had already reconciled itself to the idea of establishing an online registry of its clinical trial data as part of a settlement with the New York AG. Indeed, it was the company's announcement of plans to post some clinical data that had prompted Tom Conway to end their first meeting on June 30 so abruptly. Now, six weeks later, it looked as if the talks might once again founder over the same sticking point: the level of detail the AG's office wanted included in the company's public registry.

Firestein went through the list of demands one by one. The registry, she said, should include detailed summaries not only of all the company's Phase 3 and Phase 4 clinical trials but also of some of the safety studies that it performed on healthy volunteers. Drug companies routinely carried out these Phase 1 and Phase 2 trials to see how the target drug metabolized inside the human body (these were known as pharmacokinetic studies), what its cause of action might be, and what adverse side effects it generated. While these Phase 1 and 2 studies were sometimes submitted to the FDA, they were usually not published in peer-reviewed journals or made available to the public.

Not surprisingly, the representatives from Glaxo balked at this demand.

"Nobody had ever suggested that they publish the adverse events from pharmacokinetic studies," Firestein recalled. "So that was a huge conversation."

At their first meeting in June, Firestein had also made it clear that she wanted to set a specific standard or threshold as to which adverse side effects would be included in the posted summary for each clinical study.

But should that threshold be 5 percent, 10 percent? In other words, what percentage of patients would have to suffer that particular side effect—whether it was nausea, a headache, or suicidal behavior—for it to be included in the study summary?

This, Firestein knew, was a key issue. If Glaxo only posted adverse side effects that occurred in, say, 10 percent or more of the study participants, that might mask some serious problems with a particular drug. In one clinical trial of a popular antidepressant, 9.7 percent of the study participants had developed troubling suicidal thoughts and behaviors. So if the standard settled upon was 10 percent, some serious side effects could be hidden from public view.

"We felt there had to be a clear litmus-paper standard for what constitutes an adverse event, what constitutes a serious adverse event, and which ones you have to report," Firestein recalled. "We spent a lot of time talking about at what point does something become a serious adverse event that's reportable."

The AG team also wanted each study summary to contain detailed information on efficacy results — in other words, how the drug in question did on the study's primary and secondary outcome measures. The posted summary should also include information on whether those outcome measures had been changed once the study began.

The Glaxo negotiators weren't happy with any of these demands. "They didn't want to be told what the content of their registry should be," Firestein said. "They wanted to decide what the content would be." (In an e-mail to me, the spokesperson for the drug company declined to comment on these negotiations, saying it would be "inappropriate.")

After several hours of intense but cordial discussion — "there was no shouting or yelling," Firestein recalled — the meeting broke up. Wick said he would take the AG's demands back to corporate. He'd be in touch, he said.

Walking back to their offices, Conway remarked to Firestein, "I have a feeling this case is going to settle. I think we're going to get what we need."

Firestein managed a smile. But she felt completely drained. The intensity of the negotiations, the strain of being on the hot seat with everyone in the room judging her performance — it was all a bit much. At that particular moment, she felt as if the gray matter in her brain had turned to jelly.

The next few weeks passed in a blur. Wick called her back a few days later and agreed to some of the demands, but not others. The two attorneys negotiated by phone, talking almost every day. Firestein would relay what Wick had said to Stark, Conway, and Baker, see what they thought, and then call him back. Firestein talked with Wick, then with Dwight, then with Wick again. Each time one of the Glaxo attorneys said no, they couldn't do that, Firestein would remind him that if the AG's office took this case to trial and won, it would get that particular clause. So why not agree to it now and spare both sides the expense and hassle of a prolonged court battle?

In the end, the drug company agreed to post detailed summaries of some of their Phase 2 safety studies and all of their Phase 3 and Phase 4 drug studies that were completed after December 27, 2000, plus any earlier clinical studies that were material to a physician's medical judgment in prescribing a Glaxo drug. The drug company remained adamantly opposed, however, to the idea of publicly registering the design or protocol of any ongoing clinical studies. That had been another condition Firestein and her colleagues had proposed in their August 11 meeting, and the drugmaker seemed dead-set against it. Pretrial protocols were a closely guarded proprietary secret, the Glaxo attorneys argued. Posting them would only give competitors an unfair window into the company's pipeline of upcoming drug products.

After talking it over among themselves, the assistant attorneys general agreed to concede on the pretrial registry. Since it was not central to their complaint—which had focused on GlaxoSmithKline's incomplete disclosure of already completed drug trials—"we felt we wouldn't have been able to get that through litigation," Firestein explained. Knowing that the editors of the world's top medical journals were about to require pretrial registration as a condition for publication made their decision that much easier.

By the third week of August, Firestein and Wick had worked out the details of what GlaxoSmithKline's clinical registry would look like. It would conform to the general principles of how a drug study should be reported, laid out years ago by the International Conference on Harmonisation of Technical Requirements for Registration of Pharmaceuticals for Human Use. Known in the trade as the ICH E3 guidelines, this was a detailed guidebook to how clinical studies should be conducted and presented to regulatory authorities. But the ICH E3 guidelines said nothing about having to present such data to the public.

What Glaxo agreed to went far beyond the ICH E3 guidelines. Each study summary on its registry would contain more than twenty categories of information, including specific data on the primary and secondary outcome measures of the study, the type and severity of any adverse side effects, and whether the study had been terminated early and why.

In short, Glaxo's registry would include a great deal more substance than the brief and often spotty summaries of drug study results that the FDA and other pharmaceutical companies had thus far been willing to make public.

All that was left to resolve was the amount of money GlaxoSmith-Kline would have to put on the table to settle the lawsuit. Firestein and her colleagues had already decided not to insist on a huge fine. They were far more interested in getting the drugmaker to launch a comprehensive registry. But there had to be some money on the table. To get a sense of what the damages should be, Firestein calculated how much money might have been spent on Paxil prescriptions for children and adolescents in New York State in 2002. Firestein would not disclose to me the ballpark figure she came up with. However, data from the American Medical Association indicate that Paxil prescription sales in New York State for patients under eighteen years old came to about $5.5 million in 2002.

The Glaxo attorneys said no way.

"They didn't want to give us any money," Firestein said. Finally, both sides settled on a figure of $2.5 million. The money would go into the state coffers. Firestein finished drafting the assurance agreement and consent order that had to be filed with the Southern District Court of New York.

On Thursday, August 26, the New York attorney general's office announced it had settled its legal action against GlaxoSmithKline. Spitzer hailed the settlement as "transformational in that it will provide doctors and patients access to the clinical testing data necessary to make informed judgments." He predicted that other drug companies would follow GlaxoSmithKline's lead in posting their studies online. His prediction wasn't entirely based on wishful thinking: Earlier in the summer, Eli Lilly had announced that it would create a Web site on which it planned to post the clinical results of already approved drugs. Johnson and Johnson and Forest Labs, which were under scrutiny by the AG's office, had made similar noises, as had Merck.

COMPARED TO THE barrage of coverage that greeted the initial filing of the AG's lawsuit, news of the settlement was muted, perhaps because it came at a time when so many reporters were on vacation. The *New York Times* and the *Wall Street Journal* reported the news in short pieces buried inside; other major papers didn't mention it at all.

The day the settlement was announced, Firestein was sitting on her usual perch in Stark's office when Conway strode in. He had a cup of soda in his hand.

"Great job!" he said, raising the cup in the air. "We did it!"

Earlier in the summer, Eliot Spitzer had publicly congratulated Firestein for her work on the case. He had given her (along with fifteen other attorneys in the office) the prestigious Lefkowitz Award at a special ceremony in June. The award was named after Louis Lefkowitz, a revered former New York State attorney general who had served from 1957 to 1978. "It's the highest award you can get in this office," Spitzer explained. "You get it for doing something that exemplifies the values of this office and the public-spiritedness of the litigation we're supposed to bring on behalf of the people of New York."

At the ceremony in the New York State Supreme Court building on Foley Square, Spitzer told the assembled attorneys that the case against GlaxoSmithKline epitomized everything the New York State attorney general's office stood for. "I don't usually single out specific litigation because the litigation everybody here does is important," he said. "But this case is really, really important because it has the potential to change an entire industry's practices. This case is not about money; it is about protecting people's health."

Spitzer called Firestein up to the front of the hall, shook hands with her, and gave her the Lefkowitz certificate in a frame. There was a burst of applause, and Firestein, her face flushed red with a mixture of embarrassment and pleasure, walked back to her seat.

Yet now that the case was finally settled, Firestein felt oddly let down, almost bereft. She was glad the case was over and happy that the AG's office had prevailed, but some part of her mourned the excitement, the prolonged high she'd been on in preparing for this day. Over the past seven or eight months, she'd developed a real sense of camaraderie with Stark and even Conway and Baker. It was the kind of fellowship that developed from working around the clock on something you fervently believed in, with colleagues who had become as wedded to its success as you were. Firestein found it hard to accept that all that heady antici-pation was now over. Finis.

Stark talked about the four of them celebrating by going out to lunch at her favorite kosher restaurant, a few blocks down on Broadway. But for some reason or other, the lunch never happened. As Joe Baker re-called, "We were all too busy working on the next case."

THE PUBLIC SPOTLIGHT, of course, didn't shut off overnight. GlaxoSmithKline's public reaction to the settlement was oddly unrepentant, almost dismissive, as if the summer's legal wrangling had all been a tempest in a teapot. In a press release dated August 26, the drug company said that "although GlaxoSmithKline believes the charges made in that litigation by the Attorney General are unfounded, the company has agreed to pay the State of New York $2.5 million to avoid the high costs and time required to defend itself in protracted litigation." The release noted that the company's plans for a clinical registry had been under way "for some months" and quoted Mark Werner, senior vice president for U.S. Legal Operations, as saying, "We are pleased that the Attorney General believes the clinical trial register we have been developing will provide useful information to the medical and scientific community."

The company's disingenuous response so angered Spitzer that the following week, he lashed out at GlaxoSmithKline. "The arrogance of the [Glaxo] commentary is offensive and problematic," he said in an interview published in the *Financial Times* of London on August 31. "We are going to be watching them with an eagle's eye to see that they have abided by the terms of the settlement."

By then, New York's attorney general was no longer the only lawmaker watching the pharmaceutical industry with an eagle eye. A congressional subcommittee on oversight and investigations had decided to take the matter into its own hands.

# 19. Martin Teicher Is Vindicated, and Rose Firestein Takes a Bow, Fall 2004

Martin Teicher's office at McLean Hospital was tucked away in a hard-to-find annex behind the newer and more imposing Mailman Research Center. There was no sign on his door, and first-time visitors would walk right past it on their way to the Developmental Biopsychiatry Research Program (the official name for Teicher's research group). The group office resembled a standard doctor's waiting area, with a sofa and chair soothingly upholstered in a dark blue and green leafy pattern, a coffee table, an assortment of magazines, and the requisite New England seascape. Teicher's private office was a more modest affair, with barely enough room for a desk, a small leather couch, two thin bookcases, a file cabinet, and two chairs. On one wall, a small portrait of a frightened little boy caught the eye. The painting of a sad clown hung in another corner, and a number of framed diplomas were displayed above his desk. A mounted Westminster clock chimed to mark the passing hour. The melodious clock was the only hint of Teicher's abiding love affair with music. When he turned his sights on a medical career as a young man, music became a sideline he enjoyed whenever he could squeeze it into his busy life. The year he turned fifty, though, Teicher decided to make some changes in his life. He remarried and began devoting more time to his music. He went to a folk music festival in Texas and took a songwriting course there. By the summer of 2004, his marriage was foundering (he and his second wife would divorce in 2005), and Teicher would spend hours writing songs about love and hurt and betrayal. (He eventually posted three of the blues tunes he had written and sung himself on myspace.com, where visitors to the site could listen to his songs and see a picture of Marty playing the guitar in shades and an open-collared white shirt.)

The blues, however, were far from Teicher's thoughts when he returned to his office on the afternoon of August 20, 2004. There, he found a message from his assistant Cindy McGreenery: a reporter for the *Baltimore Sun* wanted to interview him. In the past few months, as the controversy over the SSRI antidepressants heated up and the FDA finally acknowledged that yes, there was an increased risk of suicidal behaviors from antidepressants, Teicher had suddenly become a sought-after source. Reporters from all over the country wanted to talk to the man who had first raised that possibility fourteen years ago. But this time, Teicher was careful to consult with the hospital's medical chief and PR director, and he didn't take all or even most of the press calls. He would only speak to reporters from newspapers that he knew and trusted, such as the *Boston Globe,* the *Baltimore Sun,* and the *New York Times.* At the age of fifty-three, with a receding hairline and a closely cropped salt-and-pepper beard, Teicher had become, finally, a cautious man.

The first media calls back in February 2004 had caught him by surprise. Immersed as he was in a completely different field of study — the biological effects of child abuse on brain development — Teicher simply hadn't been paying much attention to the renewed debate over the SSRI antidepressants and their link to suicidal behaviors in children. But after the first press inquiry, he started browsing the FDA Web site and reading the news coverage more closely. He found himself cheering on Andrew Mosholder, the FDA official whose initial reanalysis had so panicked his superiors that they prevented him from testifying at the February hearing. Months later, Teicher was gratified to see that Mosholder's conclusions had finally been confirmed by another FDA reviewer and published on the agency's Web site. According to that August 20 posting, FDA analyst Tarek A. Hammad had reviewed clinical data submitted to the agency for nine of the newer antidepressants: Prozac, Paxil, Zoloft, Celexa, Effexor, Remeron, Luvox, Wellbutrin, and Serzone. Hammad had found that out of every one hundred children and teenagers in those trials, two to three experienced increases in suicidal thoughts and behaviors as a result of treatment with the drug. The increase in suicidal gestures among participants who took antidepressants was 1.8 times, or nearly double, the rate of suicidal thoughts and behaviors among those taking sugar pills.

Despite such clear-cut findings, most of the comments posted on the psychiatric Web sites Teicher browsed sounded disturbingly dismissive. Some comments implied that the difference between the antidepressants and placebo on safety and efficacy grounds was not that significant; so what was all the fuss about?

Teicher knew this wasn't true. He also knew that the real risk of suicidal ideation among patients who took antidepressants was probably much higher than the trial data indicated. Not only had the adult and pediatric trials of SSRIs like Prozac, Zoloft, and Paxil specifically excluded patients who had been hospitalized for depression, but in a number of cases, children who responded poorly to the antidepressants had dropped out of the studies and had not been followed to see if they attempted to kill themselves. In serving as an expert witness against Eli Lilly back in the 1990s, Teicher had seen evidence in unsealed legal documents that several drugmakers had included as "placebo suicides" deaths that had occurred after patients had been taken off other meds to participate in these trials. So their deaths should not have been coded as suicides from placebo, but rather as deaths that occurred during the washout period before the trials began. It was the contention of experts like David Healy, among others, that if the drug companies had designed their studies to more accurately reflect the number of suicides and suicide attempts among participants, the suicidal risks from the SSRIs would have been far greater than that reported by the FDA.

In the same posting in which it announced Tarek Hammad's findings, the federal agency announced that it would be holding an advisory panel hearing on September 13 and 14 to consider mandating stronger warnings for antidepressants prescribed to minors. Even so, Teicher found it hard to believe that any real change would occur. So when he called back Julie Bell, the reporter from the *Baltimore Sun,* he couldn't hide his skepticism. "People are going to equivocate and they're going to do nothing," he told Bell.

A fast-moving juggernaut of events would soon prove him wrong. On August 26, the New York State attorney general's office settled its case with GlaxoSmithKline. Two weeks later, on September 8, the International Committee of Medical Journal Editors announced its plan to require that researchers register key aspects of the initial protocols for their studies on a public Web site if they wanted to be published in a leading medical journal. In identical editorials that ran in twelve top medical journals that month, the editors declared that this new policy would become effective starting in July 2005.

Before the media had time to absorb this development, Congress grabbed the spotlight. On September 9, the U.S. House Energy and Commerce's Subcommittee on Oversight and Investigations held a full-day hearing at which legislators, Democratic and Republican alike, excoriated the pharmaceutical industry and the FDA for withholding "vital information" about the safety and effectiveness of drugs for children and adolescents.

"What we are seeing is that the pharmaceutical industry has systematically misled physicians and patients by suppressing important data on their drugs," said Rep. Henry Waxman (D-Calif.), a member of the House subcommittee. "At the same time, the industry has encouraged physicians to use drugs that are ineffective and possibly even dangerous in one of the most vulnerable population groups, children. The industry has reaped literally billions of dollars in the process."

Waxman then announced that he and Rep. Edward Markey (D-Mass.) were planning to introduce a bill that would impose penalties on drug companies that did not register their clinical trials and the outcomes on a public Web site run by the National Institutes of Health (http://www.clinicaltrials.gov).

During the September 9 hearing, several legislators mentioned the New York AG's case as a catalyst for their concerns. One lawmaker— Rep. Peter Deutsch (D-Fla.)—even brought up a few of the damaging internal Glaxo memos that Rose Firestein had unearthed. Referring to GlaxoSmithKline's 2001 memo to its sales reps lauding Paxil's "REMARKABLE efficacy," Deutsch wanted to know whether David Wheadon, GlaxoSmithKline's senior vice president for regulatory affairs, thought Paxil did in fact have "remarkable" safety and efficacy. Wheadon, who had been corralled for the hearing along with top officials from six other drug companies, did some serious backpedaling. "We, in the case of Paxil, have not been able to discern a significant effect versus placebo . . . ," he acknowledged.

Earlier in the day, Rep. Joe Barton (R-Tex.), chairman of the Energy and Commerce Committee, had lashed out at the FDA for stonewalling his requests for information. "The conduct by the FDA has only reinforced my past sentiments that the Food and Drug Administration really stands for Foot Dragging and Alibis," Barton said.

The FDA had dropped the ball at other key times as well, Barton charged. Even though the agency had been required by law since 2002 to make summaries of all pediatric clinical trials available to the public, it had not posted the summaries of the antidepressant trials on its Web site until very recently. Of those postings, "almost all of them were made just three weeks ago after I made a personal phone call to an individual at the FDA," Barton said. "Why did it take so long for the FDA to do its job?" he asked.

The press pounced on another disturbing revelation from the hearing. In a bid to divert attention from themselves, executives from three drug companies testified that the FDA had urged them not to disclose on their SSRI product labels any information that might indicate problems with the drugs' safety. Wyeth Pharmaceuticals senior vice president Joseph Camardo said that the FDA actually reversed Wyeth's decision to amend its label for Effexor to include a warning that the antidepressant was associated with increased hostility and suicidal thinking among children.

"Why would the FDA require a company to remove stronger labeling?" demanded an incredulous Rep. Greg Walden (R-Ore.).

Dr. Janet Woodcock, the FDA's deputy commissioner for operations, was the government official on the hot seat that day. At first she tried to dodge Walden's question, replying that the FDA's job is to make the language in the drug labels "factual and based on the scientific data that is available." When Walden noted that the agency's own analysts had found scientific evidence of an increased risk of suicidal behaviors among study participants who had been prescribed the antidepressants, Woodcock responded that the FDA would be taking up those findings at its advisory meeting the following week. But that is all she would say. The head of the FDA's Center for Drug Evaluation and Research (which oversees drug labeling) was not about to venture a public opinion on the need for stronger labels just yet. Janet Woodcock had been in Washington long enough to know that top government officials who spoke out of turn didn't last long.

IN FIVE DAYS, however, Woodcock and other FDA officials were singing a different tune. On September 14, the FDA's own advisory panel (a joint gathering of its psychopharmacological drugs advisory and pediatric advisory committees) decided that physicians and patients should be warned in the strongest possible terms that antidepressants did increase the risk of suicidal thoughts and behaviors in children and adolescents. Panel members voted 15–8 in favor of the FDA's requiring that all nine antidepressants that had been reviewed carry "black box" warnings, so-called because the warnings are written in boldface type, surrounded by a black border, on the information sheet that physicians review when prescribing the drugs.

TEICHER WAS DELIGHTED to read the news on the *New York Times* Web site the next morning. He found the panel's decision to include Prozac in its black box recommendations especially satisfying. He had been worried that Eli Lilly's blockbuster drug would be given a pass. Prozac was, after all, the only antidepressant officially approved for use in children and adolescents. Its patent, of course, had lapsed in February 2001, allowing generic versions of fluoxetine to compete with the brand. Teicher couldn't help wondering: was it just a coincidence that shortly after the patent on Prozac expired, Eli Lilly laid off his ex-wife, Bev, from her research job in Indianapolis? Bev was now back in the Boston area after four years in the Midwest. By the time she returned, his son was almost through college and his daughter was finishing up her senior year of high school. They no longer needed their father to drive them around.

Teicher knew he would not soon forget what Eli Lilly and its various agents had done to him. But his concern that Prozac be included in the black box warnings was based strictly on scientific grounds. He believed that the published results of the Prozac pediatric trials had been flawed, in much the same way the Keller Paxil study had been. And he was not alone. In a 2004 article for the *British Medical Journal,* Australian researchers argued that the pediatric trials of Prozac done by Graham Emslie and his coauthors had *not* found the drug more effective than placebo on the study's primary outcome measures, only on the secondary outcomes.

The day after the FDA's advisory panel voted to recommend the black box warnings, a correspondent for the *Boston Globe* called Teicher.

Carolyn Johnson had been assigned to write a feature about the FDA panel's decision that would appear the following Tuesday in the paper's Health and Science section. Johnson wanted to know what kind of alternative therapies could be offered for pediatric depression now that the SSRIs were probably going to be black-boxed. Teicher told her what he had told other reporters: that the potential for serious side effects with the newer antidepressants didn't mean they shouldn't at times be prescribed—under close medical monitoring. Doctors, he said, are not going back to the older generation of antidepressants, which carry their own severe side effects. The SSRIs, he concluded, will continue to play a role, but they are not for everyone. "In a small population of people, the antidepressants worsen every single symptom of depression," Teicher told Johnson.

It was virtually the same conclusion he had arrived at fourteen years earlier. Teicher hadn't changed his opinion in the intervening time, but the world around him clearly had.

BACK IN MANHATTAN, Rose Firestein was also following the steady thrum of news from Washington, but not as closely. She was too busy with another case that had suddenly come to the fore. On September 7, in an unusually fast turnaround time for a New York State investigation, the AG's office reached a legal agreement with Forest Labs, the maker of Celexa. The AG agreed not to sue the New York–based drug company if it would immediately disclose its Phase 3 and Phase 4 clinical trial results on the pediatric use of Celexa and work on posting a public registry of its drug studies, using much the same template that Firestein and her colleagues had agreed upon with GlaxoSmithKline.

It was perhaps no coincidence that Dr. Lawrence Olanoff, an executive vice president of Forest Labs, was scheduled in two days' time to stand with other pharmaceutical executives before the House subcommittee's hearing on *Publication and Disclosure Issues in the Antidepressant Pediatric Clinical Trials.* And so when members of the

Subcommittee on Oversight and Investigations asked Olanoff on September 9 whether his company would support a comprehensive registry of clinical studies, the doctor was ready with his answer. He told the legislators that in accordance with his company's agreement with the New York attorney general's office, Forest Labs would be posting on-line summaries of clinical trial results for all its Phase 3 and 4 studies, as well as any pertinent safety information from completed clinical trials dating back to 2000. His timing was superb. The transcript of the hearing reveals that the legislators spent more time grilling executives from the other drug companies than they did the good doctor from Forest Labs.

The congressional inquisition finally ended at 7:08 p.m. on September 9. But the legislators weren't done. Two weeks later, the same subcommittee held another hearing on Capitol Hill, this time focusing on the FDA's treatment of one of its own medical experts, Andrew Mosholder. In the course of investigating why Mosholder had been prevented from testifying back in February, the legislators discovered that he had been subjected to an internal investigation and threatened with disciplinary action for allowing news of his gagging to be leaked to the press. Mosholder denied leaking the information and mentioned the disciplinary proceedings in his sworn statement to the congressional investigators. But his superiors at the FDA insisted that he delete that information from his statement and submit a cleaned-up version to Congress instead. Mosholder refused. At the September 23 hearing, Rep. Peter Deutsch declared that by refusing to go along, Mosholder had "thwarted a criminal act of obstruction of justice." "As it was," Deutsch said, "the FDA and its lawyers are only guilty of *attempting* to obstruct justice." (When I asked to talk to Mosholder for this book, a spokeswoman for the FDA said he was not giving interviews.)

Deutsch and a number of other legislators also blasted the agency for not acting quickly enough to protect vulnerable children. "The FDA is failing to live up to its responsibility to the American people," said

Rep. Bart Stupak (D-Mich.). "This hearing illustrates a larger problem where too often . . . medical evidence is suppressed and expert opinion is silenced. It illustrates that our system to study the effects of drugs on children is broken."

In hindsight, it is tempting to conclude that the hubbub over the SSRIs was one possible explanation for the bombshell that dropped a week later. On September 30, 2004, Merck announced it was withdrawing its bestselling painkiller, Vioxx, from the market. The news stunned doctors and consumers alike. Until that point, there had been only scattered reports about an increased risk of heart attacks and strokes among people who took Vioxx, a drug that was routinely prescribed for arthritis and had generated sales of $2.5 billion in 2003. The mainstream press might have been excused for not paying much attention to Vioxx's safety issues. The FDA itself was giving out some very mixed signals about the painkiller. Although the agency did order Merck to put a warning label on Vioxx in 2002—much watered down after Merck protested—the FDA then approved the drug for migraines in March 2004 and for use in children a few months later. The FDA's dithering on this and other drug safety issues prompted a columnist for the trade publication *Medical Marketing and Media* to write in early 2004 that the Bush administration had made the federal agency "an informal 'partner' to the industry."

On August 25, 2004, at a conference in France, FDA investigator David Graham presented an analysis showing that Vioxx was significantly more likely to increase the chance of heart attack and death from cardiac arrest than Celebrex, a painkiller that worked by a similar mechanism: blocking "bad" enzymes known as COX-2 that cause stomach inflammation and pain. Dr. Graham's presentation, however, received little press coverage. The mainstream press did not wake up to this story until September 30, when Merck made its stunning announcement. Merck said it had decided to pull Vioxx off the market after seeing preliminary results from a clinical trial being conducted to determine whether its COX-2 painkiller could prevent the recurrence of colorectal polyps. Initial results from that trial confirmed that people who used the drug had nearly twice as many serious cardiovascular problems as those on placebo. Merck stopped the trial and faced the music.

Merck may have acted with such dispatch in an effort to blunt the kind of litigation and bad publicity that had dogged the makers of SSRI antidepressants. Or perhaps the drug company did so out of a genuine desire to do the right thing. Whatever the motivation, the drug company only opened up a Pandora's box.

"Yesterday's announcement [by Merck] rekindled the debate over whether the FDA has been sufficiently aggressive in monitoring drug safety," wrote *Washington Post* reporter Marc Kaufman, one of many journalists to jump on the story.

Kaufman quoted Dr. Eric Topol, head of cardiology and chief academic officer of the Cleveland Clinic, as saying Merck's decision to pull the drug was "the right decision about three years too late." Topol was referring to a major study funded by Merck and published in the *New England Journal of Medicine* in November 2000 that found Vioxx was easier on the stomach than an older painkiller, Aleve. The study had also found a twofold to fourfold increase in the risk of heart attacks among patients taking Vioxx versus those taking Aleve. However, the study's authors did not mention that disturbing statistic in their 2000 paper; they merely noted that the incidence of heart attacks was lower in Aleve than in Vioxx and offered a reassuring explanation about Aleve's extra-protective effects, which steered attention away from Vioxx. (In 2005, the editors of *NEJM* would accuse Merck and the researchers who did that study of withholding key evidence from the paper they submitted. In fact, the journal editors said they discovered that the authors deleted heart-related safety data from a draft of the Vioxx paper just two days before submitting it to the journal for publication. The journal said it was able to determine this by reexamining a computer disk submitted with the manuscript.)

By the end of 2004, Merck would be sued on behalf of thousands of people who had had heart attacks after taking Vioxx. Congress would hold yet more hearings to investigate what Merck knew about the heart risks of Vioxx and when they knew it. And the federal Department of Justice and the SEC would initiate their own inquiries into the COX-2 painkillers, as would the New York attorney general's office.

Two weeks later, on October 15, 2004, the FDA dropped its own bombshell of sorts. The agency announced that it was going beyond the recommendations of its own advisory panel and requiring black box warnings on all thirty-two antidepressants currently on the market, old as well as new. Although the agency only had evidence showing elevated risks in nine of the newer antidepressants, FDA officials said they decided to put the warnings on all thirty-two drugs because they did not have sufficient data to clear them of similar side effects. News of this decision was almost buried by the clamor over Vioxx.

ON THE MORNING of October 28, Rose Firestein rose as usual at dawn, even though she didn't have to go to the office. She had been asked to give a presentation that day to doctors and medical researchers at a meeting of the World Health Organization. The meeting, a preliminary discussion on guidelines for an international clinical trial registry in advance of the WHO's annual meeting in Mexico City, was scheduled to begin at 9 a.m. at the Rockefeller Foundation on the East Side of Manhattan.

Sitting around the large conference table amid distinguished doctors, journal editors, and top health-policy makers from around the globe, Firestein felt like a fish out of water. What could she, an attorney with no medical background, add to the conversation? She kept her remarks brief, talking about what the AG's office had hoped to accomplish with its case against GlaxoSmithKline and what the limitations of its authority were. When she finished, she felt redundant and slightly foolish, like a footnote buried at the bottom of a page.

But then a doctor from Southeast Asia—Firestein couldn't read her name tag but she sounded as if she was from India or Pakistan—turned to her and said warmly, "We've been working on this issue for a decade and were never able to get it moving. But your lawsuit brought public attention to the issue. What you've done really moved the ball."

Several other people chimed in, saying they too sensed there was now a new opportunity to push drug companies to disclose the results of all their clinical drug trials. Firestein smiled but said nothing. As the discussion flowed around her, she basked quietly in the realization that top medical experts—many of them important officials who were making health policy in their own countries—were saying that a case she had poured her heart into had precipitated significant change, not only here but globally. It dawned on Firestein that she had finally done what she set out to do some thirty years earlier: make a difference in people's lives. A sense of pure contentment enveloped her. Tomorrow, this feeling would surely dissipate, lost in the maze of endless work, annoying commuters, and the constant heartache of being blind in a vast and oblivious city. For now, though, it would do. It would do just fine.

## Epilogue: Rose Firestein Gets Run Over and Survives, and Donna Howard Turns Out to Have Been Right All Along

ON MARCH 22, 2006, Tonya Brooks and her parents sued GlaxoSmith-Kline for failing to warn them that Paxil can make adolescents suicidal. Representing them in that lawsuit was Baum, Hedlund, Aristei, Goldman, and Menzies, the Los Angeles law firm that brought suit on behalf of dozens of other children who had killed themselves or attempted to while taking Paxil. The very same month, researchers at Glaxo-SmithKline published a paper acknowledging that they had discovered ten previously unreported cases of suicidal thoughts and behaviors among the children and adolescents who participated in the original Glaxo-funded trials of Paxil. The 2006 paper, published in the *Journal of Child and Adolescent Psychopharmacology,* was prompted by the FDA-mandated review of SSRI data. The researchers for Glaxo re-examined five double-blind, placebo-controlled trials of Paxil, including the three studies of adolescents with depression (studies 329, 377, and 701), along with two other studies of youngsters with obsessive-compulsive disorder and social anxiety disorder. They concluded that overall, "suicide-related events" occurred almost four times more often in patients taking Paxil than in those taking a sugar pill (the odds ratio was 3.86 and the relative risk was 3.76). That came to an almost 50 percent greater risk than the rate of suicidal behaviors found in the FDA's re-analysis two years earlier.

In the Keller study alone, the Glaxo reviewers identified four additional cases of possible suicidal behaviors among teenagers taking Paxil. In an e-mail to Keller and his coauthors, Regan Fong, one of the Glaxo reviewers, wrote, "Four of the 10 additional events potentially suggestive of intentional self injury, suicidal ideation or suicide attempt . . . occurred in study 329, all in the paroxetine group."

This e-mail was among the documents uncovered in the Baum Hedlund legal proceedings against GlaxoSmithKline. Those documents, together with the 2006 Glaxo paper, provide strong support for Donna Howard's assertion that the researchers for study 329 miscoded and underreported data on Paxil's impact in children and adolescents.

Keller and his coauthors, for example, reported in their 2001 paper that six patients in the paroxetine group suffered "emotional lability"— the code term for suicidal thoughts or gestures— as compared to three in the tricyclic antidepressant group and one in the placebo group. However, when the FDA insisted that GlaxoSmithKline (and other drug companies) comb through their trial data again, the number of patients in the Keller study who were suicidal jumped from six to ten (out of ninety-three participants in the Paxil arm).

Keller declined to be interviewed for this book. When asked about these discrepancies, Mary Anne Rhyne, a spokeswoman for Glaxo-SmithKline, said that "it is not productive to have this kind of patient-by-patient discussion here." She would say only that the additional cases unearthed by reviewers for Glaxo "do not change the interpretation of the results of 329."

According to several experts, that simply isn't true. Even without the addition of the mysterious patient 70, the 2006 paper by the Glaxo reviewers concluded that the adolescents taking Paxil in the Keller study were almost four times more likely to develop suicidal thoughts or behaviors than those taking placebo. That is a significant difference, and had it been published in 2001, it would have alerted physicians and the media to a dangerous side effect of Paxil.

Keller and his coauthors also chose not to do a proper statistical comparison of the patients in the Paxil group who suffered serious adverse events versus those in the placebo or imipramine group. That statistical analysis would have shown that Paxil users had five times the number of serious psychiatric effects as placebo takers and more than twice the number of those taking the older tricyclic antidepressant. Again, even without the additional unreported cases of suicidal behavior reported in 2006, such an analysis would have alerted doctors to Paxil's significant adverse effects in adolescents.

"This kind of analysis would have shown that the psychiatric issues are significantly greater in the paroxetine [Paxil] group than in the placebo group and it's a statistically significant difference," says Dr. Roger Grimson, a former biostatistician at the State University of New York (SUNY) who has advised plaintiffs in a lawsuit against Glaxo. "They didn't do that statistical analysis, and they should have."

So why weren't these comparisons made? The contention that Paxil is "generally well tolerated in this adolescent population" was one of the key findings of the 2001 Keller paper. If Keller and his coauthors had accurately reported all of the suicide-related events in their study or done a statistical comparison of serious adverse events, they would not have been able to reach that conclusion. They would not have been able to tout Paxil as a safe and well-tolerated drug. And that would have made their research sponsor, GlaxoSmithKline, very unhappy.

IN THE THREE YEARS since the New York State AG's office shone a spotlight into the black hole of drug research, there has been a growing outcry about the enormous influence the pharmaceutical industry wields over the practice of medicine. The impact of corporate money on the way doctors prescribe drugs and treat patients has become one of the most contentious issues in health care today. As articles in the nation's leading newspapers and medical journals and newsletters reveal, the pharmaceutical industry pays millions of dollars in speaking and consulting fees to physicians throughout the nation. Take, for example, a series of stories by the *New York Times* in the spring of 2007 about payments from drug companies to physicians in Minnesota (the first state to require such full disclosure). According to the *New York Times,* pharmaceutical companies paid Minnesota doctors, nurses, and other health care providers at least $57 million between 1997 (when the law was passed) and 2005. More than 25 percent of the licensed doctors in Minnesota received money from drug companies. More than one hundred doctors received more than $100,000 each from the industry, among them physicians who sit on FDA advisory panels and help craft the guidelines that other doctors rely on when prescribing drugs. It might come as no surprise to the readers of this book that psychiatry was the specialty with the highest number of doctors receiving payments from drug companies.

But the medical profession's ties to Big Pharma go beyond payments to individual doctors. In the past decade, industry money has become the single largest source of funding for the medical courses that practicing physicians need to take in order to remain accredited, according to Dr. Daniel Carlat, a professor at Tufts University School of Medicine and the editor in chief of the *Carlat Psychiatry Report.* Moreover, drugmakers routinely offer free junkets, lunches, gifts, and product samples to physicians in order to promote their wares.

Such generosity works: research shows that doctors who receive consulting or other personal income from drugmakers are more likely to report positive findings about a particular drug than researchers who don't receive money from the industry. Doctors with such financial conflicts of interest are also more likely to prescribe newer and more expensive drugs than doctors who don't have such conflicts. A *New York Times* article in May 2007, for instance, showed a distinct correlation between the financial relationships that Minnesota psychiatrists had with the makers of antipsychotic drugs like Risperdal, Zyprexa, and Seroquel and the growing use of such drugs among children in that state. According to the *Times* analysis, during the very same period (2000 to 2005) that drug company payments to Minnesota psychiatrists rose more than sixfold—to $1.6 million—the prescriptions of anti-psychotics to children in Minnesota's Medicaid program climbed more than ninefold. Those who received the most consulting speaking fees from the makers of these antipsychotics tended to prescribe the drugs most often. On average, the Minnesota psychiatrists who received at least $5,000 in personal income from the makers of these drugs appear to have written three times as many prescriptions for them as psychiatrists who received less or no money, according to the *Times* analysis.

Only a handful of states (such as Minnesota and Vermont) require drugmakers to disclose such conflicts, and even in these states, disclosures are incomplete. In Vermont, for instance, drugmakers are allowed to keep payment records private by declaring them trade secrets. In 2005, drugmakers declared 73 percent of payments to doctors in Vermont trade secrets, the *New York Times* found.

Despite such extensive coverage, many medical professionals still take money from the pharmaceutical industry—for both research and consulting gigs. While the most respected medical journals insist on the disclosure of these conflicts (in fine print at the end of the article), many other venues do not. Take, for example, the debate over whether black box warnings should be extended to antidepressant usage in young adults. In December 2006, the FDA held an advisory meeting to consider new findings that young adults between eighteen and twenty-five who took Paxil and eight other antidepressants were significantly more likely than those on placebo to report a suicide attempt, just as the research on children and adolescents had shown. At that hearing, opponents of the black box warnings on SSRIs cited preliminary results from a study showing what appeared to be a correlation between an uptick in national suicide rates among adolescents and a drop in the prescriptions of SSRIs among this age group. Several psychiatrists pointed to that apparent correlation as proof that the publicity over the

SSRIs and the black box warnings had scared physicians from prescribing these drugs. The lack of treatment, these psychiatrists argued, may have prompted more youngsters to kill themselves.

However, when this finding was published in the September 2007 issue of the *American Journal of Psychiatry,* it was roundly criticized as being erroneous. The number of suicides among adolescents under the age of nineteen did indeed climb about 14 percent (from 1,737 to 1,985) between 2003 and 2004, according to statistics from the Centers for Disease Control and Prevention. The number of prescriptions for SSRIs among adolescents, however, remained essentially unchanged from 2003 to 2004 (prescription usage didn't decline until after 2004). Thus the FDA's black box warnings cannot be blamed for the apparent increase in suicides among adolescents the year before. This discrepancy in the data was not mentioned at the December 2006 FDA hearing. Nor was it disclosed that an SSRI maker (Pfizer) paid the $30,000 cost of obtaining prescription data for the *AJP* study, or that two lead authors of this study have financial conflicts of interest: Robert Gibbons served as an expert witness for Wyeth Pharmaceuticals (the maker of Effexor, another SSRI), and Dr. J. John Mann, a professor of psychiatry at Columbia University, has been a paid consultant to at least two SSRI makers: GlaxoSmithKline and Pfizer.

Other psychiatric researchers say that the latest upturn in suicide rates does not mean anything, given the small numbers involved and the tendency of suicide rates to fluctuate from year to year. "People who are specialists in statistics know you have to look at trends over years and years," said Julie Zito, an associate professor of pharmacy and psychiatry at the University of Maryland, who has published several articles on this subject. "For instance, you'll see that the overall trend [in suicide rates among children and adults] had been going down quite a ways before the SSRIs arrived on the scene."

In the end, the FDA did extend its black box warnings on antidepressants to young adults. But it also added language to the labels warning that "depression and certain other psychiatric disorders are themselves associated with the risk of suicide." The FDA's Thomas Laughren, now director of the Division of Psychiatry Products, said the new language had been added because of the agency's concerns about the uptick in suicide rates between 2003 and 2004. (National suicide rates for 2005 and beyond had not been released when this book went to press.)

Both Zito and Dr. Peter Lurie, deputy director of the Public Citizen Health Research Group, say that including language about untreated depression in the black box cautions on antidepressants undermines the whole point of the warning. "The important thing is that the risk of suicidal ideation is higher in the treated group than in the untreated group in randomized controlled trials, and that's what the warning should be about," Lurie says. "Whether or not untreated depression also leads to suicidal ideation is misleading and irrelevant. The FDA should not have put in that kind of language because it's intended to confuse."

IN THE YEARS since the New York State attorney general's lawsuit and the Vioxx controversy precipitated public outcry, the FDA has come under considerable pressure to toughen its stance on drug safety. According to former FDA officials at a 2006 conference, the federal agency did issue more black box warnings in 2004 than it had in previous years (although most of those warnings were for antidepressants). There is also evidence that the agency has slowed down the pace at which it approves new drugs and is approving fewer new drugs. According to the most recent statistics available from the FDA's Report to the Nation, the agency approved ninety new drugs in 2004 but only fifty-eight in 2005. And in a significant policy shift, the FDA recently began requiring drug makers to study specifically whether patients become suicidal during drug trials. For the first time, makers of drugs that treat obesity, epilepsy, heart problems, and many other conditions are being asked to include a comprehensive suicide assessment in clinical trials.

Even so, the federal agency continues to come under attack from consumers and lawmakers for not doing an adequate job of ensuring the safety of drugs, particularly those already on the market. A report by the General Accounting Office (GAO) in March 2006 found that the FDA "lacks a clear and effective process for making decisions about, and providing management oversight of," drug safety issues that arise after a medicine is on the market. The GAO said the agency's drug safety office was under the thumb of the FDA's new drugs office, which receives the lion's share of funding, and had no "independent decision-making responsibility" to ensure that postmarketing safety studies were conducted on already approved drugs. An equally stinging report in September 2006 by the Institute of Medicine (IOM), a group of prestigious physicians within the National Academy of Sciences that provide advice on medical issues, described the FDA as hobbled by underfinancing, poor management, and outdated regulations. The IOM report suggested that consumer advertisements of newly approved drugs be restricted for at least two years and that such drugs carry a black triangle on their labels to warn people that their safety is not certain. (Research shows that it takes years to ascertain the safety of new drugs.) The report also said the FDA should be given the authority to issue fines, injunctions, and withdrawals when drugmakers fail—as they often do—to complete required postapproval safety studies.

In an interview in August 2006, Eliot Spitzer said he was "mystified" as to why the FDA didn't just require drug companies to disclose the results of all their clinical trials so that doctors and consumers could see for themselves how safe newly approved drugs were.

"This is something that the FDA commissioner could probably do unilaterally," Spitzer said. "I don't understand why this hasn't been done."

In November 2006, Spitzer's vigorous attacks on Big Pharma, Wall Street, and lax regulatory authorities propelled him into the New York governor's office. There, he was joined by a number of his former assistant AGs from Lower Manhattan. Joe Baker became Spitzer's deputy secretary for health policy and Tom Conway was appointed general counsel to New York State's Department of Health in Albany. In September 2007, Conway recruited Rose Firestein to work with him. Seven months later, the governor who had brought them on board resigned after a federal investigation uncovered evidence that he had paid thousands of dollars to a high-priced prostitution club.

Firestein is still working with Conway in the counsel's office of the New York Department of Health. She continues to put in impossibly long hours, toiling out of an office in Lower Manhattan.

Firestein did find time, however, to design a renovation to her kitchen in Brooklyn to make it easier for her to cook safely with her limited eyesight. "She spent nights and nights measuring down to the inch and then designing and redesigning the layout on draft paper," says her sister Janice. "The new kitchen is magnificent."

In January 2007, a car ran over Firestein's left foot as she stood near the curb waiting to cross the street in front of her apartment building. The accident broke three bones in her foot, but she only missed four days of work. For weeks she commuted to and from work in a cast up to her knee. "I've got tuition to pay for," she says simply, as if that were all that is needed to explain why, at the age of fifty-seven, Rose Firestein perseveres on behalf of the citizens of New York.

THE LAWSUIT FIRESTEIN and her colleagues brought against GlaxoSmithKline continues to bear rich fruit. In a case that garnered front-page coverage in 2007, Dr. Steven Nissen, a prominent cardiologist with the Cleveland Clinic, published new findings that show an increased risk of heart problems among patients taking Avandia, a commonly prescribed diabetes drug. (Avandia earned GlaxoSmithKline, its maker, more than $3 billion in worldwide sales in 2006.) Nissen's study, an analysis based on Glaxo's own clinical trials of Avandia, raised concerns in the medical community about the safety of the drug and renewed fears that the FDA did not act fast enough to alert the public about problems with a new drug. Nissen told reporters that he would not have been able to do his meta-analysis had it not been for the public registry that GlaxoSmithKline posted online as part of its settlement with the New York attorney general's office. The Avandia trials were among the first studies that Glaxo posted on the new database, and they popped up when Nissen googled the drug. "It was a treasure trove," he told Barry Meier of the *New York Times,* referring to the Web site that Firestein and her colleagues helped bring into being. In November 2007, the FDA put black box warnings about the increased heart risks on Avandia's label.

The New York AG's work has spawned huge ripple effects elsewhere as well. Under pressure from the International Committee of Medical Journal Editors, researchers sponsored by the drug companies are increasingly disclosing the designs of their clinical studies and results. Before the ICMJE began mandating such pretrial disclosures, the government database www.clinicaltrials.gov (the largest trial registry at the time) contained only 13,153 trials. One month after the ICMJE policy went into effect in July 2005, the number climbed to 22,714, and as of April 2007, the registry contained more than 40,000 trials, with more than 200 new trial registrations occurring weekly, according to an editorial in the *New England Journal of Medicine.* In May 2006, the World Health Organization climbed on board, calling for drug researchers worldwide to register on a public Web site the key protocols for all clinical studies involving humans before they are begun and to post a detailed summary of the results once they are completed. And some drug companies (in addition to GlaxoSmithKline and Forest Labs) are voluntarily posting the results of their clinical trials online, with varying degrees of detail.

The spark ignited by Eliot Spitzer's team seems to have burst into something of a national conflagration. While federal prosecutors (under the Clinton administration) launched a number of successful probes of pharmaceutical practices in the 1990s—the cases against Pfizer/Warner-Lambert and TAP Pharmaceutical Products being the most prominent examples—the pace of state investigations into the drug industry has picked up considerably since the New York AG's successful foray against GlaxoSmithKline. State and federal prosecutors are now looking at everything from the improper pricing of medications for Medicare and Medicaid patients (average wholesale pricing redux) to the illegal marketing of drugs. (GlaxoSmithKline eventually settled the New York AG's AWP case in the spring of 2006 for $70 million.

Many of these investigations have zeroed in on deceptive marketing ploys. In the spring of 2007, the Justice Department hit Purdue Pharma with a $600 million fine for falsely marketing the narcotic OxyContin as a safe and nonaddictive pain medicine at a time when Purdue executives knew otherwise. Eli Lilly is now facing criminal and civil cases in several states over allegations that it concealed links between its antipsychotic drug Zyprexa and diabetes and illegally promoted Zyprexa for off-label uses. And federal and state prosecutors are continuing to investigate Johnson and Johnson for allegedly engaging in the deceptive marketing of Risperdal for off-label use in children and adolescents. Texas court records unsealed in 2006 allege that Johnson and Johnson overstated the effectiveness of Risperdal and understated its risks in order to boost sales of the drug in a pediatric population.

For the first time in decades, Big Pharma is on the defensive, and judging by the amount of money it spent on lobbying and political contributions for the 2006 elections, the industry knows it. According to the Center for Responsive Politics, companies that make drugs and medical products shelled out an all-time high of $172 million in lobbying Congress, federal agencies, and other policy makers in 2006. They also disbursed an additional $19.3 million in political campaign contributions during the 2006 election cycle. In the past, such largesse has reaped enormous benefits, in the form of federal legislation and regulations that made the FDA and other federal agencies more responsive to the wishes of the drug companies. The question now is whether the Democrat-controlled Congress will rise above the siren lure.

So far the signs are not promising. In 2007, the Democrat-controlled Congress did pass legislation that would give the FDA greater enforcement powers to ensure the safety of drugs already on the market. The law, for example, gives the FDA the power to require drugmakers to undertake clinical trials of medicines that the agency has already approved and fine those who fail to do so. It also requires the FDA to reduce the number of conflict-of-interest waivers it grants to experts who serve on its advisory boards. And it requires drug companies to register the results of new clinical trials on a publicly available Web site or face stiff penalties.

"The public needs to know about the results of clinical trials on drugs," said Senator Edward Kennedy when he introduced the bill in February 2007. "Tragically, such information was not adequately available for the clinical studies of antidepressants in children."

The 2007 legislation, however, does not apply to previously completed studies of drugs already on the market. Its limitations became glaringly evident in 2008 with the news that Merck and Schering-Plough never published studies that raised questions about the health risks of their popular cholestrol drug Zetia. By failing to disclose this research, drug companies once again gave physicians and patients a misleading view of a blockbuster drug's safety and benefits.

The new law also does nothing to change one fundamental reality: the excessive reliance of the nation's premier health agency on the industry it regulates. As part of the legislation it passed in 2007, Congress renewed the Prescription Drug User Fee Act for another five years. Instead of reducing the FDA's dependence on industry, as consumer advocates and medical ethicists have urged, Congress approved an $87.4

million increase in the annual user fees the FDA can collect from the drug industry, bringing the total of industry funds for agency operations to a projected $400 million.

With the renewal of PDUFA, consumer advocates fear that a golden opportunity to truly reform the way drugs are tested and sold has been lost. "Our position is that the agency should be fully funded out of the public purse and there should be no user fees of any kind at the FDA," said Dr. Peter Lurie, deputy director of Public Citizen's Health Research Group. "With these user fees, the agency will continue to be in hock to the drug companies."

A number of prominent medical ethicists agree. In her 2004 book, *The Truth about the Drug Companies,* Dr. Marcia Angell argues that user fees from drugmakers should be abolished and more public funds allocated to support the work of the FDA and the testing of new drugs. In a 2007 editorial in the *New England Journal of Medicine,* Dr. Jerry Avorn, author of *Powerful Medicines: The Benefits, Risks, and Costs of Prescription Drugs,* also calls for a "national commitment to publicly supported studies of drug risks so that no company could take possession of critical findings for its own purposes."

Yet that is precisely what is continuing to happen. Even as medication becomes a way of life for more and more Americans, drug companies continue to control how drugs are tested, marketed, and sold in the United States. Drug trials are still largely funded by pharmaceutical companies who have a vested interest in positive research results. And many prominent doctors continue to receive millions of dollars in personal consulting income from the industry. Despite evidence to the contrary, some of these key opinion leaders persist in believing that the money they receive in no way clouds their judgment in doing research or treating patients. Such KOLs seem to feel that unlike the rest of us, they are not subject to a sad reality of human nature: money talks.

As of May 2008, Martin Keller remains the chief of psychiatry at Brown University and a KOL in good standing with Big Pharma. To this day, Keller has denied that there is anything wrong with the results of his Paxil pediatric study or the way it was conducted. In a deposition taken in September 2006 for a lawsuit against GlaxoSmith-Kline, Keller insisted that the salient conclusions of his 2001 paper were accurate: that Paxil is generally well tolerated in adolescents and is significantly more effective than placebo in the treatment of depression for adolescents.

The lingering controversy over how the 2001 Paxil study was conducted does not seem to have harmed Keller's career or his ability to attract research funding. The department he oversees at Brown received $50 million in research funding from external sources, including pharmaceutical companies and the taxpayer-funded National Institute of Mental Health, according to Keller's own testimony in the 2006 deposition. There has been no ultimate finding by any professional association or federal or state authority of wrongdoing by Keller, and his employer continues to stand by him. Responding to questions for this book, a spokesman for Brown said that "Brown takes seriously the integrity of its scientific research. Dr. Keller's research regarding Paxil complied with Brown's research standards."

None of this comes as any surprise to Donna Howard. Her experience with Martin Keller and Brown University has made her exceedingly wary of the medical establishment.

"I'm certainly not antimedication," she said. "It saved my daughter's life. But I have become so cynical about the whole medical-pharmaceutical establishment. They want to rush the drugs to market and convince you that you're depressed or that your cholesterol is higher than it should be or whatever it is—all so they can make huge profits. I think it's clear that not everyone needs that much medication."

In the spring of 2006, Howard took a job that had nothing to do with the medical community. She began working for the National Housing Partnership Foundation, a national nonprofit that provides housing and services for the poor. Her job, as the resident services manager for one of its community centers in Fall River, was to develop programs that help break the cycle of poverty.

Now in her late fifties, Howard is not particularly interested in raking up the past. She has her feet firmly planted in the present. Her large green eyes are clear and untroubled. She accepts the fact that she will always be an outsider, a renegade attempting to bring justice to deeply flawed systems. She will never make much money and she will always have to struggle with bipolar disorder. But that's okay. What matters to Howard is that she has friends and admirers in the mental health field who still turn to her for counsel and support. And if you ask her to name the one thing she is proudest of, she will say without hesitation her daughter, Maria.

Maria dropped out of community college in 2005 — "the stress was too much for her," Howard said. But her daughter is working full-time at an inn near her home. It's a supportive and welcoming environment, her mother said. Although Maria still lives with Howard and continues to take medications to manage her mental illness, she is financially and emotionally independent.

"She is doing extraordinarily well — better than anyone predicted," Howard said. "I don't come from a privileged background. I never had it in my head that she should go to Harvard. She has a healthy, independent, rewarding life and she is an extraordinary individual. She just inspires me."

Tonya Brooks, who turned twenty-one in May 2008, is doing well too. The Texan teenager who repeatedly tried to kill herself while on Paxil works full-time as a veterinary technician in Pflugerville, Texas. Now that she is off Paxil and Ambien, she says she's fine. She lives on her own with two cats and two dogs. She is still uncomfortable in social situations and knows she will never be "the life of the party."

She has learned to accept her anxieties and is not taking any medication for them. She dyed her hair an eye-catching red, and she has a boyfriend for the first time in her life. Speaking on the phone recently, she sounded happy, even bubbly. It's clear that Tonya Brooks is at peace with herself, which is all anyone in this world can really ask.

## Acknowledgments

THIS BOOK COULD NOT have been written without the assistance of the people who appear in it. I owe an enormous debt of gratitude to Donna Howard, Rose Firestein, Martin Teicher, and Tonya and Cheryl Brooks, who opened their lives to me and made themselves available to answer my questions. I'm also grateful to Donna's daughter for being part of this project.

My special thanks go to the team at the New York attorney general's office: Shirley Stark, Joe Baker, Tom Conway, Mark Violette, and Eliot Spitzer. I am grateful to the medical experts who helped tutor me, especially David Healy, Sheldon Krimsky, Arnold Relman, Marcia Angell, Jonathan Cole, Julie Zito, Malkah Notman, Jerry Avorn, Peter Lurie, and Ethan Kisch.

Karen Gievers, Bernard Perlmutter, Carol Marbin Miller, Barry Perlman, David Levoy, Janice Firestein, Linda Jorgenson, Jon Albano, Skip Murgatroyd, Joel Shames, David Gessner, Russell Ames, Robin McCall, Nils Bruzelius, Judy Foreman, Larry Tye, Stephen Solomon, and Ryan Derousseau all helped in many ways. I'd like to thank Martin Teicher's assistant, Cynthia McGreenery, who treated me kindly.

I would also like to thank my literary agent, Jim Levine, and his assistant, Lindsay Edgecombe, without whom this book would not have happened. And I am indebted to my editor, Amy Gash, whose incisive comments allowed me to see the forest without forgetting the trees. I'd also like to thank Rachel Careau, whose thoughtful copyediting saved me from myself.

I owe a special debt to the late Laura Van Dam, who knew there was a book in there somewhere and encouraged me to keep trying. I'd also like to thank Judy Foreman and Nils Bruzelius, whose wise counsel and support kept me going.

The Alicia Patterson Fellowship gave me the time I needed to complete this enterprise, for which I am deeply grateful.

I would also like to thank the friends and colleagues who took the time to read part or all of my manuscript and offer support and criticism, both equally helpful: David Rosenbaum, Sarah Scalet, and Scott Berinato. I am especially grateful to Ross Gelbspan and Michael Goldberg, who were there for me throughout the entire writing process. Their support and wise counsel kept me going.

I'd also like to thank my mother, Estelle Brager, who has taught me much about the craft of writing and whose belief in my work has been a sustaining force over the years.

Finally, I would like to thank my husband, Jim, whose unflagging support made this book possible, and my two boys, David and Jake, who bring joy to my life and whose patience with this project never ceased to amaze me.

# Notes

## Prologue

*This chapter is based on interviews with Tonya Brooks, Cheryl Brooks, and a spokeswoman for the Baum Hedlund law firm in Los Angeles, which represents the Brooks family.*

## Chapter One

*This chapter is based on interviews with Martin Teicher and Jonathan Cole.*

7, *Ms. D.* Martin H. Teicher et al., "Emergence of Intense Suicidal Preoccupation during Fluoxetine Treatment," *American Journal of Psychiatry,* 147, no. 2 (February 1990): 08.

8, *norepinephrine and dopamine* Joseph Glenmullen, *Prozac Backlash* (New York: Simon and Schuster, 2000), 10.

10, *she kill herself* Martin Teicher, letter to the Massachusetts Board of Medicine, June 12, 1992.

10, *that "deadly drug"* Teicher et al., "Suicidal Preoccupation," 208.

11, *self-destructive urges abated* Ibid.

12, *Valium and alcohol* Ibid.

## Chapter Two

*This chapter is based on interviews with Donna Howard and people who know her.*

18, *"Victor"* Brief filed in U.S. District Court in support of *Richard Doe v. New York City Department of Social Services,* September 23, 1987.

19, *extreme cases of psychosis* Ibid.

## Chapter Three

*This chapter is based on interviews with Donna Howard and people who know her.*

23, *Maria* Donna Howard and I agreed to use the middle name of her adopted daughter to protect her daughter's privacy.

## Chapter Four

*This chapter is based on interviews with Martin Teicher, Jonathan Cole, Ida Hellander, and Paul Leber, and also relies on a transcript of the September 20, 1991, FDA hearing.*

29, *Psychopharmacological Drugs* Transcript of the FDA's Psychopharmacological Drugs Advisory Committee hearing, September 20, 1991.

30, *"the country has ever seen"* R. Behar, "The Thriving Cult of Greed and Power," *Time,* May 6, 1991, 32–39.

33, *the McLean authors wrote* Martin H. Teicher et al., "Antidepressant Drugs and the Emergence of Suicidal Tendencies," *Drug Safety* 8, no. 3 (1993): 197.

35, *she told the committee* Transcript of FDA hearing, September 20, 1991, 13–15, 24–26.

36, *Moneymaker said* Ibid., 78–80.

36, *"break into his apartment"* Ibid., 81–86.

36, *"kitchen knife beside him"* Ibid., 86.

37, *Leber said* Ibid., 128–29.

37, *"working together on the suicide issue"* Exhibit 109, *Forsyth v. Eli Lilly,* Lilly memo, September 12, 1990; and Exhibit 104, *Forsyth v. Eli Lilly,* Lilly memo regarding call from Paul Leber, July 18, 1990.

37, *"injury to public health"* Transcript of FDA hearing, September 20, 1991, 129.

38, *"suicidal acts or ideation"* Ibid., 210.

38, *"a very serious disease"* Ibid., 232–33.

39, *"interpreting those data"* Ibid., 257.

39, *caused by the SSRI* David Healy, *Let Them Eat Prozac* (New York: NYU Press, 2004), 131.

39, *bestselling drugs in pharmacological history* Data from IMS Health. (From 1992 to 2000, Prozac was among the five top-selling drugs in the United States, and in 1997 it was ranked the second-bestselling drug.)

40, *"a few moments to talk"* Transcript of FDA hearing, September 20, 1991, 278.

40, *"prior to or following"* Ibid., 286.

40, *"some more to say?"* Ibid., 287

41, *shutting Teicher off* Ibid., 290.

42, *"might prefer it to be"* Paul Leber, memo to Robert Temple, ODE, "Subject: Zoloft NDA Approvable Action Recommendation," August 26, 1991.

42, *Zoloft must be approved* Paul Leber, memo to Robert Temple, director, ODE, "Subject: Recommendation to Approve NDA 19-839 (Zoloft)," December 24, 1991.

42, *annual sales of $3.4 billion* IMS Web site, "Leading Products by Global Pharmaceutical Sales, 2003," http://www.imshealth.com/.

43, *entire drug-review budget* Anna Wilde Mathews, "Druge Firms Use Financial Clout to Push Industry Agenda at FDA," *Wall Street Journal,* September 1, 2006.

44, *approximately twelve months* Philip J. Hilts, *Protecting America's Health* (New York: Knopf, 2003), 279.

44, *owned stock in Lilly* The Integrity in Science Web site, http://cspinet .org/cgi-bin/integrity.cgi/.

## Chapter Five

*This chapter is based on interviews with Rose Firestein, Tom Conway, Joe Baker, Shirley Stark, Eliot Spitzer, Joseph Sedwick Sollers, Dwight Davis, and Mark Violette, PR spokesman for the AG's office.*

49, *"repeated and persistent" fraud* People of the State of New York by Eliot Spitzer, Attorney General of the State of New York v. GlaxoSmithKline, filed in the Supreme Court of the State of New York, June 2, 2004.

## Chapter Six

*This chapter is based on interviews with Donna Howard, Alice Tangredi-Hannon, Ron Seifer, and other sources.*

68, *"reasons of noncompliance"* Martin B. Keller memo, to Ivan W. Miller, chair, Brown Institutional Review Board, "Re: Annual Review of Project Entitled: 'A Multicenter Double-Blind, Placebo Controlled Study of Paroxetine and Imipramine in Adolescents with Unipolar Major Depression,'" November 11, 1995.

70, *several thousand dollars* Alison Bass, "Brown Researcher Faced Billing Question in Past," *Boston Globe,* January 21, 1996.

70, *whistleblower's career at Brown* Alison Bass, Five Ex-Employees Allege Harassment by Brown," *Boston Globe,* January 21, 1996.

## Chapter Seven

*This chapter is based on interviews with Donna Howard and other sources.*

## Chapter Eight

*This chapter is based on interviews with Martin Teicher and other sources and also relies on a transcript of the deposition of Martin Teicher in the matter of* Greer v. Eli Lilly, *October 29 and 30, 1996.*

80, *"dismissed . . . as settled"* Glenmullen, *Prozac Backlash,* 173–76.

86, *show her that he cared* Respondent's Memorandum on Disposition in the matter of *Board of Registration in Medicine v. Martin H. Teicher,* September 5, 1997.

88, *medical board documents reveal* Ibid., 8.

88, *resulted in a mistrial* Alison Bass, "Doctor Brings Lawsuit against Lozano Attorney," *Boston Globe,* May 1, 1992.

## Chapter Nine

*This chapter is based on interviews with Rose Firestein, Tom Conway, Joe Baker, Shirley Stark, Mark Violette, Joseph Sedwick Sollers, Dwight Davis, David Healy, and Thomas Laughren.*

97, *suicides in adults* T. P. Laughren, "The Scientific and Ethical Basis for Placebo-Controlled Trials in Depression and Schizophrenia: An FDA Perspective," *European Psychiatry* 16 (2001): 418–23.

97, *wanted to kill themselves* Teicher et al., "Antidepressant Drugs," 188–212.

98, *in a press release* AMA press release, June 15, 2004, http://www .amassn.org/ama/pub/.

98, *"junk science"* Richard A. Knox, "Doctor Lashes Out in Prozac Battle," *Boston Globe,* May 15, 2000.

98, *while taking Prozac* Healy, *Let Them Eat Prozac,* 87–102.

98, *link between SSRIs and suicidal behavior* Ibid., 215–16.

99, *trust in the medical profession* Jeanne Whalen, "Doctor Defends Linking Suicide, Antidepressants," *Wall Street Journal,* July 20, 2004.

99, *$645,000 to the institute* Karen Birmingham, "Dark Clouds over Toronto Psychiatry Research," *Nature Medicine* 7, no. 6 (June 2001): 643.

## Chapter Ten

*This chapter is based on interviews with Martin Teicher, Alan Schatzberg, Stephen Goldfinger, and others who attended the 1998 annual meeting of the American Psychiatric Association (APA), along with Sheldon Krimsky and officials from the APA, Brown University officials, the Massachusetts Board of Registration in Medicine, and the National Institutes of Health.*

104, *not a reliable witness* Final Decision and Order in the matter of Martin H. Teicher, Massachusetts Board of Registration in Medicine, November 19, 1997.

106, *"above-described disadvantages"* U.S. Patent 5708035, January 13, 1998, http://www.uspto.gov/.

107, *"Optimizing Long-Term Treatment"* Program for the 1998 annual meeting of the American Psychiatric Association in Toronto.

108, *published with much fanfare* Martin B. Keller et al., "A Comparison of Nefazodone, the Cognitive Behavioral Analysis System of Pscyhotherapy, and Their Combination for the Treatment of Chronic Depression," *New England Journal of Medicine* 342 (May 18, 2000): 1462–70.

108, *"extensive financial associations"* Marcia Angell, "Is Academic Medicine for Sale?" *New England Journal of Medicine* 342 (May 18, 2000): 1516–18.

108, *testimony in a later lawsuit* Deposition of Keller in *Beverly Smith v. GlaxoSmithKline,* Sept. 7, 2006.

109, *chronically depressed patients* Martin B. Keller et al., "Maintenance Phase Efficacy of Sertraline for Chronic Depression," *Journal of the American Medical Association* 280, no. 19 (November 18, 1998): 1665–72.

111, *from the pharmaceutical industry* Bass, "Drug Companies Enrich Professor," *Boston Globe.* (This article was based on Keller's income tax returns from 1997 and 1998.)

111, *on the disclosure form* APA Disclosure Index 1998.

112, *the pharmaceutical industry* Alison Bass, "Drug Companies Enrich Professor," *Boston Globe* October 4, 1999.

112, *his tax returns* Alison Bass, "Drug Companies Enrich Professor."

112, *per patient for clinical trials* Kurt Eichenwald and Gina Kolata, "Drug Trials Hide Conflicts for Doctors," *New York Times,* May 16, 1999.

114, *"present positive findings"* Les S. Friedman and Elihu D. Richter, *Journal of General Internal Medicine* 19, no. 54 (2004): 51–56.

## Chapter Eleven

*This chapter is based on interviews with Rose Firestein, Janice Firestein, and several attorneys in Florida, including Karen Gievers, Andrea Moore, and Bernard Perlmutter.*

119, *series on the problem* Carol Marbin Miller, "Foster Kids Describe Drugs' Effect," *Miami Herald,* April 23, 2001.

120, *"concentrate on my schoolwork"* Affidavit of Leslie F., *Foster Children Bonnie L et al. v. Jeb Bush et al.,* March 2001.

120, *45 to 46 percent of foster children* Carol Marbin Miller, "Report Decried Giving Drugs to Kids," *Miami Herald,* May 11, 2001.

## Chapter Twelve

*This chapter is based on interviews with Donna Howard, Nicki Sahlin, Jim McNulty, Sheldon Krimsky, Jim Hallon of Butler Hospital, and other sources.*

127, *June 1995 progress report* Progress Report Summary on NIMH grant MH48877-04, "Lithium Prophylaxis in Adolescents with Bipolar Illness," 1995.

128, *In January 1996* Alison Bass, "State Paid School $218,000 on Falsely Billed DMH Study," *Boston Globe,* January 7, 1996.

130, *NAMI's posted annual reports* http://www.nami.org/.

132, *"cover the matter up"* Alison Bass, "Whistleblowers Question Brown Settlement," *Boston Globe,* January 12, 1999.

## Chapter Thirteen

*This chapter is based on interviews with Rose Firestein, Joe Baker, Tom Conway, Shirley Stark, Eliot Spitzer, Peter Lurie, and Julie Zito.*

141, *the Public Citizen survey* http://www.citizen.org/publications/.

142, *lobbying members of Congress* http://www.opensecrets.org/lobbyists/.

143, *Parke-Davis and Warner-Lambert* Marcia Angell, *The Truth about the Drug Companies* (New York: Random House, 2004), 157–60.

145, *an SSRI antidepressant* Daniel Safer and Julie Magno Zito, "Treatment-Emergent Adverse Effects from Serotonin Reuptake Inhibitors by Age Group," *Journal of Child and Adolescent Psychopharmacology* 16, nos. 1–2 (2006): 159–69.

145, *accompany suicidal behavior* Julie Magno Zito and Daniel J. Safer "The Efficacy and Safety of Selective Serotonin Reuptake Inhibitors for the Treatment of Depression in Children and Adolescents," in *Pharma-*

*covigilance,* 2nd ed., ed. Ronald D. Mann and Elizabeth B. Andrews (London: John Wiley and Sons, 2007).

145, *"major depressive disorder"* FDA Talk Paper, June 19, 2003, http://www.fda.gov/.

146, *"depression in adolescents"* Martin B. Keller et al., "Efficacy of Paroxetine in the Treatment of Adolescent Major Depression: A Randomized, Controlled Trial," *Journal of the American Academy of Child and Adolescent Psychiatry* 40, no. 7 (July 2001): 762–72.

148, *these dubious circumstances* Paul Edward Parker, "Brown Pays $300,170 to Settle Dispute," *Providence Journal-Bulletin,* December 30, 1998; and Bass, "Whistleblowers Question Brown Settlement."

## Chapter Fourteen

*This chapter is based on interviews with Rose Firestein, Janice Firestein, Shirley Stark, Tom Conway, Joe Baker, Ross Baldessarini, Martin Teicher, and others.*

155, *"suicidality in any of these drugs"* FDA Talk Paper, October 27, 2003, http://www.fda.gov/.

155, *among children and adolescents* Erica Goode, "British Warning on Antidepressant Use for Youth," *New York Times,* December 11, 2003; and http://www.mhra.gov.uk/.

156, *"have not been published"* Gardiner Harris, "Debate Resumes on the Safety of Depression's Wonder Drugs," *New York Times,* August 7, 2003.

157, *"the chances of positive studies"* Shankar Vedantum, "Antidepressant Makers Withhold Data on Children," *Washington Post,* January 29, 2004.

157, *agency's own public hearing* Rob Waters, "Drug Report Barred by FDA," *San Francisco Chronicle,* February 1, 2004.

158, *Pfizer, and Eli Lilly* Executive Summary, *Preliminary Report of the American College of Neuropsychopharmacology Task Force on SSRIs and Suicidal Behavior,* January 21, 2004.

159, *"induction of suicidality"* Thomas P. Laughren, memo to committee members, "Background Comments for February 2, 2004, Meeting of the Psychopharmacological Drugs Advisory Committee (PDAC) and Pediatric Subcommittee of the Anti-Infective Drugs Advisory Committee (Peds AC)," January 5, 2004.

160, *Sharav charged* Transcript of the February 2, 2004, meeting of PDAC and Peds AC, 104, http://www.fda.gov/.

160, *constituted suicidal behavior* Ibid., 349.

## Chapter Fifteen

*This chapter is based on interviews with Rose Firestein, Tom Conway, Joe Baker, Shirley Stark, Robert Milin, Marcia Angell, and Arnold Relman, among others.*

167, *"SSRI Use in Children"* Wayne Kondro and Barbara Sibbald, "Drug Company Experts Advised Staff to Withhold Data about SSRI Use in Children," *Canadian Medical Association Journal* 170, no. 5 (March 2, 2004): 783.

167, *"the profile of paroxetine"* SmithKline Beecham position piece, "SB Confidential—For Internal Use Only," attached to memo from Jackie Westaway, October 14, 1998.

168, *"negative commercial impact"* Ibid.

170, *object to the wording* Deposition of Martin B. Keller in *Smith v. GlaxoSmithKline,* September 7, 2006.

170, *Back in November 1997* Ibid.

170, *decided thumb's-down* Review of Paxil study by *Journal of the American Medical Association* reviewers, produced by GlaxoSmithKline in *Smith v. GlaxoSmithKline.*

170, *"in the discussion"* Mina Dulcan, editor of *Journal of the American Academy of Child and Adolescent Psychiatry* (*JAACAP*), letter to Martin Keller enclosing reviewers' comments, July 27, 2000, produced by GlaxoSmithKline in *Smith v. GlaxoSmithKline.*

171, *Emslie was a paid consultant Preliminary Report of the American College of Neuropsychopharmacology Task Force on SSRIs and Suicidal Behavior,* January 21, 2004.

171, *"purchase 500 reprints"* Matt Battlin, GlaxoSmithKline, e-mail to Sally Laden, April 25, 2001, produced by GlaxoSmithKline.

171, *the ACNP report* Deposition of Karen Wagner in *Smith v. GlaxoSmithKline,* March 22, 2006; Deposition of Neal Ryan in *Smith v. GlaxoSmithKline,* October 4, 2006; and 2004 *Preliminary Report of the ACNP Task Force.*

172, *"remarkable" in his memo* Zachary Hawkins, Paxil Product Management, memo to all sales representatives selling Paxil, August 16, 2001.

173, *"emergence of suicidal ideation"* FDA Talk Paper, March 22, 2004, http://www.fda.gov/.

173, *"help they deserve"* APA press release, March 23, 2004.

173, *"a really tragic outcome"* Denise Grady and Gardiner Harris, "Overprescribing Prompted Warnings on Antidepressants," *New York Times,* March 24, 2004.

174, *in treating pediatric depression* Legal complaint, *People of the State of New York by Eliot Spitzer, Attorney General of the State of New York v. GlaxoSmithKline,* filed in the Supreme Court of the State of New York, June 2, 2004.

177, *"few weeks on medication"* Mitch Parsons, MD, letter to the editor, *Journal of the American Academy of Child and Adolescent Psychiatry* 41, no. 4 (April 2002): 364.

177, *in May 2003* Jon Jureidini, PhD, and Anne Tonkin, BM, PhD, letter to the editor, *Journal of the American Academy of Child and Adolescent Psychiatry* 42, no. 5 (May 2003): 514.

## Chapter Sixteen

*This chapter is based on interviews with Rose Firestein, Tom Conway, Joe Baker, Shirley Stark, Eliot Spitzer, Barry Perlman, Tonya Brooks, Cheryl Brooks, and Jeffrey Drazen.*

179, *"Their effort to suppress"* Barbara Martinez, "Spitzer Charges Glaxo Concealed Paxil Data," *Wall Street Journal,* June 3, 2004.

180, *"Similar suits are likely"* Gardiner Harris, "New York State Official Sues Drug Maker over Test Data," *New York Times,* June 3, 2004.

180, *"data from those studies"* GlaxoSmithKline statement on PR Newswire, June 2, 2004.

180, *falling 13 percent* Jeanne Whalen and Elena Barton, "Glaxo's Earnings Decline 13%," *Wall Street Journal,* July 28, 2004.

180, *"The new wrinkle"* Harris, "Official Sues Drug Maker."

181, *"an outrageous cost"* Jeanne Whalen, "Glaxo CEO: Litigation Is 'Getting Out of Control,'" *Wall Street Journal,* June 3, 2004.

181, *"bullying in these tactics"* Robert Peston and Sylvia Preiffer, "Garnier Hits Back at Spitzer over Allegations of Fraud at GSK," *Sunday Telegraph* (London), June 6, 2004.

181, *"odds are 100 percent"* Ibid.

183, *"associated with the drug"* Kay A. Chitale, FDA consumer promotion analyst, letter to P. Kaia Agarwal, senior director, Regulatory Affairs, GlaxoSmithKline, June 11, 2004, http://www.fda.gov/cder/.

183, *aired months earlier* Jeanne Whalen, "Glaxo Is Rebuked by FDA over Ad for Paxil CR Drug," *Wall Street Journal,* June 14, 2004.

183, *"dangerous industry practice"* Jeanne Whalen, "Glaxo Releases Studies on Drug for Depression," *Wall Street Journal,* June 16, 2004.

184, *and their outcomes* Press release from the American Medical Association, June 15, 2004, http://www.ama-assn.org/ama/pub/.

185, *catch such manipulations* An-Wen Chan et al., "Empirical Evidence for Selective Reporting of Outcomes in Randomized Trials," *Journal of the American Medical Association* 291 (2004): 2457–65.

185, *"scared out of prescribing'"* Editorial in Review and Outlook section, *Wall Street Journal,* June 21, 2004.

186, *"harming innocent bystanders"* Ibid.

## Chapter Seventeen

*This chapter is based on interviews with Rose Firestein, Joseph Sedwick Sollers, Dwight Davis, Donna Howard, and other sources.*

189, *its SSRI, Celexa* Barry Meier, "A Medical Journal Quandary: How to Report on Drug Trials," *New York Times,* June 21, 2004; and Christopher Windham and Barbara Martinez, "Saga of Unpublished Drug Data Takes an Unexpected Twist," *Wall Street Journal,* June 21, 2004.

189, *children and adolescents* News Roundup, "Forest Labs Asked for Information on Trials, Promotion of Its Drugs," *Wall Street Journal,* June 30, 2004.

193, *"the study medication"* Final Clinical Report, *A Multi-Center, Double-Blind, Placebo Controlled Study of Paroxetine and Imipramine in Adolescents with Unipolar Major Depression* (study 329), November 24, 1998, 35, http://www.gsk.com/media/paroxetine.htm.

193, *the Brown study* Ibid., 277.

193, *the published 2001 Paxil study* Keller et al. "Efficacy of Paroxetine."

194, *"for non-compliance"* Martin Keller, memo to Dorinda Williams, Brown University IRB Staff Assistant, "Re: Adverse Event Report for "A Multiceter, Double-Blind, Placebo Controlled Study of Paroxetine and Imipramine in Adolescents with Unipolar Major Depression,'" October 30, 1995.

194, *memo to the Brown IRB* Martin Keller, memo to the IRBs of Brown University and Bradley and Butler Hospitals, "Re: Adverse Event in 'A Multicenter, Double-Blind, Placebo Controlled Study of Paroxetine and Imipramine in Adolescents with Unipolar Major Depression,'" January 30, 1995.

195, *for being "noncompliant"* Martin Keller, memo to Ivan W. Miller, chair of the Brown University Institutional Review Board, "Re: Annual Review of Project Entitled: 'A Multicenter Double-blind, Placebo Controlled Study of Paroxetine and Imipramine in Adolescents with Unipolar Major Depression,'" November 11, 1995.

195, *company's final report* Final Clinical Report, *A Multi-Center, Double-*

*Blind, Placebo Controlled Study of Paroxetine and Imipramine in Adolescents with Depression* (study 329), November 24, 1998, 318, http://www.gsk.com/media/paroxetine.htm.

## Chapter Eighteen

*This chapter is based on interviews with Rose Firestein, Shirley Stark, Tom Conway, Eliot Spitzer, Joe Baker, Joseph Sedwick Sollers, Dwight Davis, Mary Ann Rhyne (spokeswoman for GlaxoSmithKline), and congressional sources.*

197, *division of GlaxoSmithKline* Charles E. Grassley, chairman of the Senate Committee on Finance, letter to Christopher Viehbacher, president of U.S. Pharmaceuticals, GlaxoSmithKline, August 3, 2004, produced by GlaxoSmithKline in *Smith v. GlaxoSmithKline.*

197, *"and/or suicidal behavior"* Ibid.

197, *"some drug companies"* Ibid.

198, *drug test results* Barry Meier, "Results of Drug Trials Can Mystify Doctors through Omission," *New York Times,* July 21, 2004; *Wall Street Journal,* July 28, 2004, and August 3, 2004.

198, *an antianemia medication* Barry Meier, "Spitzer Asks Drug Maker for Off-Label Use Material," *New York Times,* August 5, 2004.

198, *reached by Mosholder* Anne Wilde Mathews, "FDA Revisits Issue of Antidepressants for Youth *Wall Street Journal,* August 5, 2004.

203, *"make informed judgments"* Gardiner Harris, "Glaxo Agrees to Post Results of Drug Trials on Web Site," *New York Times,* August 27, 2004.

205, *"The arrogance of"* Christopher Bowe, "Spitzer Sounds Further Warning to GSK," *Financial Times,* August 31, 2004.

## Chapter Nineteen

*This chapter is based on interviews with Martin Teicher, David Healy, Rose Firestein, and congressional sources.*

209, *those taking sugar pills* FDA Talk Paper, August 20, 2004, http://www.fda.gov/; and Mark Kaufman, "FDA Alters Tack on Children and Antidepressants," *Washington Post,* August 21, 2004.

210, *he told Bell.* Julie Bell, "FDA Review Renews Antidepressant Debate," *Baltimore Sun,* August 21, 2004.

211, *"dollars in the process"* "House Committee on Energy and Commerce, Subommittee on Oversight and Investigations, transcript of hearing on *Publication and Disclosure Issues in Antidepressant Pediatric Clinical Trials,* 108th Cong., 2nd sess., September 9, 2004.

211, *"placebo"* Ibid.

211, *"and Alibis," Barton said* Ibid.

211 *"FDA to do its job"* Ibid.

212, *Rep. Greg Walden* Ibid.

212, *"data that is available"* Ibid.

213, *prescribing the drugs* FDA Statement on Recommendations of the Psychopharmacologic Drugs and Pediatric Advisory Committee, September 16, 2004.

213, *on the secondary outcomes* Jon Jureidini et al., "Efficacy and Safety of Antidepressants for Children and Adolescents," *British Medical Journal* 328, no. 7444 (April 10, 2004): 879–83.

214, *Teicher told Johnson* Carolyn Johnson, "What's Next for Depressed Kids?" *Boston Globe,* September 21, 2004.

215, *"attempting to obstruct justice"* House Committee on Energy and Commerce, Subcommittee on Oversight and Investigations, transcript of hearing on *FDA's Role in Protecting the Public Health: Examining the FDA's Review of Safety and Efficacy in Antidepressant Use by Children,* 108th Cong., 2nd sess., September 23, 2004.

216, *"effects of drugs on children"* Ibid.

216, *"informal 'partner' to the industry"* Trudy Lieberman, "Bitter Pill," *Columbia Journalism Review,* July–August 2005.

216, *investigator David Graham* "Study of Pain Killer Suggests Heart Risk," Bloomberg News, August 26, 2004.

217, *jump on the story* Mark Kaufman, "Merck Withdraws Arthritis Medication," *Washington Post,* October 1, 2004.

217, *"three years too late"* Ibid.

218, *of similar side effects* Carolyn Johnson, "Suicide Warning Ordered on Drugs," *Boston Globe,* October 16, 2004.

## Epilogue

*This chapter is based on interviews with Donna Howard, Rose Firestein, Eliot Spitzer, Tom Conway, Joe Baker, Sheldon Krimsky, Arnold Relman, Ross Baldessarini, Julie Zito, Peter Lurie, Robert Gibbons, Roger Grimson, and Susan Cruzan of the FDA, among other sources.*

221, *relative risk was 3.76* Alan Apter et al., "Evaluation of Suicidal Thoughts and Behaviors in Children and Adolescents Taking Paroxetine," *Journal of Child and Adolescent Psychopharmacology* 16, no. 1–2 (March 2006): 77–89.

222, *"the paroxetine group"* Regan Fong, GlaxoSmithKline, e-mail to Martin Keller, Neal Ryan, and Karen Wagner, February 3, 2004.

222, *in the Paxil arm* Ibid.

225, *to remain accredited* Daniel Carlat, "Diagnosis: Conflict of Interest," *New York Times,* June 13, 2007.

224, *money from the industry* R. H. Perlis et al., "Industry Sponsorship and Financial Conflict of Interest in the Reporting of Clinical Trials in Psychiatry," *American Journal of Psychiatry,* 162, no. 10 (October 2005): 1957–60.

224, *children in that state* Gardiner Harris and Janet Roberts, "Doctors' Ties to Drug Makers Are Put on Close View," *New York Times,* March 21, 2007; and Joseph S. Ross et al., "Pharmaceutical Company Payments to Physicians," *Journal of the American Medical Association* 297, no. 11 (March 21, 2007): 1216–23.

225, *the* Times *analysis* Gardiner Harris et al., "Psychiatrists, Children and Drug Industry's Role," *New York Times,* May 10, 2007.

226, *In 2005, drugmakers* Harris and Roberts, "Doctors' Ties."

226, *between 2003 and 2004* Transcript of the FDA's Psychopharmacologic Drugs Advisory Committee meeting on December 13, 2006, http://www.fda.gov/.

226, *Centers for Disease Control* WISQARS Injury Mortality Report, http://www.cdc.gov/.

226, *maker of Effexor, another SSRI* Robert D. Gibbons, et al., "Early Evidence on the Effects of Regulators' Suicidality Warnings on SSRI Prescriptions and Suicide in Children and Adolescents," *American Journal of Psychiatry* 164, no. 9 (September 2007): 1356–63.

226, *Dr. J. John Mann* Executive Summary, *Preliminary Report of the American College of Neuropsychopharmacology Task Force on SSRIs and Suicidal Behavior,* January 21, 2004.

227, *only fifty-eight in 2005* CDER 2005 Report to the Nation (latest available figures), http://www.fda.gov/.

228, *already approved drugs* GAO Report on *Drug Safety,* March 2006, http://www.gao.gov/.

229, *prescribed diabetes drug* Steven E. Nissen et al., "Effect of Rosiglitazone on the Risk of Myocardial Infarction and Death from Cardiovascular Causes," *New England Journal of Medicine* 10, no. 356 (May 2007), http://www.nejm.org/.

230, *"a treasure trove"* Barry Meier, "For Drug Makers, a Downside to Full Disclosure," *New York Times,* May 23, 2007.

230, New England Journal of Medicine  Christine Laine et al., "Clinical Trial Registration: Looking Back and Moving Forward" *New England Journal of Medicine* 10, no. 1056 (June 2007): 8110, http://www.nejm.org/.

232, *2006 election cycle*  http://www.opensecrets.org/.

233, *the testing of new drugs*  Angell, *Drug Companies,* 243–44.

233, *"for its own purposes"*  Jerry Avorn, "Dangerous Deception: Hiding the Evidence of Adverse Drug Effects," *New England Journal of Medicine* 355, no. 21 (November 23, 2006): 2169–71.

234, *depression for adolescents*  Deposition of Martin Keller in *Smith v. GlaxoSmithKline,* Sept. 7, 2006.

234, *2006 deposition*  Ibid.

# Index

Index